D1711168

First and Lasting Impressions

First and Lasting Impressions

JULIUS RUDEL LOOKS BACK ON A LIFE IN MUSIC

Julius Rudel and Rebecca Paller

UNIVERSITY OF ROCHESTER PRESS

This work is a memoir. The experiences and conversations recounted here are the result of the author's recollection and are rendered as a subjective accounting of events that occurred in his life. His perceptions and opinions are entirely his own and do not represent those of the publisher or sponsors.

Copyright © 2013 by Julius Rudel and Rebecca Paller

All rights reserved. Except as permitted under current legislation, no part of this work may be photocopied, stored in a retrieval system, published, performed in public, adapted, broadcast, transmitted, recorded, or reproduced in any form or by any means, without the prior permission of the copyright owner.

First published 2013

University of Rochester Press
668 Mt. Hope Avenue, Rochester, NY 14620, USA
www.urpress.com
and Boydell & Brewer Limited
PO Box 9, Woodbridge, SuffolkIP12 3DF, UK
www.boydellandbrewer.com

ISBN-13: 978-1-58046-434-5

Library of Congress Cataloging-in-Publication Data

Rudel, Julius, author.
First and lasting impressions : Julius Rudel looks back on a life in music / Julius Rudel and Rebecca Paller.
    pages cm
Includes index.
    ISBN 978-1-58046-434-5 (hardcover : alk. paper) 1. Rudel, Julius. 2. Conductors (Music)—United States—Biography. 3. Opera producers and directors—United States—Biography. I. Paller, Rebecca, author. II. Title.
    ML422.R83A3 2013
    782.1092—dc23
    [B]
                                                                                        2012046694

A catalogue record for this title is available from the British Library.

This publication is printed on acid-free paper.
Printed in the United States of America.

To all the past company members of New York City Opera
and to the memory of Rita Rudel and Morton Baum.

CONTENTS

FOREWORD

First and Lasting Impressions reads like Julius: honest, informal, energetic, optimistic, funny—even chatty—and always fascinating.

Singlehandedly, he pulled me from Broadway to the daunting world of opera, calling me one day with a new piece by the esteemed Israeli composer Josef Tal called *Ashmedai* and saying he thought it was high time I made the move. The material was especially theatrical, so I jumped at the chance. He started a second career for me that extended to the Lyric Opera of Chicago, the Houston Grand Opera, the Met, the Teatro Colon in Buenos Aires, and the Staatsoper in Vienna. Many of these houses were scenes of Julius's earlier triumphs.

Born in Vienna, Julius immigrated to the United States, studying music here and making his conducting debut in 1944 with Johann Strauss's *The Gypsy Baron*. Quickly rising through the ranks at Fiorello La Guardia's gift to New York City—"a people's opera"—Julius became the general director of the New York City Center Opera Company, and he masterminded its watershed years, discovering and nurturing the spectacular careers of Beverly Sills, Plácido Domingo, and Norman Treigle, to name a few. Julius is a man of the theatre, and he envisioned, as the best conductors have, opera as *Gesamtkunstwerk*—total theatre.

Julius redefined what American opera could be, conducting the world premieres of Robert Kurka's *The Good Soldier Schweik* and Hugo Weisgall's *Six Characters in Search of An Author*, and the New York premiere of Lee Hoiby's *Summer and Smoke*, and commissioning operas including *The Crucible* by Robert Ward and *Lizzie Borden* by Jack Beeson. And he simultaneously introduced Broadway musicals to an opera audience at the City Center Light Opera Company: *Show Boat, Carousel* starring Barbara Cook, and an award-winning production of *Brigadoon*.

He remained general director after New York City Opera moved to the New York State Theater at Lincoln Center in February 1966, across the plaza from the Met. There were only eleven days separating the fall 1966 openings of both of those august institutions and plenty of competition between them. Good-natured (well, mostly!). I was lucky enough to get in on one of his last productions at the City Opera in the spring of 1980, an adaptation of Kurt Weill and Georg Kaiser's *Silverlake* by Hugh Wheeler, the Broadway librettist (*Sweeney Todd*), and starring Joel Grey.

The book you're about to read extends beyond the City Opera to summers in Caramoor, the opening of the Kennedy Center with Julius as its first music director, and even the Grammy Awards. His is a life dedicated to opera and music theatre.

Julius is in his nineties now, but you'd doubt it if you knew him. I wish he were still standing on the podium or sitting in the general director's office. In the vernacular, he still has the chops.

—Harold Prince

ACKNOWLEDGMENTS

We'd like to thank Jamie Rigler and the Ledler Foundation, without whose generous support this book could not have been written, and The Paley Center for Media (formerly The Museum of Television & Radio)—especially Ron Simon, David Bushman, Barry Monush, James Sheridan, and Arthur Smith of the curatorial department; vice presidents Diane Lewis and John Wolters; library services manager Jane Klain; development director Erin Gromen; and curatorial intern Bridget Johnston.

Special thanks go to Susan Woelzl, former press director and archivist of New York City Opera, for her invaluable help in putting us in touch with City Opera alumni and for reading the manuscript with us when it was still a work in progress. We are also grateful to Joan Baekeland for her thorough reading of the manuscript, and to photographers Beth Bergman and Jack Mitchell for their generosity.

We'd also like to thank the many individuals who shared their memories of New York City Opera with us or provided other invaluable help while we were writing the book:

Jack Beeson, Richard Beeson, Edward Berkeley, Martin Bernheimer, Harolyn Blackwell, Elaine Bonazzi, Elisabeth Carron, William and Irene Chapman, Peter Clark, Frank Corsaro, Dominic Cossa, Phyllis Curtin, Michael Devlin, Joan Dornemann, Jack Doulin, Cori Ellison, Matthew Epstein, Gerald Freedman, Muffy Greenough, Paul Gruber, Joshua Hecht, Lila Herbert, Ruth Hider, Barbara Hill, Christopher Jaffe, David Kanzeg, Brian Kellow, Kathleen C. Kelly at the Kennedy Center Press Office, Bettyann Holtzmann Kevles, Richard Kidwell, Rosemary Kuhlmann, Jeffrey Laikind, Gemze de Lappe, Bob Levine, Brenda Lewis, Tedrin Blair Lindsay, Barbara and David Lloyd, Saba McWilliams, Elaine Malbin, Spiro Malas and Marlena Kleinman Malas, Catherine Malfitano, Susanne Marsee, Bruce Maza, Johanna Meier, Brian Mitchell at the Houston Grand Opera, Rosalind Nadell, Florence Nelson, Maralin Niska, Martin Oppenheimer, Tim Page, Harold Prince, Regina Resnik, Frank Rizzo, Lou Rodgers, Lud Rudel, Joan Rudel Weinreich, Madeleine Rudel Grant, Anthony Rudel, Marc Scorca, Connie Shuman, Michael Steger, Richard Stilwell, Martha Moore Sykes, Robert Tuggle, Veronica Tyler, Edward Villella, Robert Walker, Jeannie Williams, and Corinne Zadik.

With appreciation also to Suzanne Guiod, editorial director of the University of Rochester Press, one of our strongest proponents when the book was but a rough draft, and to production editor Tracey Engel and managing editor Ryan Peterson.

INTRODUCTION

New Year's Eve 1976, Vienna.

The Staatsoper was ready for its traditional gala *Fledermaus* performance, and so was I. It was to be my debut in that venerable house, and although I am generally quite calm before a performance, this time I could not suppress a slightly tense feeling in the pit of my stomach. It had started to snow ever so gently but steadily, and I decided I needed to leave for the theater earlier than I usually would to allow a little extra time for travel.

Marcel Prawy, my longtime friend and the Staatsoper dramaturg, was waiting for me. I took the key from the *portier* and we walked to the conductors' lounge. And then I realized I had forgotten my tails at the hotel. What to do? It was snowing, and I wouldn't make it to the hotel and back in time. The orchestra supervisor said, "We have a whole wardrobe department. We can find one for you."

Prawy, ever resourceful, said, "No. In the conductors' lounge are several closets for staff conductors who keep their tails here. Let's see if we can find one that fits."

The security manager had an extra set of keys for these closets. We opened one after the other and inspected the tailcoats; the only one that fit was Karl Böhm's. I wore Böhm's tails for my debut, and afterward surprised him with a box of chocolates and a note thanking him for saving my performance.

❧❧

If it were not for Hitler, I may never have come to this moment in my life. I might have been perfectly content to fulfill my teenage dream of becoming a rehearsal pianist at the Vienna Staatsoper. But political events have a funny way of altering lives.

On March 12, 1938, six days after my seventeenth birthday, Hitler's hordes marched down the Ringstrasse—a sight I shall never forget. I was there, trying to be inconspicuous, walking behind the people lined up three and four deep on the street. Hitler ranted to the cheering crowd about the great future of the people of Germany, of which Austria was now the "Ostmark" (the eastern bastion). The whole Austrian nation had gone crazy, and there was a palpable hysteria in the air. Little did they know these feelings of joy wouldn't last long.

Changes were instituted within a matter of hours, particularly the deputization of young thugs as uniformed armed guards. People I knew, including some of my former school teachers, were suddenly wearing Nazi uniforms; they had been secret members of the outlawed Party all along.

The Anschluss was the second blow to my family within a short period of time. My father had died of cancer less than three months before, at the age of forty-nine. His illness had put a halt to our plans to emigrate. But the moment the Germans marched in, my mother reactivated our visa applications, and on May 25, 1938, I said good-bye to her and a few of my school friends on the platform of Vienna's Westbahnhof. I wore my best suit and my father's cuff links, along with a recently purchased "heirloom" pocket watch (which I had strict instructions to sell or pawn if I was in need of money) and a new white-gold-and-onyx ring on my left pinky—a ring that I still wear (and actually cannot take off) today. I had one suitcase and $17 in my pocket, the maximum amount of currency I was allowed to take out of the country. I was leaving behind my mother and my eight-year-old brother, Ludwig, who were unable to go until my mother's quota number came up. Quotas had been set by US law based on the place of birth of the applicant. Because I was born in Vienna, I was in a much more open quota than my mother, who was a native of Rumania. She and my brother would have to remain in Vienna until their number was called. Mother tried to be upbeat, reassuring me that she and Lud would "soon" join me in America, but none of us knew when, or if, that would be.

As the train prepared to depart, one of my friends handed me a small red book, *Vienna's Musical Sites and Landmarks.* On my journey to Paris and then to New York, I picked it up every so often to look at the pictures of the Vienna Staatsoper, my home away from home for the past four years, where two or three nights a week, I had attended operas conducted by Hans Knappertsbusch, Victor de Sabata, Wilhelm Furtwängler, and Bruno Walter in addition to those led by the house conductor, Karl Alwin—and one *Tristan* by a wunderkind named Herbert von Karajan.

I was giving up one world for another, leaving the Vienna of my youth (oh, the waltzes and the neighborhood inns that smelled of beer and sawdust!) for a sprawling city where the subways were fast and the music was carefree. George Gershwin had been dead for more than a year when I heard "I Got Plenty o' Nuttin'" for the first time on the radio and thought, *This could be a hit!*

If Vienna was the cultural crossroads of Europe, New York was the melting pot of the world, an incredible mélange of native and immigrant music and cultures. I arrived in the United States at a remarkable time, historically and culturally. Broadway musicals, popular songs, and jazz had come into their own, and American classical music and opera were on the cusp of greatness, no longer pale imitations of their European models.

The Queen Mary pulled into New York Harbor at night on June 6, 1938. I was so busy getting my papers together for the immigration officials that I almost missed seeing the Statue of Liberty, though I managed to get a glimpse of it as the ship was towed into its slip. The New York city skyline lit up the night. My mother's sister Ethel and her husband, who had immigrated a few years earlier, met me at the dock, and we drove up the West Side Highway to their apartment in the Fordham Road section of the Bronx. I stayed with Aunt Ethel, Uncle Ludwig, and their three young children until my mother and brother arrived, four months later.

I was a high school dropout with only a couple of night-school English lessons under my belt. I felt I was too old to enroll in high school in New York; I would be seventeen-and-a-half in September when the school year began. Fortunately I was a quick study; I learned English from my American cousins—who spoke *only* English—and from the radio. I pawned the watch and bought a used upright piano for $12, which my aunt permitted me to have hoisted into the apartment. My uncle, who managed a drugstore, derided me for wanting to work as a musician and advised me to find a "real job" to make money. I did as I was told, landing a job as a grocery delivery boy. Of course I was merely "bidin' my time" (in the words of another Gershwin song I heard on the radio) until my mother and brother arrived, when I knew that somehow I would find my way back into music.

Music, quite simply, was my life, and the land of opportunity was to offer me a career that I never dreamed of in the old world of Vienna.

1

EARLY LIFE IN VIENNA AND THE
SHADOW OF THE SWASTIKA

I was born in Vienna to a middle-class Jewish family with no discernible connection to music except that my maternal grandfather was a part-time cantor.

Both of my parents came from Bojan, a small town close to the city of Czernowitz, near the Russian border in the province of Bukowina—at that time, still a part of the Austro-Hungarian Empire. After World War I and the Treaty of Versailles, the region became a part of Rumania, and the Jews, rightfully fearing anti-Semitism, fled the area in droves, many of them resettling in Vienna.

The surname Rudel is not a Jewish name. (Ironically, a famous German Luftwaffe pilot during World War II named Hans Ulrich Rudel was personally decorated by Hitler.) The earliest known relative who makes an appearance in my paternal family's oral history is "Eliezer from Galicia." He was born in 1825 in Galicia, Poland, which was at that time a province of Russia. As the story goes, in order to save their son from the cholera epidemic that was sweeping Poland, Eliezer's parents sent him away from Galicia at the age of seven or eight with a wagon driver named Rudel from Bojan. Eliezer remained in Bojan with the Rudel family and took the wagon driver's name. (That's the acknowledged story, though there were murmurings the boy may have been the son of imprisoned or murdered intellectuals or revolutionary leaders, whose surname was so notorious that it could never be revealed.) Years later, Eliezer married the wagon driver's daughter, Rebecca Rachel. Together, they raised ten children, and my great-grandfather lived to the ripe old age of eighty-eight.

My paternal grandparents, Isaac and Leah Rudel, were farmers in Bojan. My father, Jakob, was born in 1888, the elder of two brothers. He was a serious, introspective boy who became a reserved, responsible adult.

My maternal grandparents, Josef and Feige Sonnenblum, were Orthodox Jews who operated a successful granary. Josef, as I mentioned, was also a *chaz-zen* (cantor). My mother, Josephine (or "Pepi" as she was called), was born in

1895, the second of six children. She was an attractive, vibrant girl, outgoing and trusting but not always the best judge of people. After my grandparents' granary was destroyed in World War I by the skirmishing Russian and Austrian armies, they moved the family to Vienna, where my grandfather bought a small neighborhood food store with a mustard factory at the rear. As a child, I would carefully scrutinize all the pickles in the large wooden barrel in my grandfather's store, ultimately choosing the perfect one— yellow, with a heady tang of garlic and vinegar. To this day there are certain smells I strongly identify with my grandparents' store and their house.

My father studied law at the university in Bukowina and served in the Austrian military during World War I as an officer in the military law office. His parents remained in Bojan; his younger brother, Nathan, who became an accountant, lived nearby in Czernowitz. I have fleeting memories of my only trip to visit my grandparents Isaac and Leah when I was a two-year-old. I can recall their farm and a house with a fenced-in yard, whitewashed walls, and a thatched roof. There's a photograph from that visit in which I'm looking serene and resting my arm on my grandfather's shoulder. I never saw them again. Isaac and Leah hid in Bojan throughout the Holocaust and survived. Leah died in 1943 and my grandfather in 1944, shortly after being reunited with my Uncle Nathan, who along with his wife, Fritzi, and their daughter, Rita, had miraculously survived the harsh conditions in a detention camp for Jews located about 100 miles from Czernowitz. Nathan, Fritzi, and Rita migrated to Israel in 1947, where I met them more than two decades later during my first guest-conducting performances in Tel Aviv.

My mother was working at the Phoenix Insurance Company in Vienna when my father took a job there in 1918 as a company lawyer. Phoenix was founded by a Jew named Wilhelm Berliner and was the only insurance company in Austria that had Jewish directors in its upper echelons. Since by Austrian law only one person per family was permitted to hold a job, my mother resigned.

My memory of my parents is that they were very much in love with each other, and there was always a good spirit in our home. My father said he fell in love with my mother the first time he saw her, when she was a schoolgirl in Bojan. He pursued her during the postwar period and into Austria. I have a bundle of affectionate letters they exchanged with each other during those years.

They were married in 1919, and I was born on March 6, 1921, in the seventeenth district, a worker's enclave called Hernals. In those days there was a housing shortage in Vienna. Our apartment was tiny, just a kitchen and a living room that doubled as a bedroom for the three of us. There was no running water in the apartment, and we shared a toilet down the hall with the four or five families living on that floor.

My mother was overly protective and wouldn't let me mingle with the kids of the neighborhood, whom she considered tough and uncouth. She would take me by streetcar to one of the elegant inner city parks so I could play with children from "better" families. Vienna is a series of concentric circles, at the center of which is the first district or Old City, where the government offices, fine shops, hotels, and palaces are located. Around that, in a circle separated by the Ringstrasse (literally, a "circle street," along which are built the Staatsoper, the Burgtheater, several of the city's museums, Parliament, and City Hall), are the middle-class districts—two to nine. Another circular road, the Gürtel (literally, a "belt"), which runs parallel to the Ringstrasse, separates the middle-class districts from the workers' districts—ten to twenty-one. Most of the Eastern European Jews who moved to Vienna after World War I settled in the second district, keeping more or less to themselves, while the more assimilated Jews lived primarily in the sixth, seventh, and eighth districts.

Ours was a fairly religious, "observant" household—we had two sets of dishes for Passover, and Mother lit the Sabbath candles at sundown on Friday nights. My father prayed every morning, and I knew from a young age that I would have a bar mitzvah when I turned thirteen. My mother's parents lived just a few blocks from us in a three-room flat with two of their children—my Aunt Gusta and Uncle Herman (the youngest of my mother's siblings). My mother's sister Ethel had married and emigrated to the United States, where she lived in New York City; her oldest brother, Abraham, had died of tuberculosis in 1924, and her oldest sister, Malke, died in 1923, leaving behind an eight-year-old son, Hans (the eldest of my first cousins), who was raised by my grandparents. Malke's story was a sad one. She was fifteen when Hans was born, and though I was told she died of pneumonia, I later suspected that she committed suicide; but since my mother habitually shielded me from bad news, I knew very little about her.

My father would usually come home for lunch, take a short nap, and then board the streetcar back to his office, where he would work until seven. On Sunday afternoons, we'd ride the streetcar to the last stop and go wandering in the Vienna Woods, stopping for *Jause* (a light afternoon snack) at five—tea for my parents and cocoa for me. Occasionally a friend would come along, but I really did not have many friends until I was six years old and we moved to our second home in one of the "better districts" and, a few years later, when I started going regularly to the Staatsoper.

In the summers we would take the train to Salzburg, where the insurance company had a beautiful summer home that overlooked the entire city for its employees. We'd usually stay for a whole month, or my mother would rent a furnished room in a small village on a placid river for a few weeks in July and August, where I would go swimming every day and my mother would be with her circle of friends (a small but tight-knit group, as I recall). Father would join us for weekends only.

As a rare treat, my mother would allow me to visit my father at work; Phoenix's main office was in the first district, less than a half-hour walk from our apartment. I loved to visit my father's imposing workplace. I was especially intrigued by a little red light in his office that would flash when the chairman of directors, Herr Berliner, wished to speak to him.

In 1927, when I was six, my parents were finally able to buy a larger apartment. We moved to the seventh district, Neubau—a good middle-class neighborhood. Moving from the workers' district to an apartment with four rooms on the third floor of 16 Kandlgasse was true aggrandizement. We never moved again.

My brother, Ludwig, was born in July 1930. I was elated because until then I had been an only child, under the moment-by-moment supervision of Mother. Father celebrated Lud's entrance into the world by giving Mother a painting of a street scene with snow by the Austrian artist Josef Dobrowsky. The painting, in shades of brown and teal, is nearly identical to another work by the same artist that hangs in Vienna's Leopold Museum. Imagine how surprised my brother and I were, many years later on one of our trips to Vienna, when we first rounded the corner of the museum gallery and came face to face with "our" painting! The Dobrowsky was one of our family's prized possessions, along with some Biedermeier furniture and jewelry that my mother managed to ship from Vienna to New York prior to her journey here. Today, all these years later, the painting hangs in my living room.

Like most apartments in Vienna in the 1930s, ours had no central heat or hot water; every room was equipped with an old-fashioned tile oven. My parents had a private bathroom built in our apartment, and installed a bathtub with a special water heater so we could take hot baths—a luxury that made our apartment more valuable. I shared a bedroom with my brother, but because of our nine-year age difference, it was not until much later in life that we became close friends.

The apartment I grew up in exists to this day; it survived the war unscathed. I visited there with my brother, my children, and my grandchildren in December 2002, on the sixty-fifth anniversary of my father's death. The present tenant, a representative from the Turkish travel industry, invited us for afternoon tea and some recollections. What I remembered as being a fairly large apartment was really quite small by American standards. I could still recall the exact spot near the window in the living room where my piano used to stand.

My earliest memories are filled with music. Although my mother and father were not musicians themselves, they enjoyed classical music and opera. When I was three, my parents bought me a half-size violin, which I happily experimented on for a few years, leading my family to believe that I might have some musical talent. I also had a very nice high voice, and would entertain people with hit tunes from operettas and films, including

Spoliansky's *Heute Nacht oder nie* (Tonight or never), in the manner of the popular tenors of the day like Jan Kiepura and Richard Tauber. My parents would sometimes trot me out to sing when they had guests for dinner, and I would happily warble away.

My grandparents knew someone who was a friend of Professor Zimbler, the concertmaster of the Vienna Symphony Orchestra—the city's "other" orchestra after the renowned Vienna Philharmonic. I played for Zimbler, and he thought I showed some talent. However, he suggested that I should postpone the violin and start on piano instead. At the time we were preparing to move from our first apartment to the larger one, so my parents bought a piano. I then had a series of ineffectual *Fraulein* who "taught" me piano—and I use the verb quite loosely. Young girls of the era often became piano teachers to augment the family income. It was considered a respectable job, and these young women always came highly recommended by Mother's friends. But none of them actually had any teacher training. They came and went, and I didn't learn much.

I did, however, gain valuable training of another sort from one of the pretty young teachers my mother had hired. I succumbed to her considerable charms when I was twelve; she taught me more about romance than about music.

Later that year my parents finally engaged a piano teacher of a much higher caliber, and I started to learn about theory and composition. After some time with him, I began studying with Alexander Klahr, who taught me the techniques of sight-reading, which of course later on became an essential component of my career. Klahr gave me grounding in everything that, up till then, I had been lacking. Concurrent with my lessons with him, I enrolled in theory courses at the Vienna Music Academy. I had begun "composing" when I was eight or nine. I based a concertino that I wrote for piano and orchestra on a Jewish chant I heard from my Grandfather Josef.

By the time I was fourteen, I had written an opera—text and music. When I was fifteen, a contest was announced in Vienna for a one-act opera. I decided to enter, and wrote the music and libretto for *Die Bauern* (The peasants), a verismo work heavily influenced by Eugen D'Albert's *Tiefland*. I actually entered *Die Bauern* into the competition in 1937—but after the Anschluss I had to withdraw it. (A few years later, when I was living in New York, I became fascinated by the Maxwell Anderson verse play *Winterset*, and I thought I'd try my hand at adapting it. It didn't progress beyond the first few pages.)

When I was fifteen, I wrote a musical with a fellow student, Joe Wisnizer (who emigrated to Israel and changed his name to Porath). It was a *pièce d'occasion*, written for the annual gala held by our parents' club. We began our collaboration in January 1937, at the time when preparations were being made for the 1939 World's Fair. Our musical was set in the Jewish Palestine Pavilion at the Fair. It was a tongue-in-cheek mystery, with a plot about a Nazi spy disguised as a European businessman who tries to blow up the pavilion. We wrote and performed the songs, including a cute duet for two British women in the pavilion crowd. I staged the show and was also the pianist.

The visual aspect of opera has always fascinated me. I still have memories of the very first time my parents took me to the opera, when I was three years old. We went to the Staatsoper for a performance of Bizet's *Carmen*, starring Maria Jeritza. In that production she had to run over a footbridge. The setting of the town square in Seville, with the bridge spanning a large part of the stage, was very imposing. I have a burnt-in visual memory of that stage and of the moment of Carmen's escape at the end of the first act.

By the time I was four, I had started building my own little "opera houses." In the beginning I used cardboard shoeboxes. My mother stitched together some old cloth so my theater would have a proper "opera" curtain. A proper curtain, of course, had to open on the diagonal, with that wonderful swoop. To this day that sight is exciting to me: the raising of the curtain means the start of another adventure.

Over the years my "theaters" became more complex and sophisticated. Soon I abandoned cardboard and moved on to wood. The last one, built when I was fourteen or fifteen, included an ornate proscenium arch that I made from a picture frame that I found in the attic.

I designed and built sets for many different operas, and was particularly obsessed with scenic transitions—especially if they had to occur in view of the audience. I was terribly disappointed the first time I saw Wagner's great opera *Parsifal*. The composer's specific instructions for the transition from the forest to the immense hall of the Grail presented a grand challenge, and I couldn't wait to see how the Staatsoper would solve the problem. To my astonishment, they simply lowered the curtain and deprived the audience of the visual component of the vast musical journey through the rocky range. When I arrived home from that performance, I started to experiment and, after many tries, solved the problem by creating a "moving sidewalk." That miniature theater, the first theater I "ran," was a crucial part of my life. When I left Vienna in 1938, that wooden box was the possession that was most difficult to leave behind.

Though opera was quickly becoming my passion, I also went to my fair share of concerts and movies as a child—I still recall being amazed that Shirley Temple spoke German so well (having no idea that there was a process called "dubbing")! I also attended the theater occasionally, and I recollect going with my mother to see Max Reinhardt's famous production of Goethe's *Faust* in Salzburg. It was performed in that remarkable space, the Felsenreitschule—a former riding school with stone arches hewn into the cliffs of Salzburg Castle. Reinhardt (with assistance from the scenery wizard Clemens Holzmeister) placed the prologue in Heaven quite literally on top of the mountain, with the "Faust city" on the audience level below. It was positively breathtaking. After the performance, walking with my mother toward the exit, we suddenly saw Max Reinhardt just inches away from us. We paid obeisance to the celebrated director, and I got his autograph for my collection.

The Claque

When I reached my thirteenth birthday, I was bar mitzvahed; I still have a copy of the engraved invitation that was sent out to family and friends. More important, once I hit that milestone birthday, my parents gave me permission to attend the opera alone. I had reached a new level of maturity! As a bar mitzvah present my Uncle Herman got me a ticket—a box seat, no less—for the world premiere of Franz Lehár's *Giuditta* at the Staatsoper, starring Jarmila Novotna and Richard Tauber and conducted by the composer. (I'm sorry to say that the work, in spite of a few good tunes, was a bit of a disappointment.) But from that moment on it was strictly standing room for me—not in the large space at the rear of the orchestra floor where most of the standees congregated, but on the fourth gallery, where there was a better overview of the stage and the pit. There were special queues in the side lobby where standees would line up for tickets. The line would form several hours before the performance depending, of course, on the popularity of the evening's stars or the opera. As soon as we purchased our tickets, we would run up the stairs, taking two or three steps at a time to get the best spots. I got to know many of the standees, including my lifelong friend Marcel Prawy, who later became a dramaturg and producer at the Volksoper and the Staatsoper. From the moment we arrived until the performance began, we engaged in lively discussion and argumentation—comparing notes on previous performances, exchanging operatic gossip, and generally showing off our knowledge. We each had our favorite stars (whose virtues we would extol); mine included Ezio Pinza, Jan Kiepura, Lotte Lehmann, Jarmila Novotna, and Charles Kullman. A few of the older standees actually got to know their idols by starting or joining existing fan clubs. From those still relatively innocent groups it was but a small step to the "professional" claque.

   Sometime in the distant past a clever aficionado perceived the commercial possibilities in making sure that singers—always insecure and easily upset when not properly appreciated by their audience—would be applauded and even cheered, no matter what. The discreet services of "enthusiasts" to initiate and guide the general public's appreciation would be offered to singers—and some proved too weak to resist. Of course the slippery slope could lead to a form of blackmail, since an enthusiast could also react negatively and thereby incite the public's disapproval—and so the poor singer needed to be protected from such predatory wolves. Numerous tales abound of performers or their "protectors" paying someone to whistle or boo their rivals. At the Staatsoper the claque was silently tolerated by the administration (of course, officially, no claque existed). In a few instances the "house" even made use of the claque for their own ends (Rudolf Bing, in his autobiography, admitted that he once used the services of a "claqueur" at the Met). It is told that when Gustav Mahler became director of the Staatsoper, he called all his first-rank singers together and made them take an oath that they would not use the claque.

Because of the distance between the two standing-room areas, there were two men in charge: one, named Stieglitz, on the orchestra level, and the other, named Schostal, in the fourth gallery. It was not long after my fifteenth birthday that I first caught the attention of Schostal—who was portly and not at all well dressed (especially in those days, when people dressed up to go to the opera). He quizzed me briefly (no doubt because of my tender age), and then accepted me into the claque. From then on when I wanted to attend a performance I would meet my "leader" at a certain spot in the lobby. He would give me a standing-room ticket and fifty *groschen* and let me know whom I was to be "working for" that night. There were usually four or five of us and he would place us strategically around the fourth gallery. He would generally initiate the applause himself, but we all had to know the music well enough to be prepared to "attack" at the proper moment—not so soon as to "step on" the singer's last note and not so late that the conductor would be forced to stop before continuing. Almost all the standees were older than me. Many were students in their late teens and early twenties, but there were also a good number of middle-aged people and even a few gray-haired veterans of the operatic wars.

The opera played ten months of the year with performances every night except Christmas Eve. The active repertoire consisted of approximately sixty operas. Since I was still attending school, I could not go more than twice a week—but even so I saw and heard a lot of performances.

I wasn't always working as a member of the claque. Sometimes I would buy my own ticket for a performance I particularly wanted to hear. I can recall booing, completely unprompted, only once. It was the first time I saw Lawrence Tibbett, whose legend had preceded him to Vienna. He seemed to be having an "off" night, and also he did not coordinate with the conductor. I was so disappointed.

On the other hand, the first time I went to *Elektra* (when I was fifteen) with Knappertsbusch conducting Rosa Pauly and a bass-baritone (a Nazi, we later found out) by the name of Alfred Jerger, whose voice and demeanor had an intensity like Norman Treigle's, I was caught off guard by the recognition scene between Orest and Elektra. At the moment when the orchestra goes berserk, I literally had to hang on to the fourth-ring railing to keep myself from jumping down into the pit to swim, to drown in that incredible sound.

It was enlightening to observe the various conductors and musical minds. We (the standees) would compare the differences in the smallest details here and there. Each of these great conductors had a style and personality all his own; there were differences in the interpretations that did not take away from the validity of what was being performed. Knappertsbusch, a favorite of the standees, was a very tall man who always sat when he conducted, but at the climax of a scene, he would stand up—this long, long figure—to emphasize the dramatic moment. His orchestra loved him, and perhaps appreciated his attitude about rehearsals. After a few minutes of rehearsing, he would stop and say, "Gentlemen. You know this music. I know this music. I'll see you tomorrow night." And the performance would be, more often than not, an inspired spontaneity. He had a well-honed sense of humor. Once a student asked him why he always used a score when the other maestros did not—and Knappertsbusch laconically responded, "I can read music." One day his students got hold of his score, eager to see what markings (what secrets!) he had written there. There was nothing written at all.

Not all conductors were of the caliber of Knappertsbusch or Bruno Walter. House conductors like Alwin and Reichenberger were perhaps not earth-shaking, but were nonetheless efficient and helpful to the singers—*routinier* in the best sense of the word.

Mahler was appointed director in 1897, three decades after the beautiful neo-Romantic-style opera house first opened. Gustav Mahler's engagement marked the beginning of a radical modernization at the Staatsoper. Prior to this time, the lights in the auditorium had always been left on during the performance. (The house was lit with candles and torches, and later on with gas, long before electricity came into the picture.) Mahler, the first conductor to have the luxury of electric lights, insisted that the auditorium be dark so that the lighting effects onstage could be perceived and appreciated.

Although Mahler's reign at the Staatsoper ended in 1907, a few of his productions still remained in the active repertoire at the time I was regularly attending opera in the 1930s. I particularly recall *Tristan und Isolde* (from 1903) and *Don Giovanni* (from 1905). The *Tristan* production was just about perfect in every way. The designer was Alfred Roller, who had apparently made such exquisite drawings that the design of *Tristan* was artwork in itself—realistic and romantic. There was one face to the whole thing; it fit together.

Don Giovanni had been given a rather austere production that was a model of simplicity. Roller's sets consisted of two gray towers—one on stage right and the other on stage left, each of which had a mid-section that opened into a balcony (and also allowed for the opening of windows and doors). It was all very flexible and moved quickly from scene to scene, thus eliminating the long waits that are the curse of so many *Don Giovanni* productions. (So often the opera has an aria that lasts five minutes, and then you have to wait five more minutes for the next scene. The exquisite Eugene Berman production at the Metropolitan Opera in the 1950s suffered from these long scene changes that sometimes took more time than the scenes themselves.)

In the early and mid-1930s, Gustav Mahler's influence still could be felt in the music I heard at the Staatsoper. Mahler had forbidden all vocal ornamentations in Mozart—not even the most natural and basic appoggiaturas were allowed. More astonishing still was the fact that Mahler had apparently never come to terms with the actual ending of *Don Giovanni* and he took it upon himself to cut it—totally eliminating the final scene of the opera, the sextet in which the survivors point up the "moral" of the story. (This one time the genius Mahler did not understand the genius Mozart.) After the Don's demise the curtain simply fell. This defiance of Mozart's and Da Ponte's wishes was still being practiced more than two and a half decades after Mahler's death. As a matter of fact, I never heard that last scene of *Don Giovanni* until I came to New York and saw the Metropolitan Opera production with Pinza and Rethberg.

Actually, thirty-year-old productions (scenery and costumes) are not all that unusual in the international opera world. In the early 1990s I conducted a series of *Bohème* performances in Copenhagen. The sets dated from 1920, and when discreetly and properly lighted, they still looked acceptably romantic. Of course in an opera like *La bohème*, shabbiness can be a virtue.

I have returned to the Vienna Staatsoper several times over the years, most recently in 2005, to conduct *Tosca*. That production, by Margherita Wallmann, was having its five-hundredth performance that very evening. Singers come and go, and they're integrated into this highly workable production that was originally staged in the 1950s—and the sets are still usable, even after five hundred performances. There is a continuity about it that speaks to the tradition. The performers are incorporated into the overall pattern—given their entrances, exits, and so on—and each person's individuality quickly becomes apparent and is encouraged. (Callas would have performed Tosca differently than Tebaldi, just as Pavarotti would have done Cavaradossi differently than Domingo.) Generally the artists are expected to be so sure of what their role demands that there is no interpretive upheaval. Very infrequently a guest star will insist on doing a bit of "business" his or her own way—in which case the assistant in charge will try to make the necessary adjustments.

Mahler was born a Jew but converted to Catholicism in order to become director of the Staatsoper. The anti-Semitism he personally faced in 1900 may not have been as blatant as it would later become, in the days leading up to World War II, yet he still encountered anti-Jewish sentiment in every nook and cranny of the Staatsoper. A colleague once told me of an incident where Mahler needed to speak to the chorus master. The chorus master was summoned to Mahler's chambers by a man who uttered, "The Jew wants you!" There were many tales of how demanding Mahler was and how hard he was on everybody—including himself. I don't think I ever consciously said, "I want to be like Mahler," but I knew his way was the right way to go.

Though I was too young to have crossed paths with my idol, I did meet his fascinating widow toward the end of her life. In fall 1962, when we were preparing our first production of Charpentier's romantic *Louise* at New York City Opera (with Arlene Saunders, John Alexander, Norman Treigle, and Claramae Turner), Alma Mahler telephoned me and asked if she could attend the dress rehearsal. Jean Morel was conducting, so I was free to sit with her. She let me know about the time when her husband was putting *Louise* into the repertory of the Vienna State Opera and he'd invited the composer to be present for the final rehearsals. Then she regaled me with tales of Mr. Charpentier's obvious infatuation with her.

In Austria the public schools were set up in such a way that everybody, beginning at age six, had to go through the first four years of school together. The next four years were spent in middle school. After that, those who would become workmen and laborers went to vocational school and were apprenticed at the end of that time, and those who intended to pursue a higher intellectual calling continued at *gymnasium* (in German the word is pronounced with a soft *g* and a long *a*, and denotes a college preparatory high school).

There were nine Jewish boys and twenty Christian boys in my class. There was religious instruction in Austria, so once a week we were separated from the boys of the Catholic and Evangelic faiths and assigned to a Jewish professor who taught us about our religious heritage. Outside of school we had virtually no contact with kids of other religions. We stuck together, and they stuck together. Once a year there was an excursion day for the whole school. On one of those class trips, the Christian kids ganged up on us on the train coming back, and started to beat us. Luckily one of the compartments on the train had a door with a lock, so we took refuge there. This happened in 1934, when I was thirteen. At that time we also began hearing reports about Jewish university students being beaten up.

I was a below-average student and could not have cared less about my studies at the gymnasium. What with my miniature theater and my composing and my piano lessons, I really had no time left for schoolwork. I constantly begged my parents to let me drop out of school so I could devote myself to the music academy during the day while continuing my nighttime education at the Staatsoper, of course. Finally my parents agreed, and I left the gymnasium after my third year there, in the spring of 1937. I immediately enrolled in additional classes at the academy, where I worked with Professor Lafitte in the piano accompanying classes and with Professor Stöhr, chairman of the theory department.

The only thing my parents insisted on was that I learn another profession as a "fallback." Finally we settled on leather crafting. I hated it because I was not good at it. I always got glue on my fingers, and in all the time I was at the leather working school I made only one acceptable little elementary *porte-monnaie* which no one would buy from me—so I kept it for myself.

By 1937 horrendous things were beginning to happen all over Europe, and our comfortable sheltered existence was over. My father was out of work— the world economic crisis and political intrigue in Austria led to the Phoenix Insurance Company's takeover by a Government-controlled company and the dismissal of all the Jewish employees including my father—and my parents were talking about emigrating to the United States. By this time my mother's family had moved to New York City. Two of her sisters were already living there, as were her brother and her father (after my grandmother Feige died in 1935, my grandfather Josef moved to the States and found a position as a cantor at a small orthodox synagogue at 89 Legion Street in Brooklyn, where he lived in a room at the back). So there was a "reception committee" ready to welcome us. We began to get our paperwork (visas, immigration papers, exit permits, etc.) in order. We had affidavits from families and friends in the States. Everyone was required to take a medical exam at the American embassy. My father, who had lost a lot of weight and did not look well, did not pass the exam; he was already ill with pancreatic cancer. Once my father was declared unacceptable, we gave up all our plans.

My father died on December 27, 1937. We were devastated, and in those first few months after his death, my mother couldn't even think of moving. But on March 13, 1938, the day after Austria was annexed by Germany, she hurried to the US consulate and reactivated our application. Now there was no cause for refusal, but we were put on waiting lists. Each prospective departee received a number according to a quota. Because I was born in Vienna, I had no problem. But my mother, who was born in Rumania, had to wait several months before her quota number came up. Since young Jewish men were especially at risk to be arrested or shipped away, she was anxious to get me out of Vienna as quickly as possible. My emigration visa came through, effective June 1, 1938, and she was determined to have me on a ship bound for America the very next day.

Since I spoke not a word of English my mother had enrolled me in late March in an adult English course at night school. The instructor utilized a rather unorthodox teaching method; instead of receiving grammar lessons, we were taught common English aphorisms, beginning with "All that glitters is not gold." (Even today I don't know exactly what that means!) After a few weeks of learning phrases like "Time flies"and "Don't cry over spilt milk," I stopped going to night school.

My train left Vienna late in the afternoon of May 25 and traveled all night to Paris. This was my first trip alone. As the train rolled out of the station I was emotionally numb. My mother had told me not to speak to anyone until I was safely across the border into Switzerland. Since we weren't allowed to take more than a small amount of currency out of the country ($17, and you needed a permit for that), my mother had bought a watch and a ring for me to sell if I needed money in an emergency.

I loved trains, and the first leg of the route west, from Vienna to Salzburg, was familiar to me from our many summer vacations. I had never been west of Salzburg, though, and the countryside after that was completely new to me. That first night, I stayed awake all night because I was too nervous to sleep. As the hours passed, I kept looking at the pocket watch. All I could think about was getting out of Austria and crossing the border into Switzerland. We reached the border early the next morning, May 26. I had an exit visa but was unable to relax until I safely got through passport control. I knew my papers were in order, but I had heard of willful acts by border guards. The process took a few minutes, but it seemed like hours before the uniformed officers stamped my passport. Once I was cleared—and before the train started again—I sent a telegram to my mother to let her know I was safe and out of Austria. I learned afterward that the telegram I sent was transmitted from the Austrian side of the border, so Mother wasn't certain if I'd actually made it out of the country. Totally unaware of how nervous I'd made her, I climbed back onto the train and watched the spectacular scenery unfurling as we crossed the Alps en route to Paris.

I arrived in Paris around six that night. Some distant relatives of my mother—the Patins—were waiting for me at the train station and welcomed me to the French capital. The first thing they had me do was send a new telegram to my frantic mother, assuring her that I'd arrived safely. The Patins' flat was too small for me to stay in, so they had booked me a room at a little hotel around the corner from their place. The Patins were very kind to me and showed me the sights of Paris during my four-day layover.

Paris was a breathless adventure after Vienna. I could not help comparing the seemingly carefree spirit of Paris with the mood of despair in Vienna. I tried to pick up one of the many pretty girls I saw as I walked through the streets of this romantic city—I was, after all, a seventeen-year-old with raging hormones—but I quickly discovered my French wasn't good enough.

I remember admiring the perfectly matched buildings that lined the wide, elegant boulevards. Not surprisingly, my favorite view was the one from the Louvre Hotel straight to the Opera House (where, thirty-five years later, I would step into the orchestra pit without any rehearsal to conduct a performance of *Il trovatore*).

On my last night in Paris, I moved to a room in a better hotel; it was included with my prepaid boat fare. The next morning, with other passengers bound for the Queen Mary, I boarded a special boat-train headed for Cherbourg, our port of embarkation. When we got there, the water was too rough for us to board the ocean liner that was waiting offshore, so we had to stay on a little boat overnight in the harbor. The following morning, June 1, we finally boarded the giant ocean liner. As I climbed the long ramp to the huge ship, I nervously kept reaching in my pocket for my third-class ticket. My cabin turned out to be a small, windowless, interior room with four berths. The boat wasn't sold out, so the other berths in my room were empty. I was as close to steerage as anyone could be on the Queen Mary, yet at least I had my own living quarters with a private bathroom.

As the boat gathered speed for the United States, I watched the Continent fade into the distance. Everything at that point indicated that Hitler would conquer all of Europe. I missed my father and I had no idea when (or, though I dared not think it, *if*) I would be reunited with Mother and Brother. I thought I would never again set foot in Vienna or Salzburg. What was ahead for me in America?

Fortunately, seventeen-year-old boys are incredibly resilient. After a few hours, a sense of adventure came over me, and I began to envision the new life that awaited me in New York. No matter that I was in third class, I was a passenger on a luxury liner! The first night on board, I gorged myself on the delicious food. I'll never forget the look the waiters gave each other as I ate course after course. They knew of the rough seas ahead. I'd never been on a boat before, and the rocking motion gave me a giant case of mal de mer. I spent the next two days of the voyage throwing up. When I recovered, I passed the time during the rest of the trip with a Jewish former schoolmate named Hirschberg who, like me, was being sent by his parents to the safety of the United States. I was overjoyed to find a familiar face—and a fellow opera lover, to boot—on board. To pass the time, we played a game of "name that tune": one of us would hum a melody and the other would identify which opera it came from.

In retrospect, my trip to the US was fairly easy and incident-free. Things were more difficult for my mother and Lud, whose US visas were to be issued on October 1. Once I had left, my gutsy mother packed some furniture and managed to secure an export permit for our household effects by "innocently" standing in the line for non-Jews (as if she didn't know that's what it was). She then somehow contrived a way to get exit visas to Italy for herself and Lud, and they traveled there in late June 1938. The border crossing went without a hitch. Though Jews without an exit visa where not allowed to depart Austria, my mother did not look Jewish and was not stopped by the Austrians. Once she arrived in Italy, however, she was not prepared to lie to the Italian immigration officer who checked her passport and asked if she was Jewish. "Yes," she replied, and though the officer was very apologetic, he told her that just that morning the German government had ordered them to no longer allow Jews to enter Italy. They took Lud and Mother off the train at the next stop, and put them and their baggage on the next train returning to Austria. Fortunately it was not a through train, and it stopped at the border, where they had to get off and wait for the *next* through train which was due to arrive in four hours.

My mother and brother pleaded and cried, knowing what awaited them if they returned to Austria. Mother threatened to kill herself if she was made to go back. Remarkably, she finally persuaded the customs officer to let her and Lud "pass through Italy" and go directly to France, if they promised to remain on the train. This time, my mother lied, dutifully promising not to get off in Italy.

But Mother and Lud did get off the train in Italy, and checked into a sanatorium in the coastal town of Abbazia, where they hid illegally for six weeks. It was a trying time for both of them, with Lud many years later describing himself as "a pain in the ass, basically, at eight." Close to the end of their stay, Lud—with more than a touch of cabin fever—was allowed to wander down to the lobby, where he met a nice young lad who spoke German. They got along so well that the boy invited Lud and Mother to go for a ride with his father. Lud persuaded Mother to accept the invitation ("Come on, *please!* I want to go out! He's such a nice boy!"). They went downstairs, only to see the boy and his father standing next to a Nazi staff car with a large swastika on it. Mother said, "You go and tell them that I'm sick. I can't go and you can't go either, and come back upstairs." Lud was not scared; he was just angry at being cooped up in that room in the sanatorium. Yet all these years later, he still marvels at the ingenuity Mother displayed during that dangerous time when, as he says, "One false move by her would have ended it for both of us."

My mother then concocted another scheme: she donned her best clothes and jewelry and went to Naples and got the Swiss consul there to help her and her "ailing son, who had just recovered from whooping cough," obtain a visa allowing them to go to a "suitable mountain town in Switzerland" where he could recover. (My mother could be most persuasive when she needed to be.) Once they arrived safely in Switzerland, my mother arranged with the US consulate to issue the visas to them in Zurich, and on October 1 they were free to board the *Île de France*, which arrived in New York on October 8, 1938. It was a joyous time when the three of us were reunited. After so many months of waiting, at last we were a family again. We rented a small apartment—the first of a series of apartments we were to have in the Bronx, near my mother's sisters.

Much to Mother's consternation, I was working as a grocery clerk when she and Lud arrived in New York. But I was also searching like mad for a school where I could continue my music studies. The first school I applied to was the Henry Street Music School, where Aaron Copland was head of the teaching staff. I submitted some of my compositions and was offered a scholarship. I also auditioned for Juilliard but didn't get in. At that time (when my mother and brother were not yet safely out of Europe) I was really in no condition to impress anyone with my piano playing.

One day three of my former classmates from Vienna—fellow émigrés—appeared, having tracked me down. One of them suggested, "Why don't you go to the Refugee Service? They will be able to help you." He gave me the address, 1560 Broadway, in the middle of Times Square, and there I went. Mark Brunswick, the composer in charge of the division for professional musicians, took a personal interest in me and arranged for me to take classes at the Greenwich House Music School, where he taught. He also gave me private lessons at his home. At Greenwich House I studied with a Mrs. Solomon, the head of the piano faculty.

To help us survive in the early months when we settled here, my mother, ever industrious, made and sold leather wallets and key holders (she had taken the course in Vienna with me). Where I failed miserably, she succeeded brilliantly. A skillful seamstress, she also worked at a corset factory and in other garment shops.

In the summer of 1939 my mother, who was having trouble providing for my brother, put Lud in the Jewish Children's Home in Newark and went to California to stay with friends and look for a husband—quite frankly, she was still young-looking and attractive. My mother did not find a husband in California, but when she returned to New York she married her boss, Joe Rappaport, the owner of a small ladies garment factory in Manhattan. Lud—after spending more than a year in the orphanage—moved in with my mother and Joe, who lived in a nice neighborhood in Brooklyn. The marriage lasted only a few years and ended in divorce.

I had many odd jobs in my first few years here. On the recommendation of Mark Brunswick, the Refugee Service arranged a job for me as a stock clerk within that organization. (Later, I worked as a switchboard operator in their Brooklyn offices.) I also worked the night shift in the railroad yards on Thirty-Fourth Street, loading freight trains. In the dead of winter I worked as a delivery boy for a drugstore on the Upper West Side (on Broadway and Eightieth, where Zabar's is today), from six p.m. until midnight. Have you ever experienced Riverside Drive in a winter gale? I don't think I stayed there for more than three or four months, but they were the coldest months I ever spent.

I also toiled for a very short time in a button factory in Newark, New Jersey. I spent a nickel each way on the subway going down to the Path train and a nickel each way on the Path to Newark. I got paid a dollar for the day, so I came out with 80¢ net profit. My job was to carry the heavy cast-iron containers with the buttons to the oven. The paint from the buttons would come off on my hands, and I had to use lye to wash them at the end of the workday. That job lasted no more than a few days—and almost ruined my hands.

I didn't have much leisure time my first two years here. When the 1939 World's Fair opened in April, some of my friends went to visit it several times, but (because of my music studies and multiple odd jobs) I attended the Fair just once, with a relative, on a very superficial "walk-through." Occasionally I went to the movies. Fred Astaire had an easy charm and elegance that I found instantly appealing, and I also remember seeing a film with the opera singer Maria Cebotari, in which she sang "Caro Nome" from *Rigoletto*. "Ah, God, I don't know what I would give if I could only conduct this music just once," I dreamt.

Conducting began to interest me more and more—and, conversely, composing interested me less and less. When it became clear in my own mind that I wanted to be a conductor, Mark Brunswick arranged a scholarship for me at the Mannes School of Music to study conducting with Carl Bamberger—another European refugee, who became my first and only conducting teacher. I also studied theory with Felix Saltzer, who taught me the "Schenker method," which offered fresh approaches to studying and interpreting music.

In those days the Mannes School (today known as Mannes College) was located in a beautiful townhouse on East Seventy-Fourth Street. It had been cofounded in 1916 by husband and wife David Mannes and Clara Damrosch Mannes—both outstanding musicians and educators. Mannes, which over the years has trained many noted musicians (including Frederica von Stade, Murray Perahia, and Richard Goode), was a godsend—smaller and more personal than Juilliard—and David and Clara were quite supportive, keeping me on scholarship during my two years there.

As part of the terms of my scholarship, I played piano for the pupils of the school's vocal teacher, Olga Eisner. They would have something prepared and we would work on it in Madame Eisner's presence. She was an inspiring teacher, and it was exciting for me. What better way to learn the repertory than by playing it? On the other hand, I hated *teaching* piano. I took on a few piano students to make some extra money during those first years in New York. One of them lived in Sheepshead Bay. It took me an hour and half to get there from my apartment in the Bronx and an hour and a half to get home. The $2 fee minus *double* round trip subway fare (the BMT and IRT were separate subway lines—requiring separate fares) really wasn't worth it.

It was at Mannes that I conducted an orchestra for the first time—the student orchestra in the school's lovely little auditorium. The two works on the program were the Mozart Symphonie Concertante and the Pergolesi *Stabat Mater*. The second I raised my baton to begin the concert I knew where my future lay, but I had not been so serene earlier in the day. My charming future wife, Rita, who was studying piano at the school, was with me on the subway ride to the auditorium, and, not understanding that I needed quiet in order to prepare for my debut, she tried to entertain me with her lively conversation. The more she talked, the more nervous I felt. Finally I enlightened her on my need for quiet.

Thanks to a recommendation by David and Clara Mannes, in April 1942 I had the unique opportunity to work with one of my idols, Robert Stolz—a popular Viennese composer and conductor of operettas and musicals who achieved world fame with his 1930 movie musical *Two Hearts in $\frac{3}{4}$ Time*. Stolz, although he was not Jewish (he had immigrated to the states for political reasons), was living in New York at the time and assembled a marvelous group of singers—German and Austrian exiles (including Ralph Herbert and Margit Bokor) from the Berlin and Vienna opera houses—to perform *Die Fledermaus* at the Pythian Temple auditorium on the Upper West Side. Stolz was to conduct, and the Manneses recommended that I serve as his assistant. I played the piano for rehearsals and was the chorus master as well.

The position did not pay, but the Hungarian entrepreneur who put together the production allowed me to be one of the onstage choristers, which paid $5 per performance (out of which I had to pay $2 a day for the rental of a tuxedo). They scheduled three performances, which quickly sold out. Another six performances were added, and the house was filled for those as well. It was "old home week" for many of us onstage and in the audience.

Robert Stolz had as a youngster played in one of Johann Strauss's own orchestras in Vienna. It was Stolz who taught me the secrets of Viennese music—those freedoms that allow you to pull back the reins a bit and then push ahead to catch up, and vice versa.

He also played a role in my career a few years later, in 1953, when I was first invited to conduct a Lewisohn Stadium concert of Viennese music in place of Stolz—who was detained in Europe for nonpayment of alimony. (The much-married Stolz, it should be noted, finally found "happily-ever-after" contentment with his fifth wife, Einzi.) The soloists for that concert were Jarmila Novotna and Charles Kullman—two of the artists whom I had so much admired and applauded from the fourth gallery in Vienna. From then on, the Viennese Concerts at Lewisohn Stadium were assigned to me.

By 1941, I had fallen madly in love with the young woman named Rita Gillis. I had met her the previous year. Early one Friday evening I was standing near the school entrance when she walked up the steps, went into one of the rooms, and started to play the piano. I followed her in and pretended to be on the school staff, asking, "Why are you here? Do you have permission?" She replied that she had arrived early for a lesson and decided to practice for a bit. I must admit I came on pretty strong. The upshot: we made a date for the following Tuesday. I had two student tickets to a concert by the pianist Robert Goldsand in Town Hall, and we met there. The concert was lovely, and when it ended we started to walk uptown. It turned out she lived in the Bronx, too. It was a warm spring night; we walked and talked nonstop all the way up to 110th Street, through Central Park, before we finally boarded the subway. We never stopped talking for the next forty-four years.

Rita, who was extremely bright and funny, had graduated from high school at fifteen and wanted desperately to continue her education. When we met, she was working as a secretary-stenographer while attending night school at City College. She was an excellent writer (the last composition I wrote was a song set to a poem by Rita called "The Shroud") with an avid interest in psychology. In 1949 she earned a masters degree in psychology from The New School—subsequently getting a PhD and teaching at MIT before becoming the Director of the Neuropsychology Department at New York's Presbyterian Hospital.

Her parents were Russian Jews—her father was from Lithuania, her mother from Georgia. Her father, Joseph, had a fine sense of humor and had studied to be a rabbi in the old country. In New York he was a garment worker and was very much involved in the formation of the International Ladies Garment Workers Union. Her mother, Rose, according to old photographs, had been a beautiful girl. She was a strong-willed matriarch who demanded respect. Interestingly, she claimed to be illiterate and supposedly could not even write her name in English. (I suspected she was pretending not to be able to read, because she was a very bright woman.) And she was always arguing and fighting with people—a very Dostoevskian trait. One day she again had an argument with her cousins. Afterward she said to her husband, "Joe, when I die, I don't want them at my funeral." Without missing a beat, he replied, "I tell you what: if they come, don't talk to them."

The first time I was introduced to Rita's mother, she took one look at me, turned on the stove, and made me sit down and eat a steak. She liked to feed me, because she saw me as this poor little refugee kid. Both of Rita's parents were very compassionate—until they found out that I wanted to marry Rita. From that moment on, I was persona non grata.

Rita and her oldest brother Ivan loved classical music. In those days, the *New York Post* had coupons that you could cut out of the paper and redeem for classical music recordings. These albums were actually first-class performances previously released on major labels (including NBC Orchestra recordings conducted by Toscanini), but on these special giveaway pressings the performers were never listed. When Rita had built up a respectable library of classical recordings, she decided she would learn to play the piano. And though she never got very far, she had an incredible sense of music and was quite a perceptive critic. Rita always had the radio turned on to classical music—WQXR, WNYC—when she was studying or cooking, which she loved to do. (She was a fantastic cook, totally self-taught and very inventive.)

We were married on June 24, 1942, in a small shul on the Grand Concourse. More than fifty people attended—mainly family, with a few of our close friends—and the music was provided by my conducting teacher, Carl Bamberger, who played a wheezy little harmonium. Rita came late to the wedding because her brother Milton had tried to persuade her to call off the wedding by offering to send her on a cruise. Her father, ever the comedian, remarked that if I played the violin, I could at least perform in courtyards. But a pianist who wanted to be a conductor? *Feh.*

My mother also had grander plans for her firstborn son—I was supposed to marry Jewish royalty, not a secretary. Although Rita's wonderful qualities were apparent to everyone else right from the start, it took many years for my mother to become fond of her.

In those first days of my marriage I was certainly not the provider, though I picked up whatever gigs I could find. I conducted the Parkchester Symphony—a semiprofessional orchestra—and gave coaching lessons for a dollar an hour. (I had to go to small claims court when one of the singers didn't pay up.) At one point I even changed my name to "Rudolfo di Giulio" for a small opera company run by Josephine La Puma. A trained singer herself, she offered the services of an opera company to any singer who wanted to coach and perform a role. The La Puma troupe was a vanity operation, and many people had to pay to perform there. But Mrs. La Puma gave me $2 each time I conducted. She asked me to take on singers who were particularly difficult to handle—those who had no business singing and were in desperate need of coaching. As the "star" conductor, I learned a lot of the standard Italian repertory there (along with other staples including *Hansel and Gretel*, which I first conducted for La Puma in 1940 and returned to several times over the years, most recently for Palm Beach Opera in 2003). All in all, working with Mrs. La Puma was a good educational experience for me.

After the attack on Pearl Harbor I was deferred from the military because of my mother and my brother—I was considered the male head of the household and the chief breadwinner.

At the end of May 1942 I was awarded my conducting diploma from Mannes, a month before my wedding. In the summer of '42 I was newly married and penniless. The United States had entered World War II, and New York's colorful mayor, Fiorello La Guardia, was a few months away from making an announcement that would revolutionize the New York cultural scene.

2

"THE PEOPLE'S OPERA" TAKES FLIGHT

The Early Years of New York City Opera

Hanging in my library, on a wall covered with mementos, is the very first flyer of New York City Opera, announcing one week of eight performances in February 1944, with tickets priced from $0.85 to $2.25. At the very bottom, last and most definitely least, I am listed as "*correpetiteur,*" in this instance a euphemism for "jack-of-all-things-no-one-else-wanted-to-do."

I had played the piano for free for a very long "trial period"—three months of auditions and rehearsals prior to that first week of performances. Like so many idealistic enterprises, this one was made up of often contradictory elements: lofty ideals and harsh pragmatism, penny-pinching in the production of the most expensive of all art forms, and the development and presentation of budding talent.

My path to the company that would be my home for the next thirty-five years began at the end of September 1943, when I noticed an item in the morning paper about the formation of the City Center of Music and Drama, scheduled to open in November in the former Mecca Temple at 133 West Fifty-Fifth Street. The Ancient Arabic Order of the Nobles of the Mystic Shrine, better known as "the Shriners," had built their Byzantine sanctuary in 1924, but a decade later began falling behind in paying their property taxes. The City of New York acquired the building in 1942 by an act of foreclosure and was converting it into another type of temple—one for the performing arts. Concerts, plays and ballets would be presented at popular prices in the almost three-thousand-seat auditorium. The project was the brainchild of City Council President Newbold Morris and councilman Morton Baum, a brilliant tax lawyer who won national acclaim in 1934 for devising New York City's first sales tax, which brought sorely needed revenue to the town during the Depression. City Center had the passionate backing of Mayor Fiorello La Guardia and the sponsorship of many of the movers and shakers in the arts (including the dramatist Elmer Rice, the actress Lillian Gish, and arts patrons extraordinaire Mrs. Lytle Hull and Gerald F. Warburg) and leaders of organized labor (including William Feinberg of

Musicians Local 802 and Jacob Potofsky, president of the local Amalgamated Clothing Workers).

This galvanized me. I had to investigate. I was twenty-two years old, a newly married refugee armed with only my conducting diploma from the Mannes School of Music and an intuition that a new cultural enterprise, in a city where the mayor had an Italian name, surely had to include some opera.

I put on my best suit and tie and took the subway to the dome-topped temple on West Fifty-Fifth Street. Arriving at my destination, I saw a rather derelict building that clearly hadn't been used for a while. I boldly walked in through the front doors and roamed around. As luck would have it, I found a door slightly ajar and entered. It was the auditorium. I went to the stage. There was a single bulb hanging down—the "ghost light." Suddenly there stood before me a formidable man—George Glasten, the building super-intendent. He was about to throw me out. I told him I was a conductor and would like to offer my services. "Go to the seventh floor. Mr. Friedgut will talk to you," he said. I took the elevator up and met Harry Friedgut, the recently appointed managing director of City Center, who asked me numerous questions about my background. He told me that they were indeed going to have an opera company at City Center and that they already had engaged a director by the name of Laszlo Halasz. It was arranged that I would meet Halasz at his apartment in the Osborne, which in those days was a particularly elegant and desirable address, a few short blocks from City Center on West Fifty-Seventh Street, catty-corner to Carnegie Hall.

The maid answered the door and took me to his study, where I couldn't help noticing a life-size oil painting of a conductor (in full tails and about to give a downbeat) hanging on the wall next to the piano. I wasn't quite sure who it was. A moment later Halasz came into the room—and I immediately saw the likeness. He's certainly not lacking in self-esteem, I thought to myself.

I played something for him on the piano, and he said, "Well, you seem to have talent, but I need to know more about your knowledge of repertory. Tomorrow afternoon I'm holding auditions. Why don't you come and play for the singers? That will give me an idea of what you know, and whether you are professional enough to be engaged." The next day I went to one of the rehearsal rooms at City Center, and for three hours played for the fifty or so singers who showed up. A few brought their own accompanists, but most couldn't afford such a luxury; so I was able to show off my accompa-nying skills quite a bit. At the end of the session, Halasz said to me, "It was not bad, but I'm not quite convinced yet. On Monday there's another set of auditions. Come and play again so I can get a better idea of your skills." I returned the following Monday, and for several weeks after that, as Halasz kept telling me he had not yet made up his mind. Each time, I tried to ask him, "How am I doing?" but he was always too busy to talk to me. This was a sample of New York City Opera policy: Try to get it for free.

Halasz kept me on the string for more than two months. He even added tasks such as counting the chorus books to make sure we had enough chorus parts, and other similar chores. Finally, a few days before Christmas, I took courage in hand and cornered him. He said, "I don't think you're ready to be the assistant conductor, but you will be the repetiteur." Oh, joy! I was accepted! I would be paid $50 a week. I gave up my few remaining coaching sessions, and looked forward to getting my first paycheck the following week, but I got nothing. The week after that, much to my chagrin and my increasing anxiety, there was again no check. At first I was too cowed to say anything, but after the holidays I asked, "What's happening with my contract?" Halasz replied, "You know, I'm not totally satisfied with you, and Mr. Friedgut really thought we should dismiss you. But I can't do that to another young musician. Your good name is as important to you as my good name is to me. So I will let you continue, but I will have to bring in someone else and your salary will have to be adjusted." (What salary? I thought to myself.) That "someone else" turned out to be Wolfgang Martin, who had been a staff conductor at the Vienna Staatsoper. I subsequently learned that Mr. Friedgut knew nothing about this matter. It was the first of many lies.

Still, in spite of the fact that the position was not quite what I had hoped for and I had not yet received a cent for my weeks of work, I was ecstatic to have any position. I was part of the boldest new arts enterprise in town; my name was printed in teeny typeface on the handbill. (Words cannot describe the pride and joy I felt seeing my name on that flyer.) I was young and eager and willing to put up with almost anything that came my way. As for the occasional misgivings I was beginning to have about Halasz, I pushed them to the back of my mind. He was my boss, and I would work my hardest to prove to him how valuable I was.

Born in Hungary in 1905, Halasz had begun his career as an assistant conductor to George Szell and then as an assistant to Arturo Toscanini and Bruno Walter at the Salzburg Festival. When Toscanini moved to New York in 1936 to conduct the NBC Symphony, he brought along Halasz as his assistant. It was Toscanini who recommended him to the Grand Opera of St. Louis, where Halasz was appointed chorus master in 1937 and artistic director two years later. When the St. Louis company closed during World War II, Halasz inherited the company's scenery and costumes, a "dowry" that made him quite appealing to the City Center board members. He came to the attention of Jean Dalrymple, the director of publicity and public relations for City Center. Her client Grace Moore had sung Tosca in St. Louis, and Jean had been impressed with both Halasz's conducting and the production itself, which she pronounced "first-rate." La Guardia, who respected Jean's opinions, was so determined that City Center should have an "opera for the people" that he made the initial phone call to St. Louis to secure Halasz along with the company's sets and costumes.

Halasz was quite handsome, smart, and cunning, but would habitually trip himself up because of his seeming generosity with the truth. He also had a quick temper. I spent a lot of time smoothing over offenses he had committed and placating the singers, designers, stage directors, and others who had been the targets of his erratic behavior. Yet in those first few months of rehearsals, we saw only occasional glimpses of Halasz's temper. For the most part, we were a large, extended family working hard to put on operas that would dazzle New Yorkers who couldn't afford to go to the Metropolitan Opera.

The official opening of the center took place on December 11, 1943— Mayor La Guardia's birthday. It was a concert by the New York Philharmonic, conducted by Artur Rodzinski. Lawrence Tibett was the soloist, and the program ended with Gershwin's *An American in Paris*, which brought the cheering crowd to its feet. Or so I heard from the announcer on the radio; I was home with a high fever, listening to the concert on WNYC.

Two days later, City Center presented its first dramatic offering when Gertrude Lawrence starred in a revival of the Broadway hit *Susan and God* by Rachel Crothers. The play, which ran for five days, was fairly well received yet did not play to capacity houses, even with Lawrence's "star power." (I had seen her a few years before in *Lady in the Dark* and thought she was a most beguiling performer.) For *Susan and God* and at every subsequent City Center event over the next year and a half, free tickets were made available to members of the armed forces. Many of them came from small American towns and were seeing their first play, concert, or opera. They were among our most enthusiastic audience members. (It's a cruel irony that for some of them, en route to Europe, it was also the last theatrical experience of their lives.)

After the New Year, we began opera rehearsals in earnest, working under less than optimal conditions in one of the cramped rehearsal rooms in the basement or on the fifth floor of City Center. I shared rehearsal-pianist duties with assistant conductor James Sample (son-in-law of the famous French conductor Pierre Monteux). We had numerous vocal rehearsals but minimal full-company rehearsals because of their prohibitive cost (another indication of things to come). The orchestra is one of the most expensive parts of an opera company. I remember watching a performance of the Stivanello Opera Company at the Brooklyn Academy in the early 1940s. Before the second act Stivanello himself stepped before the curtain, looking every bit the old-school Italian maestro with a big hat and a gigantic bow-tie as he harangued the half-empty auditorium: "You see, today I have a trombone. If you don't come, we won't have him the next time!"

In those early days of City Opera, the orchestra was remarkably solid in spite of the shortage of rehearsals. This was largely due to the fact that our orchestra manager was Joseph Fabbroni, who was also the contractor for the RCA Victor Record Company. He had a pool of excellent musicians at his disposal—and shrewdly used his RCA position (and the enticement of future recording opportunities) to lure first-class players to City Opera.

Counting on the superiority of our musicians, we developed a formula for the budget for orchestra rehearsals. If a production was new, then naturally there had to be adequate rehearsal time. If a piece hadn't been done for a season or more we would usually have one run-through with the orchestra—but if it had been in the repertory the season before, there simply was no orchestra rehearsal.

Our chorus was made up of fifty young freelance singers. Their leader, Irving Landau, had been the conductor of the Radio City Music Hall Glee Club and worked admirably to create a unified, flexible sound. Regrettably he left the company a few months later, one of the earliest casualties of Halasz's reign. Others on the staff left in anger and disgust, but I doggedly stayed on and on. This was "do or die" for me. I couldn't dream of leaving this opportunity.

Halasz was not an easy man to work for. His modus operandi could be demoralizing and damaging to young artists' self-esteem. It was not uncommon for him to humiliate company members and to pit singers against each other. In a rehearsal for *The Gypsy Baron* in October 1944, Polyna Stoska, who was making her company debut as Saffi, had some rather interesting ideas about how she wanted to interpret the role. Halasz refused to listen to what she had to say and rudely barked, "If you don't want to do it my way, Brenda is sitting here. She knows the part." Brenda was Brenda Lewis, who had played Saffi in our road tour of *Gypsy Baron* and later became one of our company's leading sopranos. Brenda would have no part of the maestro's baiting and quietly walked out of the room. (The road tour had been under the auspices of the famous impresario Sol Hurok. We rehearsed the road company first, in late August and September, opening the tour in Hartford as our "home" cast got ready for an October opening at City Center.)

He once proudly told me his philosophy, "Divide and conquer is the only way to run a company"—to which I responded that I didn't see how that advice would be particularly useful to me. Another time he said, "Julius, always play them out against each other." He was certainly good at doing that.

Looking back on it all these years later, I can't help but wonder if Halasz devised all those unpleasant management techniques in part to compensate for the fact that he was not a great conductor. His beat was not clear—the running joke among our company members was that he conducted as though wielding a soup ladle in each hand.

Halasz's strengths lay in other areas. He was a brilliant pianist and a superb vocal coach from whom I learned how to teach a singer a role from scratch, and, equally important, how to look for subtleties in a musical text. He certainly knew voices and quickly recognized talent, with one notable exception—Robert Merrill. (The young baritone auditioned for our first season. Halasz did not find him a particularly interesting performer and did not hire him.) But Halasz did have a knack for drawing up a budget and actually meeting it—no small feat in the arts world. No matter how reprehensible his behavior might have been, he still deserves much of the credit for bringing New York City Opera into being.

For that first season of eight performances (plus a special matinee for children) in seven days, we had a roster of twenty-four singers, whittled down from the nearly one thousand who had auditioned, and a budget of $30,462.73. Halasz chose a nice mixture of operas and performers so that new, young artists would sing alongside seasoned veterans like Dusolina Giannini (who performed the title role in our opening night *Tosca*), George Czaplicki (Scarpia in *Tosca* and Escamillo in *Carmen*), and Jennie Tourel (Carmen). In addition to *Tosca* and *Carmen*, the third opera of our opening season was Flotow's *Martha*, which Halasz wanted sung in English and performed in the style of a Broadway musical. The title role went to Ethel Barrymore Colt (daughter of the famous actress Ethel Barrymore), who gave a solid performance.

Regina Resnik and Martha Lipton were among the other rising young singers who performed that first season. (Regina, who was then a soprano, sang Frasquita and Micaela on alternate nights in *Carmen*. In 1958, by which time Regina was an acclaimed star and I had been promoted to general director of the company, I invited her back to sing the title role, which she did to much acclaim.)

The stage director for all three operas was Hans Wolmuth. He had worked with Halasz in St. Louis, and his stagings were solid and "correct," if not especially imaginative. Richard Rychtarik, a German émigré, had designed the first-class sets we inherited from St. Louis; he acted as City Opera's first in-house scenic designer (he was succeeded by Heinz Condell, another émigré, who stayed with us for many years) and in addition, for the first couple of seasons served as the company's technical director. (Having the same person double as technical director and designer was a cost-effective measure.) Hans Sondheimer, another German émigré and a master of stagecraft, also joined the company in 1944, initially as lighting designer and later as technical director—a position he held until 1980. Hans was a brilliant craftsman and was much loved by our performers as well as by the stagehands. He had a number of idiosyncrasies and one particularly disarming negativism. Anytime he would be asked to produce a special effect, he would say, "No, it can't be done." And then he would of course proceed to do it! There is a huge advantage to having a director who knows how to use various elements from one show for another. We had certain "neutrals" which worked in multiple operas: staircases, furniture, platforms, backdrops, tables, and chairs.

We did the same thing with costumes—thanks to the resourcefulness of our longtime costume chief Edgar Joseph—altering them slightly to serve in different operas set in the same era.

On February 21, 1944, before a packed house, Halasz gave the downbeat for *Tosca*. The first person seen by the audience was the Sacristan, played by Emile Renan (who sang all kinds of character roles—even a dog named "Fox" in *The Good Soldier Schweik* in our first American season). Mario Berini was a splendid Cavaradossi; the audience cheered his opening aria, "Recondita armonia," and was duly captivated by the villainous George Czaplicki and especially by Ms. Giannini, a striking woman with a rich voice and real Italian temperament. I had first applauded her at the Vienna Staatsoper when I was a teenager. She was the sister of composer Vittorio Giannini, whose *Taming of the Shrew* and *Servant of Two Masters*—the latter a world premiere—I would later produce at City Opera.

On opening night I was backstage, giving entrances and cues, conducting the offstage chorus and orchestra, giving pitches, and doing whatever else needed to be done. That night, it was pure trial by fire, but in the second performance of *Tosca*, it was a *lack* of fire: the guns of the firing squad failed to go off in the final scene, and poor Mr. Berini was obliged to fall down dead . . . by his own hand. At the time I was mortified. But the gun snafu was merely one of a number of embarrassing moments that have occurred during performances. (There was the time a chicken got loose onstage and ran into the orchestra pit during the first act of a New York City Opera *Manon* performance, wreaking havoc in the violin section and nipping at the women's stockings; and the time at the Met when I conducted the same opera and Renée Fleming was accompanied by the dogs.) Since New York performers were not, by law, permitted to use loaded firearms onstage in the 1940s—and by "loaded" I mean loaded with "blanks" rather than actual bullets—we had supers walk on with unloaded guns while a stagehand stood in the wings with the real McCoy. At the proper moment, when the firing squad was shooting Cavaradossi, I gave a cue to the stagehand to shoot the gun but—as luck would have it—it didn't discharge. No shot. No death. When the curtain fell I berated the stagehand for not having the gun properly prepared. He explained that it had jammed. "Look at this," he said, and of course it went off at that instant. Most of the audience was still in the house, putting on their coats, and there was a lot of good-natured applause and laughter.

Our opening week flew by and was deemed a success by the public and the press. *Time* magazine wrote that the City Opera productions of *Tosca*, *Martha*, and *Carmen* "set a new standard of quality in the popular-priced operatic field."

Even during that first week, our trio of productions was distinguished from the fare presented by the touring companies that Stivanello and others brought to town—companies that advertised "*Aida* with ten horses, two lions, and five elephants." The emphasis of those companies was on cheap spectacle. Right from the start, we put the accent on singing and dramatic values.

I enjoyed my work backstage and was soon adept at it, only occasionally impinging on someone else's territory. One night during our second season, as the conductor was starting the second act of *La bohème*, I noticed there was no stagehand to pull up the curtain. The orchestra was playing, so I instinctively ran over to the curtain and pulled it myself. I got into real hot water with the stagehands' union, which informed me in no uncertain terms that if I were to "pull that stunt" again, it would be curtains for me—I would no longer be permitted backstage.

At the end of the one-week season, I finally received my first paycheck. When I saw the amount—$50—I went to Friedgut and complained, "For all these weeks of rehearsals, $50 is not very nice." Mr. Friedgut managed to get me another $10, bringing my compensation to a grand total of $60 for almost five months of work. Fortunately Rita had a job writing a handbook for newly recruited soldiers on how to load and operate a gun. In those early days of our marriage, we were practically penniless yet somehow managed to squeak by, mainly on Rita's weekly paycheck of $25.

The rent on our very small apartment at Ninety-Third Street and Columbus Avenue was $52 a month. On Sundays when I wasn't working, we would pack sandwiches and drive our old jalopy to Indian Point in Westchester County (many years before this picturesque town on the Hudson River became notorious for its nuclear power plant). If we wanted to go to the movies, we would return some empty milk bottles for the deposit money. We also had a wonderful physician, Dr. Mucelli—an unpretentious but incredibly astute general practitioner who charged a flat rate of $2 a visit. His waiting room was always overflowing with families. A native of Italy, he loved opera and classical music. When I developed a very high fever on the opening day of City Center in December 1943, Dr. Mucelli immediately phoned in a prescription to my neighborhood drugstore and got me back on my feet within forty-eight hours.

My wife was a remarkable woman with an incredible mind, a keen sense of humor, a love of music, and a fondness for wordplay that she passed on to our children, Joan, Madeleine, and Tony. She loved classical music and opera, and throughout our marriage she was both my biggest cheerleader and my severest critic—reveling in the highs of my career and empathizing to a fault with the lows. During the early years of our marriage, though I was too proud (and too embarrassed) to tell her details about the humiliations I endured from Halasz, Rita could always sense when I had been through an especially rough day at City Center.

That first season in February was so successful that the City Center board scheduled a second season for May. We had no repertory, and not a single artist had yet been signed, but in those early days of City Center, our seasons were initiated and enacted at a breakneck pace. Today it would take at least two years to accomplish what we were able to do back then in just three months. In our first year of operations, we thus had three seasons: one week in the winter, two weeks in the spring, and three in the fall. After that, we went to two seasons a year—spring and fall.

I had apparently proved my worth to Halasz. For the company's second season, which ran from May 1 to May 14, I was paid for four weeks of work: two weeks of rehearsals and two of performances. Also, when James Sample left the company at the end of the second season, I inherited his duties, starting with the job of planning rehearsal schedules. This task, which is very much like doing a jigsaw puzzle, really has no counterpart outside of opera; you have to keep the cast members, choruses, ballet, and orchestra simultaneously at work preparing up to ten different operas at a time—allowing extra rehearsals for premieres or for singers with problems (not to mention transferring artists from a dress rehearsal for one opera to a coaching session for another while making sure they don't wear out their voices before opening night), ensuring that the stage is free for staging and technical rehearsals, and on and on. The person who handles rehearsal schedules needs to know the repertoire and the abilities of the performers and creative team members inside and out.

I seemed to have an innate ability to do the scheduling—a fact that Halasz no doubt recognized. In 1945, I was joined by John White, a fellow Viennese, and together we assumed all the administrative work connected with the daily running of the house for several years. (We were later joined by Felix Popper, who arrived at City Opera in 1948 as a coach and was promoted to music administrator when I became director in 1957.)

Of course the term "daily running" is a bit misleading, since in those days the company was dormant for much of the year (although the administrative offices never closed). But when we were rehearsing and performing, I was literally living at City Center from ten o'clock in the morning till eleven o'clock at night. These were to become my "regular hours" for the next three-and-a-half decades. Dinner at home often consisted of a cold sandwich at midnight; the children had, of course, eaten earlier with Rita. ("Family life" did not exist for us as it did for "normal" families.)

For the second season Halasz enlarged the repertory immediately—doubling the number of productions from three to six by adding *La bohème, La traviata,* and the double bill of *Cavalleria rusticana* and *Pagliacci.* The *Bohème* cast included Mario Berini and Irma González, a young soprano from Mexico City who gave a very touching performance, especially in Mimì's death scene. Our first Violetta was Dorothy Kirsten, playing opposite John Hamill as Alfredo and Mack Harrell as Germont. Kirsten, a protégée of Grace

Moore, was soon to go on to stardom at the Met. She was very attractive, with a beautiful voice—a real "American" performer. Halasz mounted *Manon Lescaut* for her, and the reception was splendid. That work opened our third season on November 9, 1944.

I made my conducting debut during that third season. Halasz was so pleased with my preparation for *The Gypsy Baron* that he gave me the last performance as a gift. The date of my debut will stay with me forever: November 25, 1944—the last scheduled performance of *The Gypsy Baron*. Halasz had dangled the carrot in front of me a few weeks before, telling me that he would conduct the opening night of the Strauss operetta and then turn the reins over to Thomas Martin and perhaps me. (Tommy Martin was to become well known a few years later for the very fine English translations of operas he collaborated on with his wife, Ruth.)

My debut went wonderfully well. I had not the slightest fear or apprehension as I mounted the podium in my rented tails, absolutely set on the task of conducting *Gypsy Baron*. The performance, which featured Marguerite Piazza as Saffi and Stanley Carlson as Zsupan, had good spirit. As a matter of fact, I enjoyed it so much that I almost felt like I was part of the audience. Simply being thrown into a performance without an orchestra rehearsal is the well-established European route for opera conductors—and it's actually the best way to get out there and do your thing. I amassed most of my regular repertory by "taking over" performances. (This held true throughout my career; in most opera houses except for Covent Garden, I went in "cold" and conducted a performance, after which we would talk about future engagements.)

Gypsy Baron was a bona fide success, helped in no small way by its built-in audience of German exiles and thousands of others with a fondness for Strauss operettas. The reviews were glowing, and box office sales were so phenomenal that two additional weeks of performances were added at the end of the season, with Tommy Martin and me sharing the conducting.

Of course, what Halasz gave he could also take away.

When he got angry, he would punish me by not letting me conduct a performance he had promised me. I remember in particular a *Manon Lescaut* performance during our spring 1945 season. In the third act there's a lovely moment when a lamplighter comes onstage and turns off the street light. I was backstage giving the light cue, but I couldn't see the stage, which was crowded with choristers. I guessed the cue from the music. Unfortunately I guessed wrong, and the light went off when the lamplighter had already withdrawn his hand. This got a laugh. Halasz was furious with me. At the end of the act, he came backstage to yell at me, and as punishment he took away a performance of *Cavalleria rusticana* that I was scheduled to conduct later in the season.

Gradually, as we added more repertory, we increased the length of our seasons. The spring 1945 season was three weeks long, opening with *The Flying Dutchman*. City Opera's first attempt at Wagner, directed by José Ruben and designed by Rychtarik, drew a crowd and received fairly good reviews. The Dutchman was Frederick Destal, whom I remembered fondly from the Vienna Staatsoper. The opening night, April 12, 1945, was marred by the news of the death earlier that day of President Franklin Delano Roosevelt, who had suffered a massive cerebral hemorrhage. America's longest-serving president, who had led the nation through the Great Depression and World War II, was dead. When European victory was declared a month later, I was working as the prompter and chorus master for the Philadelphia Opera Company during a week of performances. Our victory over Germany certainly brought everything to a momentary halt; there was jubilant celebration that night.

On the second night of our fall 1945 season, baritone Todd Duncan (who had created the role of Porgy in *Porgy and Bess*) sang the role of Tonio in *Pagliacci*, and New York City Opera became the first major opera company to break the color barrier—a decade before Marian Anderson sang at the Met. Camilla Williams arrived on our stage the next season for an extraordinary portrayal of *Madama Butterfly*, and Lawrence Winters and Robert McFerrin followed. Early on, City Opera also employed black solo performers, chorus members, and orchestra members (Elaine Jones was our timpanist for many years before moving to the San Francisco Opera orchestra), and our company's first world premiere, in March 1949, was *Troubled Island*, an opera by a black composer, William Grant Still, with a libretto by Langston Hughes. This enlightened policy certainly is to Halasz's eternal credit.

I initially became acquainted with the operettas of Gilbert and Sullivan in 1941, when my future wife, a member of the City College Glee Club, introduced me to the director of the group, who in turn invited me to conduct a production of *The Mikado* for them. Although at that time I had only the vaguest knowledge of Gilbert and Sullivan, I said yes, of course. Then I took a look at the score. I thought the music was lovely, though at first I was totally bewildered by the dialogue (with its social bite and *veddy* British humor). The three performances in the City College downtown auditorium were to be accompanied by two pianists, but I was at the time working with the semi-professional Parkchester Symphony, and I thought it would be a real coup to bring the orchestra with me to City College to accompany the student singers. It all came together beautifully, and everyone was pleased.

A few years later, Halasz gave me a reward for a well-prepared *Bartered Bride*, entrusting me with full responsibility for the production of *The Pirates of Penzance*, the first Gilbert and Sullivan work to enter our repertory. Though it was practically unheard of to give a new production to an assistant conductor, I guess he didn't think the work was important enough to conduct it himself—and quite frankly I don't think he understood "G&S" at all. It was almost as strange to him as it had initially been to me. I jumped at the chance to conduct *Pirates*, since I had begun to appreciate their peculiar brand of humor and I adored the music.

At some point after the first few seasons I received a small raise, bringing my income to $60 a week, and by the end of the decade I had graduated to the grand sum of $65. But since I was only paid for rehearsal and performance weeks, at best I received fifteen to twenty paychecks a year—not enough to live on.

The City Center drama department, under the aegis of Jean Dalrymple, had to employ the union minimum of four musicians, even for a straight play, so the orchestra manager (Fabbroni, a compassionate guy who knew I could use the extra money) would sometimes hire me to play for a scene change or an introduction. I saw a lot of wonderful theater, and I still have vivid recollections of Margaret Webster's production of Shaw's *The Devil's Disciple* with Maurice Evans and Dennis King. That was one time I never left the pit; the third-act confrontation between the two men was so delicious that I watched it every night.

In the late 1940s I also occasionally acted as a piano accompanist for singers on recital tours. I remember accompanying Brenda Lewis during an especially harsh New England winter. To make some extra income after the birth of my daughter Joan, I went on the road with the popular Swedish tenor Set Svanholm in a cross-country recital tour that went as far west as Phoenix. I enjoyed working with him very much. He had a clear, bright voice, and an amiable stage presence. We performed Schubert and Brahms, an aria from *Der Freischütz*, and of course some Wagner.

Our last concert was in Pittsburgh. We were trying to finish in time to catch the 11:35 train to New York. We accomplished this by calling for a cab during intermission. Then, while I gathered the music and our belongings, Mr. Svanholm accompanied himself for the encore, a couple of charming Swedish folksongs. He bowed and ceremoniously exited the stage, and we ran like hell for the cab—arriving at the station in the knick of time.

In the spring of 1945, the Third Street Music School Settlement was looking for a new director. David Mannes recommended me for the job. The school—a red brick oasis in the middle of the crowded Lower East Side—was founded in 1894, and for half of its existence had been run by Melzar Chaffee, a violinist who was now well past the age of retirement. He looked like Rip Van Winkle, complete with a long white beard. The position paid $3,600 a year—enough so that Rita could quit her job and go to school full-time. I accepted the offer.

I worked hard to resuscitate the school. Many outstanding musicians had studied there; at the time of my arrival, the student body included the pianist Anthony di Bonaventura and the violinist Sidney Harth, both of whom went on to major careers. I started an opera department and brought in new faculty members: Carlton Gauld to head the voice department and John White for languages; New York Philharmonic concertmaster Mishel

Piastro; and several other fine musicians. The fact that the institution was a settlement school and not a professional school meant there was no activity during the day—it was in operation only in the evenings and on weekends. Taking advantage of the G.I. Bill of Rights, I opened the school in the daytime to veterans who wanted to pursue music as a career, which also meant more income for the school and better use of its facilities. I also started a concert series that was broadcast on WNYC.

For the most part, my duties at the Third Street Music School did not conflict with my work at City Opera, and the stagehands were kind enough to let me park my ten-year-old Plymouth on the Fifty-Sixth Street exit side of the theater, so I could easily drive back and forth between City Center and the music school. During the summer and winter months, when I was not on the City Opera payroll, I would still spend considerable time at City Center, stopping there first thing in the morning for a few hours to take care of any administrative work and, if necessary, returning in the evening. Halasz knew about my other job. But, as if to establish his prior claim on my time, sometimes he would phone me while I was down on Third Street and order me to come uptown pronto to do some minor task at City Opera that could have waited until the following day.

Everything went well at the school for the first six years of my directorship. Things started to go downhill in 1951, when I invited the pianist Ray Lev, an alumna of the school, to play at a benefit concert. A fogey on the board protested, claiming that Miss Lev was a Communist—and from that moment on my relationship with the board changed. They viewed me with suspicion. McCarthyism was in its heyday, and my contract was not renewed.

By then City Opera had entered a new chapter.

3

THE FLYING BATON

A Company in Transition

The first few years after World War II were a heady time for the country, and the overall enthusiasm couldn't help but trickle down to the performing arts. New York City Opera had established itself as an innovative, gutsy opera troupe, and miraculously, our company's first general director, Laszlo Halasz, was able to work within the confines of a minuscule budget while bringing fine singers, conductors, directors, and designers into our ranks. We were producing a nice mixture of staples and lesser-known operas—building up a repertory, the backbone of any opera company. And we were building a cadre of talented performers through open auditions. Anybody could come in; they did not need an agent or a friend or a relative. We had everyone fill out an audition form. Occasionally the answers were funny—intentionally or not. Under the section marked "Experience" one singer wrote: "Plenty." Another informed us, "I was told I sing in the key of F." We kept a file on each person who auditioned. Those who were not interesting or qualified, we would of course not hear again. But we encouraged many to come back in a few months or a year for another audition.

After the war, Europe was closing its doors to American artists, and we gained the services of some first-class American singers, including the baritone Frank Guarrera (who was with us for only one season before being snapped up by the Met) and bass James Pease. If there was a single defining moment for the company, it occurred during the fall 1946 season, when Halasz—with the enthusiastic encouragement of Morton Baum—mounted the first US professional performance of Richard Strauss's delicious *Ariadne auf Naxos*. Baum had seen *Ariadne* on one of his trips to Europe and loved the opera. The production was a huge success, prompting Richard Strauss to write a complimentary letter to Halasz. (As flattering as this may sound, it was not entirely guileless. Strauss would often praise conductors of his work, telling each one, "Only you understand how to conduct my music," hoping his operas would be brought back into the repertory the next season—which, of course, meant more royalties for the composer.)

Halasz engaged Leopold Sachse—a man of the theater who had been general manager of the German State Opera in Hamburg prior to Nazism— to direct *Ariadne.* We did the first part (the prologue) in English translation and the "opera seria" in the original German of the poet Hugo von Hofmannsthal. The audience liked this bilingual approach. Before every performance, Sachse, who was affable yet superstitious, would give each cast member a penny for good luck. *Ariadne,* designed by our house designer Heinz Condell, was particularly well cast: Ella Flesch, a member in exile of the Vienna Staatsoper, in the title role; Polyna Stoska as the Composer; Virginia McWatters as Zerbinetta; Ralph Herbert as Harlequin; and the Greek tenor Vasso Argyris, also a member of the Vienna Staatsoper, in his company debut as Bacchus. The combination of experienced performers and fresh young faces was always typical of our company.

Salome proved to be an artistic and popular success during our spring 1947 season, and it made a star of twenty-six-year-old Brenda Lewis. It was directed by Sachse, who actually demonstrated "The Dance of the Seven Veils." I can still see that shaggy old bear shimmying around the stage. Ramón Vinay and Winifred Heidt had made their joint City Opera debuts in *Carmen* during our fall 1945 season, in our hand-me-down production from St. Louis that was directed with fresh eyes by Sachse. It included the best staging of the last act I've ever seen. Don José's stabbing of Carmen was so clearly motivated: she had laughed in his face and walked away—as though saying, "You'll never be able to do it." That laugh made him spin around and stab her in the back, letting our audience see her surprised and contorted face at the exact moment when the cold steel of his knife "pierced" her body.

Another feather in our cap was our first production of *Aida*, in 1948, with Camilla Williams and the rising tenor Ramón Vinay. (Vinay, a good actor with a strong personality and strong voice, performed the title role in Toscanini's NBC Symphony *Otello* broadcast in 1947.) It was directed by Komisarjevsky, the exalted Russian theater director.

Laszlo Halasz was capable of showing the occasional kindness to his employees; one year he gave me a score of *Faust* for my birthday, which he had inscribed to me. But his temper could erupt at any time. If he didn't like the way I played the piano during a rehearsal he would push me off the chair and sit down himself and play—as if he had to show off. Over the years Halasz had alienated many New York City Opera company members— both singers and creative staff—with his duplicity. It was not uncommon for Halasz to ask two or more singers to learn a certain role, and then wait until the eleventh hour to announce who would sing the first performance. Some (like the Canadian tenor Leopold Simoneau) couldn't take it and quit. Others (including soprano Ann Ayars) tried to bring legal action against him.

One of the most outrageous examples of this modus operandi occurred during our fall 1948 season, when Halasz replaced Rosalind Nadell—who had been with our company since our first season—with Frances Bible as Cherubino in *The Marriage of Figaro*. He broke the news to Nadell at the final dress rehearsal, taking her aside after the first act and saying, "Rosie, if I let you do this, you'll be a flop. You don't want to be a flop, do you?" Nadell, shocked but undeterred, insisted she wanted to do the role, but to no avail; Halasz had already made up his mind. Artistically he was right—Bible was superb as Cherubino, her breakthrough role—but humanly he was dead wrong; the final casting should have been done weeks earlier.

In fall 1950, when *Die Meistersinger* entered the company's repertory, Halasz kept four sopranos in limbo until a few days before the opening. Although it was a foregone conclusion that Frances Yeend would sing the role of Eva at the premiere, Halasz went through the motions of auditioning three other sopranos—Ellen Faull, Leona Scheuneman, and Wilma Spence. Of course the role went to Yeend. (Frances, in addition to having a really beautiful voice, also had a good sense of humor. One night in *La traviata*, the stagehand forgot to put on her desk the little bell that Violetta used to summon Annina—so Miss Yeend picked up the inkwell and sang, "Ding-a-ling-a-ling!")

There is a rather amusing story connected with that first *Meistersinger* performance. Though New York City Opera traditionally did not use a prompter, Frances was a little bit slow in her German and needed the occasional helpful word, so Halasz told me to put one of our assistant conductors—Helmut Wolfes—inside Hans Sachs's house during the second act to prompt her during the long duet with Sachs. Wolfes, an experienced German coach and a rather large man, was hidden behind the door of Sachs's house—but somehow it didn't seem to work very well and Frances was inventing a large number of "German-sounding words." When the act ended, I ran into the cobbler's house to find out what had gone wrong. Wolfes was blissfully asleep.

New York City Opera received international attention during our spring 1948 season, when Komisarjevsky designed and directed a production of *Pelléas et Mélisande* starring Maggie Teyte, who had coached with Debussy himself for the role and had sung it many times in Europe. Pelléas was to be Theodor Uppman, a young American baritone from California who went on to create the title roles in Britten's *Billy Budd* at Covent Garden and Carlisle Floyd's *The Passion of Jonathan Wade* at our company. But Ted fell ill on opening night and his understudy, Fernand Martel, saved the day by substituting for him. Ms. Teyte was sixty at the time of her City Opera debut, and our lighting designer, being chivalrous, kept the stage as dark as possible. Her acting was a bit old-fashioned but nevertheless contained moments of absolute beauty, and Carlton Gauld was a commanding Goulaud. The conductor was Jean Morel, who received abundant praise. Music critic Olin Downes of the *New York Times* spoke of the "euphonious and elegant" sound Morel obtained from the orchestra.

Morel was beloved on both sides of the footlights. He was a real French-man, charming and lithe, and the orchestra and chorus loved him. I also assisted him during rehearsals for *Faust, Carmen*, and in spring 1949, for a fanciful new production of *The Tales of Hoffmann* with Robert Rounseville resplendent as the poet Hoffmann (a role he reprised in Michael Powell's famous film of the opera); Carlton Gauld properly imposing as the three vil-lains; and Virginia MacWatters, Wilma Spence, and Ann Ayars (who was also in the Michael Powell film) well cast as Hoffmann's three loves.

A young conductor in training naturally watches his "bosses" like a hawk, learning and adopting the best qualities of the conductors he most admires. I was fortunate at City Opera to have two conductors to look up to: Morel for the French works and Rosenstock for the Germanic reper-toire. (Both represented the Grand Tradition, as did two other conducting giants, Reiner and Monteux, whom I count among my "non-teacher teach-ers"; in summer I used to sneak into Lewisohn Stadium in the mornings and watch these two masters rehearse the New York Philharmonic.) Morel was free and elegant, with a light touch, while Rosenstock was much more of a disciplinarian—but both confirmed my deep belief that a good perfor-mance begins with a good conductor.

A German exile who (through a series of twists and turns) was detained in Japan for much of World War II, Rosenstock made his company debut in 1948, conducting a brilliant *Marriage of Figaro*; he also conducted our first *Rosenkavalier*, in fall 1949—for which we had a European Marschallin, Maria Reining. Rosenstock was respected by our singers and orchestra mem-bers, but not loved. He took offense easily—and when he was angry, his face turned bright red. He was rather small in stature, which he made up for with a sizeable Napoleonic complex.

In my dual capacity as music administrator and assistant conductor I scheduled myself whenever possible to play rehearsals for Rosenstock and Morel and assisted with other preparations for their operas, which meant I was in close contact with both men. Observing them day after day in rehears-als and in performances gave me tremendous insights into the art of opera conducting.

When it came to the Italian repertory, I had a strong advocate in the per-son of conductor Giorgio Polacco—retired by the time I first met him in the 1950s, when he was in his early eighties and residing in New York. He loved our company, and came frequently to City Center. Although I had no par-ticular background in Italian opera, Maestro Polacco came backstage to con-gratulate me on my "authentic" conducting of a performance of *Rigoletto*. He took me under his wing and we became friends; I would often turn to him for advice, especially while I prepared to conduct my first *Trovatore* in 1956.

I took immense pride in our company's large repertory; in a five-week season we would present at least ten works, double- and triple-cast for practical reasons. We scheduled eight performances a week, more than any other opera company in the world did. Between Friday evening and Sunday evening we performed five different operas, which allowed ten hours per opera for mounting, performing, and dismounting. We were a real repertory company.

What exactly does an assistant conductor do? My duties consisted of coaching singers and teaching them their roles, and playing the piano for most rehearsals (solo rehearsals, chorus rehearsals, staging rehearsals, technical rehearsals, and final rehearsals). In the evenings—except when I was conducting or rehearsing another opera—I would be on "stage duty," which meant giving entrances, exits, light cues, and curtain cues, and conducting the offstage singers and instrumentalists. In those days before closed-circuit television, we would have to make a little hole in the scenery and peek through to see the conductor in the pit and coordinate our beats. Occasionally one of the performers onstage would stand directly in front of the hole in the set and block my sightline—in which case I'd operate on instinct only (which is what happened when the lamplighter failed to extinguish the lamp at the right moment in *Manon Lescaut*).

Assistant conductors have always loved operas with food, such as *Tosca*. No sooner would the curtain come down on the second act than the assistants would converge on the stage to scavenge the "leftovers" from Scarpia's last supper. The stagehands used to laugh at us, perhaps a bit contemptuously. But for us it was a free meal.

In my capacity as music administrator I had to plan the overall rehearsal schedule for the entire season: the main rehearsals, in which I tried to give everyone enough "onstage time," and the smaller individual coaching sessions. It was a tough balancing act, as time onstage was so limited. I also had to accommodate daily requests from staff members: "Mr. X doesn't know his role yet, and we also need some more coaching time for Miss Y."

I always checked up on singers making company debuts and role debuts and watched the performances even when I wasn't conducting. Every single facet of running the company was of concern to me.

In 1951 Laszlo Halasz dug his own grave. Years of objectionable behavior culminated in a dustup with the City Center board of directors when—against their express wishes—he scheduled the world premiere of *The Dybbuk* during our fall 1951 season. A dybbuk, in Jewish folklore, is a demon that enters the body of a living person and controls that person's behavior. In this instance, a demon seemed to be controlling Halasz's behavior. When Morton Baum informed him that the company did not have enough funds in place for a production of *The Dybbuk*, Halasz announced his resignation in protest, six weeks before the spring 1951 season opening.

Halasz's loyal secretary, Jessica Colfer, persuaded me and many others on the administration staff—including John White, Tom Martin, Jean Morel, Joseph Rosenstock, and Lee Shaynen—to sign a similar resignation letter. An obvious strong-arm tactic, but Halasz had played his cards wrong. Morton Baum warned all of us in no uncertain terms that the opera company would continue with or without us, even if Baum himself had to take over the directorship. His bluff called, Halasz withdrew his resignation, and so did the rest of us. The spring season took place as scheduled—but Halasz's days were now numbered.

Baum and Morris and a majority of the members of the City Center board wanted *The Dybbuk* to remain shelved for fiscal reasons. But when David Dubinsky and Jacob Potofsky, the heads of two very powerful unions (the International Ladies' Garment Workers' Union and the Amalgamated Garment Workers' Union) and members of the City Center board since its formation, each gave $12,500 from their organizations for this new production, Halasz, without clearing it with Baum and Morris, scheduled the world premiere of the Tamkin opera for the upcoming fall season.

The Dybbuk premiered at City Opera on October 4, 1951. It was not at all a bad work. David Tamkin was a proficient composer—and I mean that in a positive sense—and *The Dybbuk* had a very fine cast including Patricia Neway, Robert Rounseville, and Carlton Gauld, with Irving Pichel (a prestigious film actor and director) directing and Rosenstock conducting. The intensity of Rounseville and Neway's performances was something to behold, especially in the moment when Leah (Neway)—overtaken by the Dybbuk—begins to sing in the voice of the boy Channon (Rounseville). He sang offstage and she mouthed the words so exactly that it seemed that his voice was coming out of her body. It was a truly bloodcurdling moment.

In any other season, the Tamkin opera would have come and gone, and perhaps been remembered as a noble effort. But because of the circumstances surrounding its premiere (word had spread that Halasz had produced it against the explicit instructions of the board), *The Dybbuk* became a cause célèbre, with the press coming down squarely on the side of artistic freedom. Tickets for the five scheduled performances sold well, as so often happens for the world premieres of "novelties." As tensions mounted, Halasz's behavior became more and more nasty and vindictive, and throughout the fall season he brought many an artist to tears during rehearsals. By that time I had quit speaking to him altogether.

The final straw broke when Halasz took yet another performance away from me. I had invited several friends and a prospective agent to this particular performance, and it was very embarrassing for me to have to notify them that it would not be taking place. After that, I communicated with Halasz only through his secretary, Jessica Colfer. Halasz of course pretended that everything was fine, which prompted one staff member to observe that

Halasz was making "bonne mine à mauvais jeu," as the Marschallin says to Ochs in *Der Rosenkavalier* (a phrase which translates as, "putting a good face on a bad situation"). The season's other new production, Wolf-Ferrari's comic opera *I quatro rusteghi*, was to be the last opera mounted under Halasz's directorship.

Halasz's shenanigans finally got to me; at last I, too, was ready to leave. On November 9, 1951, I wrote Morton Baum the following letter:

> It is almost eight years now that I have been associated with the New York City Opera Company. I have had the gratifying experience of watching it grow, contributing to its growth, and developing professionally with it. There have been many times in the past when conditions have seemed intolerable and demoralizing. To resign often seemed my only recourse but the devotion I felt for the venture and your kind encouragement always carried me through. It is this same intense devotion to the high ideals of the City Center which makes this final step imperative now.
>
> With great regret I hereby inform you of my resignation from all duties connected with the New York City Opera Company effective at the end of the present season (December 10). It is impossible any longer to work constructively in the atmosphere created by the present director. His persistent vengefulness, maliciousness, high pressuring and generally bad treatment of virtually every member of the company can no longer be endured. When I accepted the additional duties of assistant director, at your suggestions and against the advice of my colleagues, it was with complete awareness of these "directorial techniques," but with the honest hope of providing a counterbalance and altering conditions for the better. I have become increasingly aware that this is impossible under Mr. Halasz. Every attempt on my part to present the other side of the picture to him is construed as disloyalty, as playing up to the "opposition," of being in "cahoots" with them, and of "letting the morale of the company slip by pussyfooting."
>
> I no longer wish to have my name professionally associated with the present directorship, nor can I further endure the insults, humiliations, embarrassments and blows to my self-respect which I have silently absorbed these many years. My deep and sincere belief in the City Center as an institution and as an ideal I have attested to by very long hours of hard work and personal sacrifice, which I don't for a moment regret. I only hope that the present deplorable conditions may not stifle its further growth.
>
> I shall always be thankful for the opportunity I have had to participate in the establishment and development of the City Center, and grateful to you personally for your share in my association with the company.

Yours very sincerely,
Julius Rudel

There was no time for Baum to respond. A scant two weeks later, Halasz's temper got out of hand once again—and so began "The Tale of The Flying Baton."

For seven consecutive years, from 1947 to 1953, New York City Opera traveled to Chicago, which had lost its own opera company. On the way there or back we would stop for performances in smaller cities, including Milwaukee and Detroit. When we played Detroit, our roster was "beefed up" with guest artists like Richard Tucker, Jussi Bjoerling, Hilde Gueden, or Eileen Farrell (whom I conducted in an exciting *Trovatore*; she was a joy to work with—so natural, so musical, so much fun!). In Detroit we also had a strange tradition: Milton Cross, the longtime Metropolitan Opera Saturday afternoon radio broadcast announcer, was engaged by our local sponsors. He would be seated in the first lower box on stage left, and before each act he'd stand and tell the audience the story of the opera as if it were a broadcast! It was all a bit *Bourgeois gentilhomme*. But this presentation actually helped sell tickets for the five-thousand-seat Masonic Auditorium, and our local sponsors insisted on it as part of their contract.

The tour always began after our New York fall season ended. We traveled by train, which in those days meant a sixteen- or seventeen-hour trip, and took along a basic chorus of thirty and a "Mozart-size orchestra" of thirty-two, adding local freelance musicians and choristers in Chicago, as needed, for works by Verdi and Puccini and the other operas that demanded larger forces. These local musicians needed to be taken through their music. Halasz disliked being bothered with this, so the task naturally became part of my job. (Have you ever heard the score of *Bohème* played with just one flute, one trumpet, two fiddles, and a bass?)

In the weeks following the premiere of *The Dybbuk*, everyone could feel the "unquiet," and a number of singers wrote letters of complaint to the board. On November 24, 1951, Halasz conducted a performance of *Madama Butterfly* in Chicago. At one point in the prelude to the third act, his beat was so unclear that the orchestra fell apart, and in anger Halasz threw his baton at the concertmaster, Alfred Bruening. Of all places, it had to happen in Chicago—the lion's den of James Petrillo, president of the American Federation of Musicians as well as the boss of "Local 10" of Chicago. Four days later, as patrons began filing in for a performance of *Carmen*, Petrillo suddenly appeared backstage with Halasz and asked the orchestra members to meet with him in the musicians' lounge, where he demanded that Halasz apologize. Halasz refused, claiming that the baton had accidentally flown out of his hand, and that he had nothing to apologize for: the entire incident had been a misunderstanding. (I had witnessed the incident from the wings, and had seen him hurl the baton with force; it had most definitely not been a "slip.")

"They will not start playing unless you apologize," Petrillo insisted. We all sat there, waiting, until Petrillo finally found the diplomatic solution. He asked Halasz, "If you *had* thrown the baton, would you apologize?" To which Halasz responded, "Of course," whereupon all faces were saved and the performance could start. The story was picked up the following morning by the

New York Times, where it appeared on the front page. The next day, November 30, a follow-up article in the *Times* quoted an angry Petrillo as saying, "If that guy throws one more baton or anything else, out he goes."

Halasz was dismissed by the board three weeks later—on December 21, 1951.

During the next few weeks Joseph Rosenstock was named acting director of City Opera, and an article in the *New York Times* from January 23, 1952, announced his appointment to the position of general director. We immediately went into high gear, planning the spring season that would open March 20, 1952, and feature the company premieres of Berg's *Wozzeck* and Menotti's *Amahl and the Night Visitors* (which had premiered the previous Christmas Eve on NBC television to much fanfare), to be directed by the composer and conducted by the brilliant twenty-two-year-old Thomas Schippers—a discovery of Menotti's. There was also a brief mention in the *Times* story that Jean Morel had resigned from the company. (Morel had been offered the directorship after Halasz's dismissal and was thoroughly outraged: "I have neither the vices nor the attributes for an opera director," he retorted. He refused to return to New York City Opera during Rosenstock's tenure.)

Rosenstock was an excellent conductor, with limits. His conducting was precise and clear, but also a bit rigid, giving singers little leeway—and he was unbending when it came to tempi rubati. (Walter Cassel, an affable artist who got along with everyone, once nearly came to blows with Rosenstock over the delivery of a passage in *The Marriage of Figaro*.) In truth, all Rosenstock cared about was the art of conducting. He was a "kapellmeister," and I use that word without malice. He was not a "people person," and was not interested in or even capable of doing administrative work. In fact, he paid so little attention to it that John White and I soon took over many of his duties. A year earlier, Halasz had delegated some artists' negotiations to me. I remember the very first contract I negotiated, for a promising tenor named David Poleri who turned out to be a bit too temperamental for his own good. In November 1953 Poleri made opera history—in Chicago, no less!—when, during the final act of *Carmen*, he snarled to Rosenstock, who was conducting, "Sing it yourself!" and stormed off the stage, leaving poor Gloria Lane to die on her own. (She took Carmen's fan and rammed it into herself as if she were committing hara-kiri.)

The press was very upset about Halasz's dismissal, and aimed their slings and arrows directly at the diminutive Rosenstock. He brought *Wozzeck* into the company repertory on April 3, 1952, with Marko Rothmueller (who had starred in the Covent Garden and Buenos Aires premieres of the Berg opera) in the title role and Pat Neway as Marie. It was a fine performance of *Wozzeck* that should have been a triumph, but the New York press reaction was unduly brutal. Olin Downes of the *New York Times* roundly chastised Komisarjevsky's physical production (a double stage with different levels upon which the action took place) and Rothmueller's performance, and went on to make a dig at Rosenstock for flying the baritone "back and forth" from Europe to appear in the production.

The press was kinder during our Fall 1952 season, when Rosenstock, in a real coup, invited the venerable Italian conductor Tullio Serafin to lead the opening night *Tosca* as well as *Aida, La traviata,* and Ravel's *L'heure Espagnole.* Serafin, seventy-four years old at the time, had been a mainstay at the Metropolitan Opera for several years but had not been heard in New York since he left the Met over a salary dispute in 1935.

Our opening-night Tosca was Serafin's protégée Anne McKnight, an American soprano who also sang Aida for our company a few days later. She had a beautiful voice but was not an especially gifted actress. Still, there was an air of excitement during all of the performances that Serafin led for us that season; he conducted with verve and sensitivity.

Serafin signed a contract to return the following season—spring 1953—but he canceled at the last minute, sending a letter from his doctor forbidding him to travel. It turned out to be a phony excuse; he had gotten a lucrative recording contract. (Miraculously he "got well" in time to conduct at the San Francisco Opera in fall 1953.)

Rosenstock scrambled to reassign the operas Serafin was supposed to conduct. He took *La Cenerentola,* which turned out to be a huge hit for our company and for him personally, and I got a good number of performances as well, including my first *Tosca,* which I conducted—naturally—without a rehearsal. I had originally prepared *Tosca* for Halasz, so I knew the opera well. On the day of the performance, a typically busy day, I arrived in time for a ten o'clock coaching with Norman Treigle, who was making his company debut as Colline the following day. I wanted to make certain he was well prepared, and he certainly was. After that I had an ensemble rehearsal followed by lunch—crackers and cheese and tea at my desk. In the afternoon I had several short meetings (with various members of our creative and administrative staff) and then a chorus rehearsal from three to five, at which time Rita joined me and we went across the street to the coffee shop Francine's and had a sandwich. After that I changed into my tails (or, as I liked to say, "put on my work clothes"), and Rita took her seat in the audience.

The principal singers—Anne McKnight, Walter Cassel, and Jon Crain—were in great shape, and the orchestra reacted to my smallest indication. I was in seventh heaven.

During his four years as General Director, Rosenstock brought eighteen new productions into our company repertory. Among them was the world premiere of Aaron Copland's *The Tender Land*—a melodic but tepid work that has had a considerable afterlife in high schools and conservatories. Rosenstock also introduced the US stage premiere of Von Einem's *The*

Trial, which brought director Otto Preminger into the operatic horizon but is mostly remembered for Phyllis Curtin's splendid debut in a trio of diverse roles.

The biggest success during Rosenstock's tenure was the *Cenerentola* in spring 1953, conducted by Rosenstock when Serafin failed to return and imaginatively directed by Otto Erhardt. Frances Bible was vocally perfect in the title role. So was the rest of the cast, which included Riccardo Manning as Prince Ramiro and George Gaynes (taking a few nights off from playing a leading role in the Broadway hit *Wonderful Town*) as Dandini.

A pair of operas that had premiered on Broadway a few years earlier also entered our repertory during Rosenstock's tenure: Menotti's *The Consul* (which Tommy Schippers conducted, with Menotti directing and Pat Neway recreating her Broadway triumph in the role of Magda) and Blitzstein's *Regina*, directed by Bobby Lewis (who had staged the Broadway premiere) and starring Brenda Lewis as the venal title character. Interestingly, Brenda had played the role of Regina's gentle sister-in-law Birdie in the original Broadway production. Both of these works were revived several times and became closely identified with our company.

Rosenstock assigned me the conducting duties for *Regina;* it was an honor for me to be given a new production. The following spring, in April 1954, I was given *Show Boat*. The critics attacked City Opera for producing something as frivolous as *Show Boat*, and for once I had to agree with them. It's a musical comedy that broaches serious issues such as racial prejudice, but, even though some of the Kern and Hammerstein songs are gorgeous, the show lacks the musical weight of works by Blitzstein, Menotti, or Weill. Morton Baum knew that *Show Boat* would draw large audiences—which would be good for our box office. He was right, of course.

In January 1955, a tense situation arose when Joseph Rosenstock's three-year contract came up for renewal. Lincoln Kirstein, who held dual positions as general director of Balanchine's New York City Ballet and managing director of City Center, opposed his reappointment. When the City Center board voted thirteen to twelve in favor of retaining Rosenstock, Kirstein angrily resigned from the board and from the managing directorship of City Center, and subsequently gave a series of interviews to the press in which he was critical of City Center and Rosenstock.

If Rosenstock had been unpopular with the press before Kirstein's resignation, he became even more unpopular afterward. It was a vicious circle, since the bad press led to poor box office and depleted morale within the company. On December 18, 1955, after meeting with Morton Baum, Rosenstock announced he would resign at the end of the spring 1956 season. As a parting gift to me, he assigned me a new production of *Il trovatore*. No one knew that Rosenstock's successor would, during a single season at the helm, very nearly lead the company to utter ruin.

The internationally recognized conductor Erich Leinsdorf had achieved much acclaim at the Metropolitan Opera (conducting the German repertory after Artur Bodanzky's sudden death in 1939) and also had served, briefly, as music director of the Cleveland Orchestra. He and John White knew each other well from Vienna, where they had been schoolmates. John sounded out Leinsdorf, who as it turned out was very interested in returning to Manhattan after nine seasons as music director of the Rochester Philharmonic.

With the board's blessing, Leinsdorf was approached more formally about the directorship in the fall of 1955. He accepted. On December 28 the press announced Leinsdorf's appointment as general director.

Leinsdorf came to New York City Opera with a "Grand Plan." He decided to turn everything around—and he did just that. In doing so, he managed to repeat many of the mistakes that had been made before. He announced his goal to present more performances of fewer operas, fewer singers with more work for each (i.e., no more double casting of operas), and fewer conductors each with more authority over his own productions. He invited Jean Morel back to the company in the position of music director, and Morel accepted. Most significantly, Leinsdorf brought in the Broadway producer-designer Leo Kerz for the newly created position of art director.

Kerz designed a single-unit set that would be used for every opera. It consisted of two concentric turntables, set at an angle, that could be moved into any number of positions. There were also two very large screens—walls on which there would be projections. The idea was to create a modern look that would afford a sense of visual satisfaction to our audiences. It didn't turn out that way at all. The unit set caused all sorts of upheavals, because the stage was raked at such a steep angle that it was difficult for the singers to maneuver. Although the turntable, which cost an exorbitant amount of money, worked fairly well for Frank Martin's *The Tempest*, it was totally unsuitable for a repertory company. Many of the singers soon found a descriptive name for it: "Lazy Susan." In addition to mounting six new productions on this set, we also had to completely restage the five tried-and-true works that were returning to the repertory that season (while our trusty old sets were put in storage): *Traviata, Fledermaus, Carmen, Bohème,* and *Rigoletto*.

As I soon realized, Leinsdorf's reign as general director put my own job in jeopardy. Surely Leinsdorf would have liked to bring in his own music administrator, but obviously he was stuck with me. In April 1956 I had a phone call out of the blue from a board member of Houston Grand Opera. He wanted to know if I was interested in the directorship of their company, and offered to fly me to Houston for two days of interviews. I accepted, telling not a soul except for Rita, and flew to Houston.

Everyone there was very nice, and I knew there was potential for repertory building and for luring top-notch singers and directors. The financial situation there was quite bright, since a number of Houston's wealthy citizens had already given huge amounts of money to the company. I would have a great deal of autonomy there, and of course my salary would be several times what it was at City Center. They gave me a "test," asking me to prepare a budget for an entire season by the following morning. "I'll be back in two hours," I said, and presented them with a detailed budget that apparently pleased them. After the interview, I called Rita from the hotel and said, "I don't know what to do. I have this offer here. I can't imagine us moving to Houston." Rita and I decided I should "sleep on it and decide in the morning." I then called John White and filled him in on what was happening to me. At the end of our conversation I said, "I'll think about it." The next morning I woke up with the certain knowledge that Texas was not where my future lay. I thanked the committee for selecting me but politely told them I didn't think I could accept the position.

Once back in New York, I went straight to the office to tell John White of my decision. He looked very embarrassed—and soon enough I found out why. He had broken my confidence and told Leinsdorf not only that I had gone to Houston, but also that I had accepted the job. Leinsdorf had immediately engaged another person for my position, and it seemed I was altogether out of a job. I wrote a strong letter of protest to Leinsdorf—to no avail. I knew the only person who could help me was Morton Baum, so I telephoned him and told him the whole story. It was only because of Baum's intervention that I retained my job and received a conducting assignment for the fall 1956 season: two performances of *Rigoletto*.

Leinsdorf's pompous response to me, in a letter dated July 5, 1956, began:

Dear Mr. Rudel:

Until I received your letter of June 29th, I was not aware that the Houston project is off—or, isn't it off?

I should like to establish first the fact that I have been fully apprised of your most valuable work for the New York City Opera. Thus, when you, in great haste, under unusual conditions, phoned John White that you were taking on the Houston Opera, the 7th floor was moving with unusual dispatch to fill the gap left by your resignation.

As our personal interview took place two days after your telephone call and then the decision in Houston was still pending, I did not tell you I had the first day after your call already made a number of arrangements to assign the opera which had been "yours" to someone else and also proceeded to make conditional arrangements for your replacement in the administrative department.

Under those circumstances, you will unquestionably be able to understand that your letter of the 29th is not a harmonious element as you (a) did not in any way notify me of the status of the Houston matter and (b) reproached me for not assigning "Susannah" to you.

I must prepare you for some disappointments in these matters: I have assigned both "Traviata" and "Susannah," but I am perfectly happy to turn over to you the New York performance of "Rigoletto" which I had assigned to myself. However, I have promised Detroit and Mr. Bjoerling that I would do the opening there. In Detroit, you would have the "Trovatore" performance with Eileen Farrell.

I am afraid that in the financial matter, I cannot do anything . . .

With my best wishes for a good summer, I am

Yours very sincerely,
Erich Leinsdorf

I was furious that John White had taken as fait acompli something that I was contemplating (something I had shared with him in strictest confidence). I'm still not sure why he told Leinsdorf I was moving to Houston. I suspect his sense of catastrophe had something to do with it. He loved to be the bearer of bad tidings.

The season opened with Offenbach's *Orpheus in the Underworld*, which did not go over well with critics or audiences. Kerz's production was dreary and joyless, when *Orpheus* called for something fluffy, airy, even a little frivolous. In addition, it was performed in a tasteless and bad English translation.

The next company premiere, Ambrose Thomas's *Mignon*, at least was musically first rate thanks to Frances Bible, Beverly Sills, and particularly Jean Morel. *Susannah*, which Leinsdorf conducted, was the one success of the season; in addition to Curtin's definitive performance in the title role, it gave Norman Treigle his first big role with our company. *The Tempest* sold so few tickets that we actually had to cancel several performances, and our audiences hated Orff's *The Moon*. It was a total disaster, and the company was demoralized. The season ended with a huge deficit, and when we returned from our annual fall tour to the Midwest, rumor had it that New York City Opera was about be dissolved. Worst of all, administrators from the Metropolitan Opera were looking at our books—and there was talk that the Met would be taking over City Opera and making us their "junior company."

Things couldn't get much worse.

4

A LIGHTER MUSE

Broadway Musicals

I need to digress a bit here to talk about another love of mine: a lighter muse, the Broadway musical. Even before I got to this country, I enjoyed the American idiom. I was not familiar with a lot of American music, but I had heard some show tunes, including Shirley Temple singing, in perfect German, "Animal Crackers in My Soup," and Fred Astaire in his lighthearted and catchy "Top Hat, White Tie, and Tails." When I arrived in New York in 1938, I heard songs by Gershwin, Rodgers, Porter, and other Broadway composers for the first time on the radio program *Your Hit Parade*. The music made quite an impression on me. I was astounded by Gershwin's range and seriousness of purpose, but I also enjoyed the easier rhythms of Sinatra and Crosby.

Within less than a year, I started going to the Met on standing room and attending the theater whenever I could—mostly plays presented by the WPA (Works Progress Administration) where you paid a quarter for a seat. I can still remember *Native Son* with Canada Lee. It was harrowing, and I was spellbound. But of course I was drawn particularly to the musicals.

In 1947 I saw two Broadway shows that would become integral to my own career: *Street Scene* and *Brigadoon*. They were worlds apart in spirit and tone, yet each made a deep impression on me. Both composers, Kurt Weill and Frederick Loewe, were German born. Each, in his music, had adjusted to and accepted the American idiom.

I never believed there was a clear-cut divide between opera and musical theater. If opera is "sophisticated" or "complicated" music, then there is no demarcation between the very best operas and musicals. An American opera is nothing more or less than a lyric work for the stage with thought-provoking musical content written by someone who lives in America.

It is not really important to classify musical dramas as opera, operetta, musical comedy, or music drama. For the audience, the only question is: Is it good or is it bad? Gian Carlo Menotti had several Broadway successes in the 1940s and 1950s, including the Pulitzer Prize-winning *The Consul* and

∨ *The Saint of Bleecker Street.* Menotti, like Weill, was a European transplant who lived and wrote in this country. He told me the word "opera" was box office poison, and this was why he chose to bill his works as *musical dramas* and premiere them on Broadway.

Frank Loesser was—like Bernstein and Sondheim (born eight and twenty years, respectively, after Loesser)—a serious composer and a fully trained musician. He began his radiant musical comedy *Guys and Dolls* with a fugue—the catchy, brilliant "Fugue for Tinhorns"—and gave Sarah Brown and Miss Adelaide a moment of bitonality in their second-act duet, "Marry the Man Today." While *Guys and Dolls* will almost certainly never be done at the Met or the Royal Opera in London, I still feel strongly that this classic American show and many other Broadway musicals are a bridge to opera. Some recent shows like *Spring Awakening* (2007) have had pretensions beyond their capabilities; but others, like *The Scottsboro Boys* (2010), might have led audiences to opera. Unfortunately, *The Scottsboro Boys* closed after only a few weeks. (This striking Kander and Ebb show should have found a really hip audience—but didn't.)

In 1949, when summer "straw hat" companies were in their heyday, a man by the name of St. John Terrell opened a "music tent" in Lambertville, New Jersey, where musicals and operettas were performed in the round. It was such a success that the next year several new music tents were opened. The formula worked. Musicals were presented in rented tents, with the stage in the center and the audience seated on all sides. There were two main poles, and quarter poles on which the lights were mounted.

The orchestra pit was actually a ditch on one side of the stage. A good stage director knew how to move the singers in all directions so that no section of the audience ever felt neglected. There was a nice collegial competition between the various theaters on the East Coast, with Wallingford, Cohasset, Beverly, Hyannis, Lambertville, and others vying to present artistically successful shows in a physically challenging venue.

In early 1952 I heard of a job opening for the upcoming summer at a new tent—the Neptune Music Circus in Asbury Park, New Jersey. I contacted the theater, and couldn't believe my good fortune when, after a short interview, they hired me as their music director for the season. (What better way to have summer employment while escaping the hot city streets of New York and providing some fun for my family? And I got paid for ten weeks in a row, a rare occurrence.) Rita and I rented a house and—with our two young daughters, Joan and Madeleine—moved to the Jersey Shore for the summer. The season opened with Romberg's *Desert Song.* Because of excessive rain earlier in the day, we were not fully ready; the toilets had overflowed, and they barely got everything cleaned up in time for curtain. *Desert Song* was followed by *The Chocolate Soldier, Carousel, Bloomer Girl, Brigadoon, Annie Get Your Gun, The Red Mill, The Merry Widow,* and *Kiss Me, Kate.* This schedule was typical of those at music tents across the country, which had varying seasons of eight to ten weeks.

Asbury Park was my first hands-on exposure to musical theater. Everything was very well organized. Director Glenn Jordan staged all the shows with a quiet efficiency. There was a chorus of a dozen; six dancers; and an orchestra of nine or ten; plus a conductor, choreographer, and scenic designer (the costumes were rented from New York costume houses). Some performers were engaged for the summer, and the leading stars were "jobbed in." We'd perform one week's show while rehearsing the next, which meant we had twenty-seven hours to put on a show: five hours' rehearsal for five days, plus two hours of rehearsal on matinee days (and if you weren't ready, tough!). It may not have been the most profound reading, but it was always professional—and if you were working with a good director (i.e., one who was disciplined and organized), you were okay. I was lucky with Jordan—he was organized and usually had the show blocked by Friday, so we actually had several run-throughs before Monday's opening.

The experience I got at that theater was invaluable. I learned about "timing," how to support a scene, how to lead into a "number," how to pace soft music under dialogue to help set the mood, and how to provide effective scene endings. In addition, I gained a whole new vocabulary. At City Opera rehearsals after that summer I would amuse the orchestra with such questions as "Will you give me a button at the end here?" or "Would you give me a fall-off in the brass?"

Soon after this, I got my start as a dramatic director, at the South Shore Music Circus in Cohasset. David Marshall Holtzmann, a theatrical lawyer (for Gertrude Lawrence and other stars) and part owner of the Cape Cod Melody Tent in Hyannis, almost always attended rehearsals for productions of these summer stock companies. I worked in the summer of 1953 as music director in Cohasset before moving, with a raise in salary, to Hyannis the next year. During auditions David, who was almost always present, noticed my dramatic proclivities and asked me if I would be interested in assisting the stage director, Ernie Sarracino, a fine character actor who played featured roles in some of the shows. "Of course!" was my quick response. I got along very well with Ernie, who didn't mind one bit if I "assisted" with his direction. And boy did I ever assist! That's how I got my feet wet in the directorial department.

I would do anything and everything that needed to be done to ensure a good performance—sometimes even eliminating or combining characters when necessary. (David Holtzmann's daughter, Bettyann Kevles, has said that *Anything Goes* was "much better" and sped along quite nicely when we cut it down to fewer speaking roles!) Holtzmann was so involved with the theater that he would even come to auditions for the women's chorus. We used to joke that "if it were up to David Holtzmann, we would be auditioning with a tape measure."

The Holtzmanns became really wonderful friends (our families remain close to this day), and I returned to Hyannis for two more idyllic summers.

The summer of 1954 ended, with a bang, quite literally, when the big-top canvas tent blew away during Hurricane Carol. We were doing the last show of the season, *High Button Shoes,* and I had not been happy with the opening night performance, so I called the company together for a rehearsal on Tuesday morning. It was raining when we arrived; by noon the weather was horrible and getting worse by the minute. Soon it became really frightening: the wind began to lift the poles of the tent (on which were mounted the lights for the show), then dropped them with a thud, smashing the glass bulbs. Everyone pitched in and made a valiant effort to hold down the tent. We were strong, but the weather was stronger. By late afternoon the tent was totally destroyed, and the entire company (over forty actors and musicians) was sent home five days early with our week's salaries, traveling expenses, and a small bonus. We made plans to open the 1955 season with Jule Styne's *High Button Shoes.*

My final summer in Hyannis was in 1956. The "music circus" phenomenon lasted only a few more years and then disappeared as mysteriously as it appeared. But it was a great training ground and tryout for many talented performers, and led to some lasting alliances. I'm thinking in particular of Hal Linden and his wife. They fell in love at Hyannis, when he was in the chorus and she was a dancer.

It was in the spring of 1953 that I got to conduct Marc Blitzstein's *Regina.* Just as Halasz had not been familiar with Gilbert and Sullivan when he "gave" me *Pirates of Penzance* in 1946, Maestro Rosenstock was not acquainted with Blitzstein's work. It's a beautiful musical drama based on Lillian Hellman's *The Little Foxes.* We engaged director Bobby Lewis (who had ingeniously directed the Broadway premiere) and rented the sets and costumes from the original Broadway production. In addition, our own Brenda Lewis, who had originated the role of the fragile Birdie in *Regina* on Broadway, did an about-face and gave a powerhouse portrayal of the mendacious, heartless Regina. I loved the music, from the touching "Rain Quartet" to the rousing "Dixieland Angel Band" number, and our larger orchestral forces made the score sound more operatic than it had on Broadway.

In addition to my work in summer theater, I also began to get bookings to conduct summer symphony concerts. In 1953 I conducted my first concert at Grant Park in Chicago and made my debut at New York City's Lewisohn Stadium. The stadium held a longstanding series of summer concerts hosted by the magnanimous Minnie Guggenheimer. She introduced each concert with a cheery "Hello, everybody!" followed by an endearing quip about the weather or the size of the crowd. She was known for her malapropisms and mispronunciations, once referring to "Ezio Pinza Bass" (momentarily confusing the famed singer with a species of fish). For the annual

Viennese Night program, which I conducted, the soloists were two singers I had cheered years before from my spot in the fourth ring of the Vienna Staatsoper, Jarmila Novotna and Charles Kullman. It was quite overwhelming to be collaborating onstage with two stars I had long admired from afar. In addition, this was my first appearance conducting the members of the New York Philharmonic; the program included bits and snatches from Johann Strauss, Kalman, and Lehár. It was a fun night, reviewed by Harold C. Schonberg in the *New York Times*: "Not much can be said about the young conductor's musical stature from a program of this nature. But one did observe a clear beat, a no-nonsense attitude, a forthright musical approach and a reliable, well-proportioned accompaniment." I returned to Lewisohn Stadium annually for the next decade, conducting stars like Renata Tebaldi (who ended the concert with a charming rendition of "I Could Have Danced All Night") and even sharing a double bill with Harry Belafonte.

In 1954 we welcomed a new resident company to City Center, and I was their conductor. New York City Light Opera was founded as an offshoot of New York City Opera, with a mandate to mount re-creations of the best works of the American musical stage. Morton Baum agreed to the formation of the Light Opera in large part to placate the unions, who were bargaining for longer engagements for their members. (Performers were paid union minimums. The success of many of the Light Opera productions meant extra income that went to cover City Opera's deficit.) The director of the Light Opera was William Hammerstein, whose father was Oscar Hammerstein II—which meant, of course, that we'd have easier access to Rodgers and Hammerstein's shows and could save on production costs by renting sets and costumes from the original Broadway or touring productions.

The Light Opera opened in May 1954 with two productions plucked from the spring 1954 City Opera season—*Die Fledermaus* and Kern and Hammerstein's *Show Boat.*(Since we had already produced *Fledermaus* and *Show Boat* for City Opera, we had two-thirds of the repertory for the Light Opera season already under our belts.) The third work was *Carousel*. Each show was scheduled to run for two weeks, but *Carousel* was such a hit that we extended it for nine additional weeks—and I had to ask my colleague Fred Dvonch to take over the conducting duties in late June when I left for Hyannis. Baum was most pleasantly surprised by the box office results.

Our gifted cast for *Carousel* included Jo Sullivan, who gave a captivating, touching performance as Julie Jordan. (Two years later she was cast opposite Robert Weede in Loesser's most operatic musical, *The Most Happy Fella*, and in true fairy-tale fashion, ended up falling in love with and marrying the show's composer, Frank Loesser.) The role of Julie's friend Carrie Pipperidge was played by newcomer Barbara Cook, who was a delight to work with. Truth seemed to emanate from her—there was nothing phony, nothing false. I recall the moment in *Carousel* when Jigger was showing her the so-called fireman's trick. He had her on his shoulder and was about to take her into the woods when her fiance, Enoch Snow, angrily confronted them: "What are you doing, coming out of the woods with this fella?" The way in which Barbara responded, "He wasn't taking me out of the woods, he was taking me *into* the woods! Oh I didn't mean that," was convincingly sweet and innocent.

Her voice was sweet, but in her beguiling number "Mr. Snow," there was no opportunity to show it off. I had no idea how fabulous her technique was until two years later—when Barbara gave an astonishing rendition of "Glitter and Be Gay" in Bernstein's *Candide.* She was *very* disciplined and had the goods to be an opera singer. I don't know where she was taught, but she had that certain something that really can't be taught: knowing just how much to give without detracting from the total.

Barbara's *Candide* costar, the New York City Opera tenor Robert Rounseville, was another performer who had the vocal goods to go back and forth between the opera house and Broadway. That ability to successfully "cross over" is rare. For every Eileen Farrell who was born with the special knack to sing Arlen and Gershwin standards, there are dozens of singers who sound stilted and unnatural when they launch into "Someone to Watch Over Me."

A side note to *Carousel,* which we brought back to City Center Light Opera yet again in September 1957 (this time with Barbara Cook as Julie): I had seen and enjoyed the original Broadway production with John Raitt, and felt thoroughly comfortable conducting it. But when Richard Rodgers came to the first rehearsal in August 1957, he was a bit upset with some of my tempi—with a certain "operatic freedom" that I gave them. "Wait a minute," he said, thereby bringing the rehearsal to a halt. Then he indicated to me what he wanted—a strict, steady beat. I gave him what he asked for. Several months later, when we took the production to the 1958 World's Fair in Brussels, I recall that once again I took some artistic license with my tempi—and this time Rodgers didn't seem to mind.

Rodgers's favorite conductor was Fred Dvonch, who won a Tony Award for conducting *The Sound of Music.* Fred was a very methodical conductor with a strong beat, while I like to conduct with a little more freedom.(Interestingly, when the coda starts in a Strauss waltz, many conductors—including me—increase the tempo. Strauss himself did not do this.) But Rodgers and I became friends, anyway, and I did conduct a very successful production of *Oklahoma!* for the Light Opera.

A versatile conductor should be able to conduct anything that comes his way. Still, it is good to have a light, flexible hand for musical theater—understanding where a singer needs more breath, where a dancer needs more time. Although I was never a "ballet conductor" per se, I always enjoyed working with superb dancers like Gemze de Lappe and Edward Villella who occasionally performed in our Light Opera productions.

One day in the summer of 1955, when I was conducting Cole Porter's *Kiss Me, Kate* in Hyannis, I had a surprise visitor after the performance. It was Marcel Prawy, a friend I hadn't seen since we both were standees at the Vienna Staatsoper, twenty years before. He had become dramaturg of the Volksoper and was producing the first Broadway musical to be performed there: Cole Porter's masterful *Kiss Me, Kate*.

"How would you like to conduct *Kiss Me, Kate* in Vienna?" Prawy asked.

This was going to be a whole lot more than just "Another Op'nin', Another Show."

5

BRUSH UP YOUR SHAKESPEARE
AND RETURN TO VIENNA

On New Year's Day, 1956, I arrived in Vienna in the late afternoon. The Four Power Agreement had just been signed, and Austria was restored to its pre–World War II size. It was dreary, damp, and cloudy, and the airport appeared to be nothing more than a couple of Quonset huts. The first thing I saw was a dilapidated bus with a driver in a leather coat—a brown leather coat, no less. I had an apprehensive feeling about returning to the city of my birth for the first time since the war, but I was scheduled to start rehearsals the next day. I was contracted to conduct *Kiss Me, Kate* and *Carmen*— and a lone performance of *Cavalleria rusticana* and *Pagliacci* with Helge Roswaenge—at the Volksoper.

All these years later, I still get a slightly queasy feeling when my plane lands in Vienna. But today, as in 1956, the feeling is soon replaced by a sense of exhilaration and a desire to revisit the haunts of my youth. On that first trip back, I stayed in a pensione run by friends of mine, and Rita joined me ten days prior to the opening.

But I seem to be getting a bit ahead of myself here.

In the summer of 1955, Marcel Prawy—my old colleague from the opera claque in Vienna—showed up unannounced at the Music Tent in Hyannis, Massachusetts. After catching up on old times (Prawy's story was an especially interesting one—he had emigrated to the United States in 1939, fought in the American army, and returned to Austria in 1946 as a "military civilian" of the US forces), he asked if I would be interested in returning to Vienna to conduct the first complete American musical ever presented there, which he was going to produce. The venue was the Volksoper, where Marcel was the newly appointed dramaturge. The show was *Kiss Me, Kate*.

I accepted the job with some ambivalent feelings about returning to Vienna but with great enthusiasm and a feeling of pride at being asked to conduct the show. For several years Prawy had been trying to convince the Austrian Ministry of Education, under whose supervision the state theaters operate, that American musicals had a valid place on the Austrian stage. After he had done sufficient convincing to get the production green-lighted, there were still many diehards who were staunchly opposed to the idea of

Broadway coming to Vienna. Right up through opening night, there were vociferous doubts and derision from the press and others (including a contingent of classically trained musicians). Though the differences between American musical comedy and the Viennese operetta were significant—the Cole Porter swing versus the three-quarter-time sway, and the sassy, idiomatic comedy of Sam and Bella Spewack versus the "gemütliche witz"—I was sure that the show would work in Vienna, because it's a masterful work with wonderful music.

Luckily the venture, from the outset, had the enthusiastic support of two very important people: Ernest Marboe, the forward-thinking superintendent of the state theaters, and Franz Salmhofer, the director of the Volksoper. As it turned out, *Kiss Me, Kate* was a far bigger success than anyone (except perhaps Prawy) could have anticipated, but getting it on the boards presented some problems that are funnier in retrospect than they were during those frenzied weeks of rehearsal.

In those days, because of work regulations, there could be no rehearsals between two and six p.m., and evenings were impossible for rehearsals, because the musicians and singers had to be on hand for performances in the regular Volksoper repertory. This restriction on rehearsal time was hardly simplified by strict union rules fixing a maximum number of rehearsals in which a musician could engage each month. Because of this, the musicians were rotated, with the result that the orchestra never had precisely the same personnel at any two gatherings. As rehearsals progressed, I tried to remain relatively unruffled as musicians came and went—but I shall never forget my shock when, at the ninth performance of the show, I walked into the pit and saw a strange man in the concertmaster's chair.

In sheer size, the orchestra was formidable. There were close to fifty players—twice the size of an orchestra in a Broadway house—and this was due only in part to the enlarged string section. Where, for example, one American musician would have doubled on clarinet, saxophone, flute, and oboe, in Vienna we needed a different man for each. Prawy brought in the Hans Neubauer Orchestra—a small jazz group whose leader played the piano for *Kiss Me, Kate* (and in the prelude to the second act actually played an improvisational solo!).

Not every one of the orchestra members was at first delighted with Cole Porter's music; there were rumors of "sabotage," although I personally did not encounter such a thing. To the credit of all these musicians, they soon caught on and were a splendid pit orchestra—stopping the show every night with "S'ist Viel Zu Heiss" (Too darn hot).

Since Prawy was determined to make this as thoroughly a Volksoper production as possible, only three American singers were imported—Brenda Lewis, Olive Moorefield, and Hubert Dilworth (who, interestingly, went on to become Leontyne Price's longtime personal manager). They played, respectively, Lilli Vanessi/Katharine, Lois Lane/Bianca, and Paul. All three were tremendously successful in their roles—speaking German with the requisite Viennese touch—and for the most part were respected by their Viennese colleagues. They probably accomplished more in the way of international goodwill than three-score diplomats or senators on a mission.

The Volksoper is state subsidized and is therefore able to maintain a huge chorus—about eighty members—to whom the work offers the security of a lifetime career with seniority benefits and pensions. As a result, many of the chorus members were no longer either very chic or very agile. We therefore selected for the chorus of *Kiss Me, Kate* only the youngest, most attractive and slimmest individuals—ending up with a chorus of thirty, which is generous for a Broadway show. (Pounds for kilos, this was "more" chorus than Broadway has ever seen.)

To have the singers moving and the dancers singing was nearly akin to a revolution in Viennese production, yet every one of the singers and dancers enjoyed his or her "dual function" tremendously. Actually the chorus members had to do some unlearning, for they read the score too meticulously, too straight. In my best bathtub baritone, I tried to demonstrate how I'd like the songs to be performed, but they would protest, "Here is an eighth-note." I finally told them, "Don't believe everything you read," and took the music away.

The physical production was lavish to the point where the lavishness sometimes threatened to get in the way of the show. Typical of the care and expense that went into it was the setting for "Too Darn Hot." This number takes about five minutes (not counting the tumultuous applause and foot-stamping that followed it every night), and the scenery for it was used nowhere else in the show. On Broadway it consisted of a simple drop. At the Volksoper we were provided with a solid wood wall about a foot thick, hung from three pipes and complete with a superstructure and fire escape on which one could easily walk. The fact that only one person ever walked on it seemed inconsequential; as a matter of fact, during one particularly trying rehearsal we mordantly concluded that if the show were a flop, we could all live in the set for quite a while. To handle the massive scenery, the services of more than fifty stagehands were required (twice the number of stagehands for a Broadway show), making for more personnel backstage than onstage. The stagehands had to move in high gear; to keep them on their toes, wherever I had thirty seconds of bridge music, I reported to the designer and director that I had only ten seconds. When the show opened, the critics were overwhelmed by what they considered its breathtaking pace!

There is no doubt in my mind that this 1956 production of *Kiss Me, Kate* had a major effect on the subsequent staging of operetta and musical theater productions in Vienna. It served to acquaint the Viennese with the use of music of many different forms in a single show, with the careful integration of music and book, with the sustaining of a constant performance without long pauses, and with the use of a singing chorus that is in motion all the time—always participating, never simply standing around. Much of the credit for the success of our production goes to the inventive stage director Heinz Rosen. Our only disagreement occurred when he wanted to interpolate "Night and Day" (from another Porter show, *Gay Divorce*)—an idea that I firmly nixed.

There were times when we worried about the effect that some spots in the libretto would have on a European audience. One example was the song "Wunderbar." Would Vienna take it as satire or as an insult? Would the Viennese resent having fun poked at their favorite type of love song? We tried changing it several times, but ended up delivering it exactly as Porter intended, and I was happy to see that the Viennese could laugh at themselves. We were afraid, too, that the number "I Hate Men" would be considered too unladylike, but after much debate and experimentation Brenda Lewis performed it as Porter originally composed it and scored a howling success. Her spirited playing was infectious.

Our leading man, Fred Liewehr, one of the most revered dramatic actors of the famous Burgtheater and the possessor of a lovely voice (he had sung Eisenstein in *Fledermaus* at the Staatsoper), helped set the mood for everyone and ultimately garnered a good portion of the laughs each night. He and Brenda Lewis had a ball fighting with each other.

The comedians cast as the gangsters were typically rotund, *gemütlich* comics of the physical comedy school of humor, and, true to the tradition of Viennese operetta, they did some ad libbing during their spots in the show. Still, "Brush Up Your Shakespeare" brought down the house there as it always does in the States.

Viennese audiences—then and now—are not all that different from American audiences. Those moments which move American audiences to applause or laughter also move the Viennese, despite the tremendous difference in their encounters with Broadway musicals. Whenever we permitted the book or music to stand as written, we were successful. Of course all this is tremendously to the credit of Cole Porter and the Spewacks, for their show is sheer perfection and was a smart choice of Prawy's. Whenever our stage director, Heinz Rosen, tried to change something in rehearsal (usually when he was attempting to second-guess the reaction of that hypothetically different Viennese audience), the effect was all the worse, and we ended up going back to the original.

At the time of the production, everyone asked me, "How could *Kate* survive translation into German?" They needn't have worried because Prawy's translation was brilliant; the German he used was intelligent and bright rather than rarefied. For example, in "Where Is the Life That Late I Led?" Petruchio sings in the original, "Where are you Lisa, / You gave a new meaning to the leaning Tow'r of Pisa." In German it went, "Wo bist du Lisa, wie selig wir schliefen hinter'm schiefen Turm von Pisa" (How blissfully we slept behind the Leaning Tower of Pisa). Prawy even managed to keep the vowel sounds similar, as evidenced by his translation of those catchy lines, "Brush up your Shakespeare, / Start quoting him now, / Brush up your Shakespeare, / and the women you will wow," which was turned into "Schlag nach bei Shakespeare, / Dort steht es genau, / Schlag nach bei Shakespeare, / Und du siegst bei jeder Frau."

I still remember the first orchestra reading of "Too Darn Hot," which is a terrific, jazzy number. That particular rehearsal happened to be in the Staatsoper rather than the Volksoper—no doubt because of some double scheduling. When we finished the number, the first cellist said with great dramatic emphasis: "And these walls are still standing." I replied, "Listen my fellow, they said that after Krenek's *Jonny spielt auf.* They said it before and they'll say it again." *Jonny spielt auf* (Johnny strikes up the band) is a 1929 jazz-inflected opera by the Austrian-born composer Ernst Krenek, who was forced to escape to the United States after his music was banned by the Nazis.

All three American cast members did the lyrics for the encores (of which there were many) in English, and it floored us to learn that Miss Lewis had 'em laughing just as loud to the English version of "I Hate Men" as to the German. It seemed that ten years of American occupation had provided the Viennese with sufficient basic English so they could understand such slightly risqué lines as "'Tis he who'll have the fun and thee the baby" or "His business is the business which he gives his secretary."

We were fine-tuning right up until opening night—as a matter of fact, we actually postponed the premiere by a week so we could get everything right.

The opening night was a great success, and *Kiss Me, Kate* at the Volksoper turned out to be a runaway hit. The erudite men who had opposed Prawy's producing a musical with government funds quickly changed their tune when they saw the box-office receipts. The "barbarian importation" sold out quickly, and after running for three nights a week in February and March, it was held over and ran "en suite" for four additional weeks. *Kiss Me, Kate*, which remains today in the Volksoper repertory, opened the doors to productions of all kinds of musicals, from Rodgers to Sondheim. (Brenda Lewis and I were asked to return to the Volksoper the following year for *Annie Get Your Gun*; she went but I declined.)

The critics who had been skeptical before the opening couldn't come up with enough superlatives for *Kate*. One likened the arrival of the Porter show to Offenbach's introduction of his first operetta to Vienna. Another exclaimed, "The operetta is dead; long live the musical."

But I think the attitude of the Viennese theatergoers was perhaps best expressed by the critic who wrote, quite simply, "Kiss Me, Kate—again and again and again."

Still, there was a fly in the ointment. Anti-Semitism was still very much present in the country. So much had transpired since I had been forced to flee Vienna two decades earlier, yet I could see for the most part there had been little change in attitude toward the Jews, and it would take many more visits before I did not feel as if everyone I met was an enemy in disguise. During the run of the show I had several unsettling encounters, and our director, Rosen, told me that one day he found a swastika in his dressing room. Also, it didn't surprise me one whit to hear Brenda Lewis tell of a moment during rehearsals when the dressers and wig people were hanging out in her dressing room (which had a space heater—there was no heat in the hallways) and suddenly the talk turned to Marcel Prawy. "Ah, er ist ein Jude," someone said, to which Brenda responded, in German, "*I* am a Jew." Brenda's dresser fell to her knees in apology—but from that moment on, "the relationship chilled," said Brenda.

The world had changed and there was no going back to Vienna's turn-of-the-century charm.

Still, I enjoyed bringing a bit of classic Broadway to the Old World, and all in all it was a triumphant trip. Viennese audiences embraced the American musical, and the great success of *Kiss Me, Kate* sweetened my return to the country that had exiled me half a lifetime before.

6

INHERITING THE WIND

In December 1956, following the failure of the fall season, Leinsdorf resigned after the company's return from Chicago. It looked very much like the end of New York City Opera. Committees were formed, and there were many phone calls and desperate meetings. Clearly I was part of management, yet my sympathy was very much with the members of the company. Mostly I stayed away from the activities.

A group of singers including Norman Treigle, Phyllis Curtin, Cornell MacNeil, Michael Pollock, and David Lloyd enlisted the efforts of other City Opera members and pleaded with the board to hire a director from within the company's ranks. They wrote a letter to the board members, imploring them to not abandon such an important cultural asset as City Opera, and sent a copy of the letter to the *New York Times*. In addition they met with Newbold Morris and Morton Baum and presented a strong case for the appointment of an insider: "Why look for an outsider to take over the company when you could have Julius—who has risen through the ranks and could run it better than anyone else?" (Or as Morris himself later quipped: "We were tired of prima donna conductors, and Rudel was the only one who knew where the scenery was buried.")

On the evening of January 17, 1957, Rita and I were home getting dressed to attend a performance of a Broadway play. The phone rang, and it was Newbold Morris, casually asking me what I was doing that evening. "I'm going to *Inherit the Wind*," I told him, to which Morris replied, "You just have!"

I received the appointment to the general directorship of New York City Opera less than two months before my thirty-sixth birthday. After I got over the initial shock, my appointment to the top seemed like a natural thing to me. I had no hubris, perhaps because I had no idea what the future held.

Morton Baum sat me down and gave me the grim financial facts. He also told me this was the "final try" the board would make to save the company. The spring 1957 season had already been canceled; the fall season was scheduled to open on October 9 and to run for five weeks, with approximately thirty-five performances. What this meant was that I had nine months to put together a five-week season and get City Opera back on its feet. Coincidentally Rita and I were preparing for the birth of our third child.

The next few weeks were a blur of feverish activity as I made a list of works and performances and came up with a budget for our "make-or-break season." I was positively consumed by the challenge, spending every waking hour and even my alleged sleeping hours planning each detail of my first season. (I kept a notebook on my nightstand for jotting down an endless to-do list.) There was never enough time—which, over the years, has been another motto of City Opera. I agonized over repertory and casting, ultimately deciding on twelve operas and forty-one performances.

The first hammer blow came a few days later. John White, with whom I had worked so closely for more than a decade on all day-to-day administrative tasks, had suffered a nervous breakdown; he blamed himself for bringing on the Leinsdorf disaster and causing the demise of the company. John was hospitalized at St. Vincent's in Greenwich Village, where he received electric shock treatments. I went to visit him now and then, but he was in absolutely no condition to work. Morton Baum urged me to replace him, but I refused. John was the person at City Opera who was closest to me and even though he had been completely off the mark in the Houston matter, we worked well together. I was used to his idiosyncrasies; his acerbic wit didn't bother me. Rather than replace him, I made the choice to go it alone until he was well enough to return to work.

My first order of business was to get rid of the ridiculous single-unit "Lazy Susan" set and retrieve some of our old but serviceable scenery from storage.

Morton Baum and I met several times in February and March to discuss the repertory. I knew that we needed to make a bold statement during my first season, yet I had no real budget to speak of. I considered two operas for opening night: *Turandot* (a favorite of mine from childhood) and *Eugene Onegin*. I finally decided on *Turandot*, which I had conducted once before—a single performance Halasz gave to me in spring 1950 (another bone thrown my way for having prepared the production for him flawlessly).

In the midst of all this I was pulled in yet another direction: in March and April there were rehearsals and performances of the City Center Light Opera production of Lerner and Loewe's *Brigadoon*. The producer, Jean Dalrymple, had taken over the company when Bill Hammerstein left, and now she asked me to be the Light Opera's musical director. I agreed, as a goodwill gesture from one department head to another. *Brigadoon* opened on March 27, 1957, to tumultuous acclaim, with Brooks Atkinson of the *New York Times* praising the production, the "uniformly excellent" cast (including David Atkinson, Jeff Douglas, Virginia Bosler, Helen Gallagher, and Robert Rounseville); Agnes de Mille's choreography; and my own contribution:

"[The score] is played with color and conviction by an excellent orchestra of thirty-two instrumentalists, conducted with obvious authority by Julius Rudel."

Brigadoon was a bona fide hit, and though we had to close on schedule after two weeks, we were able to transfer the production lock, stock, and barrel to Broadway's Adelphi Theatre for an additional four-week run. (Subsequently the Light Opera was to revive the Lerner and Loewe show *four* more times over the next decade—in 1961, '62, '64, and '67, with New York City Ballet's Edward Villella joining the cast and becoming the star of the show with his breathtaking "Sword Dance." As a completely unexpected bonus, I was pleased to receive a Tony Award nomination for Best Conductor for the 1962 revival. In addition, in May 1963 we were invited to perform excerpts from *Brigadoon* in the East Room of the White House at a State Dinner for the King of Morocco, during which President Kennedy delivered a charming welcoming speech in French to the guest of honor. Sally Ann Howes, Eddie Villella, and other cast members made the trip to Washington, but there was not enough room for the orchestra; I had to prerecord the music earlier in the day with the Marine Corps Band, which turned out to be a first-rate ensemble.)

I still hadn't filled all the positions for the fall 1957 season. I wanted to get an Italian conductor—as knowledgeable of the Italian performance style as Morel and Rosenstock were with the French and German styles. I booked a trip to Milan. Morton Baum told me in no uncertain terms that City Center didn't have the money to reimburse me, so I decided to pay for the trip myself. It was money well spent. During my ten-day journey I met with several conductors and was quite impressed with one in particular—Arturo Basile—to whom I offered a contract. He was the real deal: an authentic maestro who was familiar with the traditions of Italian opera. (He had a successful track record with the public and with the press.) The trip to Italy was even more rewarding than I had expected. Among the promising singers I heard there was a young tenor who so impressed me that I engaged him for the leading role of Calaf in *Turandot*. His name was Giuseppe Gismondo; he was handsome, with an exotic, noble face and a dark, seductive voice.

While I was in Italy the *New York Times* got hold of some of my plans and published an article that took the wind out of my sails—disclosing that the new productions for the fall season would include Verdi's *Macbeth*, which had never been performed in New York, and Mozart's *Abduction from the Seraglio*. No casting was listed, and the final paragraph ominously stated, "Whether the City Opera has a spring season will depend on the success of the fall season."

The heat was on for me to make a miracle.

The Abduction from the Seraglio, one of our new productions, was a gift from Lincoln Kirstein, the cofounder and general director of Balanchine's New

York City Ballet. In February he had called and offered me the sets and costumes for a production of *Abduction* that he had produced the previous May in Stratford, Connecticut. I knew that Lincoln had once fancied the directorship of City Opera for himself, and I needed to know he was offering me this gift in a spirit of friendship, without strings attached. He made it clear that he was doing just that, and I happily accepted the gift. The costumes and sets were simple but stylish; the production was successful, and we revived it many times.

Another gift came by way of Jean Dalrymple. She offered me a double bill of Manuel de Falla operas to be conducted by José Iturbi, the flashy pianist best known for his appearances in a number of Hollywood musicals. Jean and Iturbi had been romantically involved for several years while she was his publicist, and she wanted to show the world that he was a "serious" conductor. I proposed a concert version of a De Falla double bill, but Iturbi and Jean demanded a full-scale production and would settle for nothing less. There ensued a search for scenery. We ended up borrowing the sets for the two one-act operas, *La vida breve* and *El amor brujo*, from the Barcelona Opera Company, whose general director at the time was none other than Laszlo Halasz. (I'm not certain how Jean managed this feat; Halasz was still bitter over his firing from the directorship of City Opera in 1951—he had sued City Center following his dismissal—and he had no great love for me, either.) My budget had no provision for a stage director, and in a moment of temporary insanity I agreed to let Jean herself direct the double bill. Little did I know she would spend a small fortune on costumes and a guest lighting director (when our own resident lighting director, Hans Sondheimer, could have done a much better job). The production, though musically first-rate, was a dramatic shambles. I had to jump in and direct the chorus at the final dress rehearsal, as Jean had apparently not told them where to be (or what to do) onstage.

To balance the repertory I also planned our first production of Lehar's *The Merry Widow* (with Beverly Sills and Robert Rounseville in the leading roles), keeping projected costs at a minimum by agreeing to share the Light Opera Company's scenery and costumes. During my trip, I had made a stop in Paris. *My Fair Lady* composer Frederick Loewe was living the high life in Paris, now that his show was the hottest ticket on Broadway. I paid a visit to his lavish suite at the Plaza Athenee to ask his permission to let *My Fair Lady* conductor Franz Allers take some nights off from that show to conduct our *Merry Widow*. When Fritz Loewe finally emerged from the hotel gambling room, where he had lost a good deal of money (which didn't seem to faze him one iota), he graciously agreed to my request.

Although I very much wanted to include *Macbeth* in my first season, I didn't put it on my initial proposal to the board. There was simply no money to produce it properly. I showed Morton Baum the lineup prior to the board meeting, and he said, "Julius, you need something more. It's not enough yet. Go ahead, do the *Macbeth*. I'll get you the money."

These were words that I heard more than once from Morton: "Don't worry, I'll get you the money." And somehow he always did.

When Baum okayed *Macbeth*, I was ready for it and knew I could cast it strongly. We had within our ranks the perfect baritone for the title role: Cornell MacNeil. "Mac" had it all—a large baritone voice of unending power from bottom to top, a wonderful stage presence, and good theatrical instincts. I was certain he would create a sensation, and I could surround him with a well-nigh ideal cast led by Irene Jordan as a steely-voiced Lady Macbeth.

On my return from Europe I was overjoyed to see our small staff working so intensely. The singers were being coached, and chorus rehearsals began in due course during the summer.

I've always felt the title role in *Turandot*, Puccini's final opera, should be sung, not screamed; just because Turandot is an "ice princess" doesn't mean she needs to sing piercingly. I wanted Frances Yeend to do the role. It took a lot of convincing, but she finally accepted the part and ultimately delivered a very beautiful performance. Adele Addison was a touching, heartbreaking Liu and Joshua Hecht a noble Timur. For the role of Calaf one needs a real Italianate tenor. The totally unknown Giuseppe Gismondo made a strong impression as Calaf; his voice was ravishing and he had thrilling top notes, to boot. I believe he would have had a major career—but after two seasons with us, he mysteriously disappeared.

Turandot opened October 9. The night before, I managed to get some sleep, but Rita was wide awake nervously tossing and turning all night. The next morning, when I walked into City Center, I was struck by a certain air of exuberance in the building, even in the administrative offices on the seventh floor. The day flew by as I tended to various administrative tasks, rehearsed *Susannah*, and looked in on other rehearsals and meetings.

A few minutes before the performance began, I went backstage to talk to the choristers. "Make the first five minutes sensational," I told them. They did—and then maintained that intensity until the final curtain.

The next day's *New York Times* review, written by Howard Taubman, tells the story:

> The New York City Opera Company began its new season at City Center last night with a remarkably fine *Turandot*. Puccini's last opera is a challenge to the greatest opera houses, and one shuddered in advance at this company's temerity. But under the guidance of its new general director, Julius Rudel, the City Center troupe carried it off with high honors.

The feat was all the more notable because the company was rising from the ashes of grave artistic and economic troubles, which caused the cancellation of the last spring season. If this *Turandot* is any indication, morale has been re-established and the new season will be lively.

The second night of the season, I conducted *Susannah*, the only opera left over from Leinsdorf's season, with Phyllis Curtin and Norman Treigle. Since we had gotten rid of the turntable set, I asked our house designer Andreas Nomikos to design a new set and brought in Marcella Cisney to direct the opera. Though I was not pleased with the resulting production, Curtin and Treigle once again gave definitive performances and Carlisle Floyd's opera was fast becoming one of our company's staples.

Less than two months before *Macbeth* was scheduled to open, Cornell MacNeil's manager called me, appealing to our friendship and the importance of "career building"—Mac's career, that is. Mac had been offered a contract by Lyric Opera of Chicago, which then, as now, had a star-studded roster and paid its artists handsomely. Mac wanted a release from his contract. I was very angry about this turn of events, but I wasn't going to hold Mac captive. (Over the years, the temptation was always there. We lost a number of singers who were making careers at City Opera to other companies, usually to the Met. Many became stars while others, like Beverly Bower and Laurel Hurley, got lost.)

I had to find a Macbeth quickly—no easy task, as precious few baritones know the part.

In the course of our regular auditions, we had heard William Chapman, and we liked him very much. I had conducted him in the summer of 1956 in *The King and I* at the Cape Cod Melody Tent in Hyannis. That had turned out very well—he had impressed me with his powerful baritone voice and charismatic stage presence—so we had signed him at City Opera for a couple of Escamillos. When he came to sign his contract, Bill casually asked if he could understudy MacNeil in *Macbeth*. Just as casually, I replied, "Sure." He was indeed sent from heaven. Now I had to persuade the conductor, Basile—who at first was dubious—that Bill could pull off the role of the Scottish king. But Margaret Webster, the director, had no doubts.

There was good chemistry between Bill and Irene Jordan—and during rehearsals, when he needed a bit of support, Peggy Webster instilled confidence in Bill by sitting down next to him and soothingly reassuring him how perfect his voice was for the role.

Bill Chapman was eager to absorb, to learn, to do. He epitomized the New York City Opera ideal. Those were the days when the challenge was extended to everybody. The vibes were good. My days were exhilarating, filled with artistic and administrative activities, and no fixed boundaries between the two. Within five minutes I might have two meetings: one with a stage director and another with our chorus master. Then I would coach a small group or ensemble for an hour, and go straight into an orchestra rehearsal. It was a crazy existence, yet we all seemed to thrive on it.

Macbeth received excellent reviews and caused a stir. Apparently the great baritone Leonard Warren came to one of our performances and then went to see Rudolf Bing—and the next thing we knew *Macbeth* was on the Met schedule for the 1958–59 season. Bill Chapman did such a fine job on Fifty-Fifth Street that he was invited to sing Macbeth at the opening of Menotti's Spoleto Festival in Italy in June 1958.

That first season, we could do no wrong. Audiences and critics turned out in good numbers, and we finished on budget. We were already in close discussions with the Ford Foundation about plans for our first American Season.

7

ALL-AMERICAN

In the spring of 1948, the company was in its fourth year, and it was time for an American opera. Halasz chose a double bill of Gian Carlo Menotti's *The Old Maid and the Thief* and *Amelia Goes to the Ball* (the Italian-born Menotti, who had studied music at the Curtis Institute in Philadelphia, was the "American of choice" at the moment). I prepared both operas for Halasz, and as reward for a job well done, he allowed me to conduct the final performance that season of *Amelia*, a sparkling comedy with Marguerite Piazza and Walter Cassel in the leading roles.

The following year, in his quest for recognition, Halasz took the company on a giant leap into legitimacy with a world premiere: *Troubled Island*, an opera written by the distinguished African American composer William Grant Still with a libretto by the equally distinguished poet Langston Hughes.

Troubled Island, which premiered on March 31, 1949, dealt with the rise and fall of the leader of the Haitian Revolution, Jean-Jacques Dessalines. By then City Opera had already broken the color barrier, so it seemed odd that a white singer, Robert Weede, was chosen to play the leading role, which he performed in blackface. I later learned that Still himself had wanted Weede for the leading role and that he had been in favor of an interracial cast for *Troubled Island* because he considered his work an "American" opera rather than a "Negro" opera.

All brilliant planning was useless; the work was not a success, and *Troubled Island* was given no subsequent productions after its premiere. Some have said this was because of racism and political maneuvering. Speaking from firsthand knowledge—I conducted the final of three performances of the opera, and I still have my copy of the score—I beg to differ. *Troubled Island*, though a noble effort, was musically and dramatically weak. It was an imitation of a European-style opera and it did not have the strength and professional substance of some of Still's other compositions. (One particularly sharp tongue described it as "stillborn.")

City Opera's second world premiere was David Tamkin's *The Dybbuk* in October 1951. This one did not succeed for other reasons. It was an interesting effort to dramatize a classic Jewish tale, but today it is remembered mainly for being the "hot button" production that led to Halasz's dismissal. The next world premiere, under Rosenstock's aegis, had all the makings of a hit. It was Copland's *The Tender Land* (1954), staged by Jerome Robbins and conducted by Thomas Schippers. Though there were some lovely moments in the opera (for example, "Laurie's Song"), I found it to be pale and lacking in real conflict. Nevertheless it has found a home in various school and conservatory productions.

The single solitary hit of Erich Leinsdorf's season as General Director was the New York premiere of Carlisle Floyd's *Susannah*, starring Phyllis Curtin and Norman Treigle. Phyllis had created the title role in the opera's first production at Florida State University in February 1955, and she was responsible for bringing the work to the attention of Leinsdorf.

Born in Florida and the son of a Methodist preacher, Floyd was just twenty-six when he composed *Susannah*. Prior to that, he had never actually seen an opera performance. He wrote the libretto for *Susannah* himself—and it is masterful. A modern adaptation of the apocryphal story of Susannah and the Elders, the opera makes use of authentic folk themes as well as Floyd's own inventions. It's a melodious, beautifully written work, without a single unnecessary word or note, that quickly became a signature piece for our company and a personal favorite of mine. I've conducted it many times over the years, most recently at Lyric Opera of Chicago in 2002. In November 2009 I conducted the "revival scene" from *Susannah* (with Samuel Ramey wonderful as the itinerant evangelist Blitch) at City Opera's opening night gala. Once again I was struck by the naturalness of the music and dramatic action. It's an opera that never fails to move an audience.

After my appointment, my meetings with Morton Baum continued with greater frequency, and they were always exciting and stimulating; the man amazed me with his love of the arts and his broad knowledge of music. He liked to attend rehearsals (strictly as an observer), and after one of them, he came home with me and stopped in to say hello to Rita. He walked over to the piano, sat down, and saw the score of *Pagliacci* lying there. Without looking at the page he started to sing Silvio's little aria to Nedda. He had a respectable, musical voice.

I knew that Morton Baum had been in close discussions with W. McNeil ("Mac") Lowry of the Ford Foundation, and that the Foundation had only recently begun to give money to arts organizations for special projects. "The Ford Foundation is interested in helping us in some way," Baum told me, "but they said it has to be something special—it cannot be the usual 'deficit financing.' I want you to meet Mac Lowry."

Baum introduced me to Mac, and the two of us had an instant rapport. Mac was a wonderful guy—eager to help but constrained by the Ford Foundation's rules and guidelines. Over the next few months we saw each other at social gatherings and arts events, and it wasn't long before Mac and his wife, Elsa, began to attend concerts and plays with Rita and me. Morton Baum, Mac, and I also met informally now and then to talk about opera.

Our conversations sometimes turned to the subject of American opera. If our audiences were willing to embrace *Susannah* and the operas of Menotti, and if New York City Opera was indeed "The People's Opera," shouldn't we perform more works by American composers? Why not try to distinguish ourselves from the other American opera companies that stuck to "the golden dozen" operas—*Bohème, Aida, Faust,* and so forth. Though the Met many years before had embarked on a mission to produce American operas—culminating with a trio of works that were very popular in their day: Deems Taylor's *The King's Henchman* (1927) and *Peter Ibbetson* (1931), and Louis Gruenberg's *The Emperor Jones* (1933)—the effort was dropped when the company's longtime general manager Gatti-Casazza (an Italian who spoke very little English yet understood the responsibility of the Met to cultivate the work of Americans!) retired in 1935. By the 1950s, the only groups tackling American works with some regularity were the opera classes of conservatories across the country.

In one of my informal meetings with Baum and Lowry in March 1957, I blurted out a bit flippantly, "I bet you I could find enough American works to fill a whole season."

Those were the magic words.

I proposed that we present ten American operas during a five-week season. It may have been a bit of braggadocio on my part, but this seemed to be exactly the sort of project the Ford Foundation was looking for. Mac liked the idea and encouraged me to run with it. As soon as the plan had shape and aim, Mac was more than happy to support us. We drew up a proper proposal, and the Ford Foundation awarded us an initial grant of $100,000 for an "American Season" of opera.

Our American Season in spring 1958 was the first season of opera ever underwritten by a private foundation, and the fact that the Ford Foundation was universally recognized gave us a certain cachet. I was acutely aware of the fact that we were breaking new ground, both artistically and financially; this partnership was an enormous investment in time, talent, and money. An entire American Season—ten operas in a five-week period. Were we trailblazing pioneers?—or self-deluded Don Quixotes?

Word got out quickly about our plans, and I was inundated with manuscripts and suggestion letters from composers (or their managers) and music publishers. The publishers of course were very much in my corner. For them the American Season was an important statement.

Not everyone was happy. There were scoffers who denied the existence of such a thing as "American opera"; deficit-dreading types who feared we would be playing to empty houses; timid traditionalists, including one woman who politely inquired, "But aren't you going to include *Bohème?*"; and foreign-language lovers who wanted to know whether this all-American season would be sung in English. I received an ominous-looking postcard with black lettering that said: "Even with the Ford grant you're going to lose your shirt; there isn't a melody in the lot." It was signed "R.H." (I banished the fleeting thought that the cryptic signature stood for Rodgers and Hammerstein.)

Morton Baum gave me carte blanche in planning the American Season, because he knew I would not abuse the privilege. I felt a bit like the sorcerer's apprentice; I had no idea what I had started until I was deluged with scores. For months I waded through, ate with, lived with, and even went to sleep with more than two hundred works. (Plus, in addition to planning the American Season, I had to plan our impending fall 1958 repertory season, which included the US premiere of Strauss's *Die schweigsame Frau*, to be performed in English as *The Silent Woman*.) Some of the compositions were handwritten (a few were nearly illegible), while others had been out of print for years. I even took a look at Frederick Converse's *Pipe of Desire*, which had been given its world premiere at the Metropolitan Opera nearly fifty years earlier; I would have liked to produce Howard Hanson's *Merry Mount*, which had also premiered at the Met (in 1934), but the forces it required were beyond our means.

The themes of the libretti were varied; a survey of them could easily fill a book. Victor Borge would have had a field day with some of the storylines. I recall that one was about electronics and had a leading role for "Alternating Current"—to be *danced* by a mezzo-soprano. Many of these works were merely "faux European" but occasionally the spark of the muse became visible.

Slowly a repertory began to emerge, and one day in mid-December 1957, the crowning piece appeared: it was *The Good Soldier Schweik.* The music was by the wildly talented thirty-five-year-old composer Robert Kurka—who tragically had died just a few days earlier of leukemia. The opera was brought to my attention by Nelson Sykes, a gifted public relations man and opera buff who founded and led the New York City Opera Guild with his wife, Martha Moore Sykes. Nelson arranged for me to meet with Kurka's widow during the last week of December, and she brought along the complete score. I was instantly taken with it and we worked swiftly to get the rights to produce it.

Based on the famous antiwar novel of the same name by Jaroslav Hašek— the episodic tale of a soldier who gets entangled in military bureaucracy during World War I—Kurka's adaptation is true to the tone of the book: tongue-in-cheek, almost slapstick in sections. The libretto by Lewis Allen (the pseudonym used by Abel Meeropol, who had written the anti-lynching song "Strange Fruit," which became a chapter in black American history) was well-crafted, and the opera had been brilliantly orchestrated for winds, brass, and percussion—no strings—by the composer himself (though the last few pages were orchestrated by Kurka's friend Hershy Kay). *Schweik* had a real "military band" feel to it, which is important to the nature of the piece, and I looked forward to conducting it.

Fifty years ago we could mount a work—from stem to stern—in three or four months. I first saw the score to Kurka's opera in December, and the premiere occurred four months later—on April 23, 1958. Today it takes several years from the time an opera is planned to its much-hyped opening night. Enough said.

I invited Carmen Capalbo, who had directed the hit 1955 Off-Broadway production of *The Threepenny Opera*, to direct *Schweik*. He was a sensitive director, fine in his work with the individual performers though not as skillful with the physical pacing of the opera. The production, which needed to move breezily, was a bit clunky. We had only three onstage rehearsals (technical, piano dress, and orchestra dress), which was par for the course—and the "final dress" was a mess. We had to stop several times and wait for stage adjustments that should have been taken care of days before.

Amazingly, the opening night went smoothly, with the audience in our camp the entire time. Tenor Norman Kelley was perfect for the title role, which Kurka had written with him in mind. Squat of build, he was both smart alecky and seemingly simple-minded. Baritone David Atkinson as Lt. Henry Lukash was properly debonair (and the perfect foil for Kelley), and the large cast showed off the strengths of our company. Among the excellent performers who assayed small roles in *Schweik* were George S. Irving (who was bound for a long Broadway career), Chester Ludgin, Joshua Hecht, Emile Renan, and Arthur Newman. *Schweik*, then and now (it has been performed with some regularity in Europe and was also successfully revived at Glimmerglass in 2003), is an opera that seems to speak to people.

Everyone in our company took on several roles that first American Season. Joshua Hecht, who was only twenty-eight years old, convincingly played the much older William Jennings Bryan in *The Ballad of Baby Doe* one night and Horace Giddens in *Regina* the next, plus Elder Ott in *Susannah* and a Psychiatrist in *Schweik*. Hecht, like Norman Treigle (and, going back to my childhood, a Viennese bass named Richard Mayr who sang the greatest Gurnemanz I ever heard), was the kind of performer who felt himself *being* the role and could completely immerse himself in a character. Hecht and his colleagues epitomized what City Opera was all about. Our company was so versatile, it seemed anybody could do anything.

Schweik was the first work in our repertory to utilize film footage, a technique that Frank Corsaro would later exploit to stunning effect in Janáček's *The Makropoulos Affair* and Korngold's *Die tote Stadt*. For this initial, somewhat primitive, use of film, we got a city permit and rode through Central Park in the back of Nelson Sykes's convertible one late-winter day, shooting black-and-white footage of Norman Kelley walking through the crowd in his soldier's uniform.

While planning the American Season, I was always mindful of money or, more accurately, the *lack* of it. When I scheduled Vittorio Giannini's *The Taming of the Shrew*, a delightful opera starring Walter Cassel and Phyllis Curtin as Petruchio and Kate, I knew I could produce it much more cost-effectively if I used the scenery, by Watson Barratt, and costumes from City Center Light Opera's production of *Kiss Me, Kate*. (I was to utilize this method numerous times. For our fall 1965 season we used the same Howard Bay set—with minor tinkering—for Strauss's *Capriccio* that we had used in '64 for Lee Hoiby's *Natalia Petrovna*.) Giannini was born in America of Italian parents. The lyric heritage from Italy was beautifully clear in everything he wrote, yet his voice was very much his own, his music a very personal statement.

Two of the best examples of American opera—*Street Scene* and *Lost in the Stars*—were written by Kurt Weill, who was born in Germany but arrived in this country and embraced everything the US had to offer. I never got to meet Weill (though I was to become friendly with his widow, the famous Lotte Lenya, who invited me to become a charter board member of the Kurt Weill Foundation), yet I always felt a special kinship with him—and not just because we were both Jewish refugees from the German territories. We were both of the opinion that Broadway presented the wave of the future, the direction in which American opera was heading and the direction in which it *should* be heading.

I was certain I could make a powerful statement by programming Weill's *Lost in the Stars* and Blitzstein's *Regina* for our American Season. These two operas had been given their Broadway premieres on successive nights in 1949. *Lost in the Stars* is based on *Cry, the Beloved Country*, Alan Paton's towering novel about apartheid in South Africa. *Regina* is adapted from Lillian Hellman's play *The Little Foxes*, about two greedy brothers and their even greedier sister. I planned to conduct *Lost in the Stars* and extended an invitation to Samuel Krachmalnick to do the honors for *Regina*. I had conducted *Regina* in its first City Opera incarnation in 1953, and I must admit it was tough for me to hand it over to another conductor, but Krachmalnick did a fine job with the opera and the subsequent LP. We had extremely strong casting for each show: for *Lost in the Stars*, Lawrence Winters as the pastor Stephen Kumalo; young Shirley Carter (who became better known as Shirley Verrett) as Irina, the girl in love with Kumalo's ill-fated son; and the very young Louis Gossett in the nonsinging role of the doomed boy, Absalom. For the other speaking roles, we went outside of the company and invited Rosetta LeNoire, who had founded the interracial AMAS Theater; Douglas Turner Ward, the creator of the Negro Ensemble Company; famed choral director Eva Jessye; Godfrey Cambridge, who was already making his mark on the comedy world; and an eight-year-old kid named Patti Austin as Nita.

José Quintero, who had become a hot property after the success of *The Iceman Cometh* at Circle in the Square, accepted our offer to direct *Lost in the Stars*. He couldn't read a note of music but familiarized himself with the opera by listening repeatedly to the original cast recording. A little side note: The second act of *Lost in the Stars* begins with a harrowing, complex choral scene with double chorus. Quintero never rehearsed it. One day I asked him when he was planning to stage the scene and he gave me a blank look. It turned out he didn't know anything about the number, as it wasn't on the recording. We played it for him, and he staged it quickly and movingly. The entire production was spare and affecting and altogether luminous.

Lost in the Stars is one of the most shattering works I have ever conducted. I could never look up onstage at the end of the final scene with the two old men facing each other and waiting for the moment of Absalom's execution. It was too heartbreaking. It still is. In 2008, fifty years after I first conducted *Lost in the Stars* at City Opera, I conducted it again at the Virginia Festival and at Opera Theater Pittsburgh. The new production was passionately directed by Jonathan Eaton, with a powerful cast led by Herbert Perry as Stephen Kumalo—and Perry's twin brother, Eugene, as Absalom. In reassessment, the score has gained in stature, and the "Fear" number has taken on a whole new meaning in today's society.

We were extremely lucky to have Brenda Lewis reprise the title role of the malevolent villainess in *Regina*. For our 1958 revival, Joshua Hecht was her ailing husband, Horace; and George S. Irving and Emile Renan were her evil brothers, with Elisabeth Carron (who made her City Opera debut in fall 1957 as a very moving Cio-Cio San in *Madama Butterfly*) giving a touching portrayal of the gentle Birdie.

Our *Regina* cast was superb, but we were not as fortunate in our choice of directors. The Broadway scenery we had borrowed for our 1953 production was gone, so as long as we needed a new designer (Howard Bay) we also opted for a new director. We looked for someone that all of us—including *Regina*'s strongly opinionated composer, Marc Blitzstein—could agree on. That someone turned out to be Herman Shumlin, who had directed the original Broadway production of *The Little Foxes*; he proceeded to direct *Regina* as if he were directing the Hellman play. He was totally stymied by the music, and rehearsals were often traumatic. Some of the music, most notably the ragtime "Angel Band," ended up being cut, as Shumlin literally did not know what to do with it. I still can't believe that Blitzstein agreed to cut that marvelous moment from the show. It seemed to me that he was betraying himself by agreeing to Shumlin's request. (I had hoped to produce Blitzstein's *Sacco and Vanzetti* at New York City Opera. But Marc opted to take it to the Met instead. He told me this news at the party for *The Cradle Will Rock*, Blitzstein's 1937 landmark agitprop musical, which opened our third American Season in February 1960. "Very well. Good luck. Try your wings,"

I told him. *Sacco and Vanzetti* was nowhere near completion at the time of Blitzstein's murder in Martinique in January 1964.)

For our first American Season, we also brought back a double bill of Menotti works, *The Old Maid and the Thief* and *The Medium*, along with Floyd's *Susannah.*

In addition, I found two other one-act operas that seemed eminently worthy: Mark Bucci's *Tale for a Deaf Ear* and Leonard Bernstein's *Trouble in Tahiti* (which he later made into a full evening's opera—*A Quiet Place*). *Tahiti*, a look at a disintegrating urban marriage, bubbles with jazzy energy but leaves a slightly bitter aftertaste. The Bucci work also deals with a bickering couple who lack the spirituality to remake their relationship. Back to back, the two works were quite effective. As a special bonus, I asked Bernstein to conduct the first of three performances of his opera—which turned out to be a highlight of the festival.

At this point the season was nearly complete, but we still needed an opera for opening night. I decided on Douglas Moore's *The Ballad of Baby Doe*, which had garnered a lot of positive attention two years earlier at its world premiere at Central City Opera. Based on a true story of the late-nineteenth-century silver baron Horace Tabor and his mistress Elizabeth ("Baby") Doe, Moore's opera had all the necessary attributes for a festive opening—including John LaTouche's poetic yet so-true-to-life libretto. I thought it would present our company in our best light, and I was confident it would fill seats. It did.

Beverly Sills was ideal as Baby Doe, and Walter Cassel as Horace Tabor repeated his Central City role for us. He *was* Tabor—and gave the most touching portrayal imaginable. Martha Lipton rejoined the company to recreate her Central City role as Tabor's long-suffering first wife, Augusta. (Our company's subsequent recording with Sills, Cassel, and Frances Bible is one for the ages.)

There was a special atmosphere on opening night, April 3, 1958—a sense of closeness between the audience and the performers that was to remain during the entire season. There were audible sobs in the audience during the final scene, when Walter Cassel's Horace—now a broken man and dying—sang to Beverly Sills, "You were always the real thing, Baby." And at the end, after Sills had floated that final gorgeous note for all eternity, the applause was deafening.

The next morning at breakfast, I opened the *New York Times* to read Howard Taubman's review of *The Ballad of Baby Doe*. It was good enough. Next I opened the *Herald Tribune* and went straight to the music pages. There was nothing there. Nothing. I was outraged that the editors didn't think it was important enough to report on. As I closed the paper, I glanced at the front page. The review was there, and it was a rave. "American Opera Hailed Here" was the headline, and music critic Jay S. Harrison began his review with: "The first opera season in history devoted exclusively to American works opened last night at the City Center with one of the few operas that is authentically American in style, spirit and subject. . . . If any others are the equal of *Baby Doe*, which has not been seen locally before, native opera will have arrived like a clap of thunder on a still spring night." The American Season had begun in triumph!

Six days and two productions later, *Lost in the Stars* opened; ticket sales were so strong for this show that we added an extra week of performances to the end of the season.

With two productions opening each week, we literally rehearsed day and night in every available space in City Center—occasionally we even borrowed the keys to the NBC Studios on West Fifty-Sixth Street. (Felix Popper, our music administrator, was also on the staff of NBC Opera, and Peter Herman Adler—NBC Opera's artistic director—was conducting our production of *The Taming of the Shrew*.) Lunch and dinner were "grab as grab can," and sometimes rehearsals would run way past midnight.

Our American Season ended most successfully, and our company celebrated. It was exhausting yet exhilarating, and we all knew that something special had taken place. (The conductor Giorgio Polacco, who had worked at the Met and as the principal conductor of the Chicago Opera Company, would come backstage after nearly every performance of our American Season and congratulate us: "Un altro miracolo," he would say.) Yet for me it was modified rapture. One swallow does not a summer make, and one American Season does not a statement make. We needed to build on our success.

A few days after the season ended, Howard Taubman of the *Times* praised our achievement, writing that the Ford Foundation's investment was "wise and creative, and deserves to be renewed." Those words gave Morton Baum and me the confidence to go back to Mac Lowry and plead our case: "We have enough operas for a second season and for a national tour." Mac was with us all the way. Sympathetic and understanding of our artistic vision, he went above and beyond the call of duty of a foundation executive, becoming a friend and a champion to our cause.

In October 1958 the Ford Foundation officially awarded us $310,000 for a second American Season (which we immediately scheduled for spring 1959) and a tour the following year. City Center would itself absorb the cost of an abbreviated third American Season that preceded the tour (which would give us a chance to perform for our New York audience all four operas that would go on tour).

In addition, a few thousand dollars of the grant was earmarked for a program that brought thirty fledgling composers and librettists to New York to observe the workings of our company firsthand. Chosen on the strength of their submissions, they came from all over the country. Some had never before set foot in an opera house. This program was a particular point of pride for me.

Beginning in 1959 (and continuing through the mid-1970s) the Ford Foundation also awarded City Opera money to commission and perform new operas; among those works were Robert Ward's *The Crucible* and Jack Beeson's *Lizzie Borden*, the two most successful new American operas to grace our stage.

I can't stress enough how important Mac Lowry's vision of arts funding was to City Opera—and to the entire cultural scene in America. Mac Lowry was a unique individual, whose influence on arts funding was gargantuan. He began his career as an English professor and in 1953 joined the Ford Foundation as head of its education department—becoming the director of the foundation's arts and humanities programs in 1957. On Mac's advice, the Ford Foundation began to support the arts in a modest way—our grant was one of the earliest—before expanding its arts program in 1962.

Morton Baum, too, was one of a kind in his total dedication to City Center and in the way he shepherded the center's opera, ballet, and light opera companies. We had a wonderful, close working relationship. I could call him at any hour of the day or night, and he was always ready with advice, guidance, and leadership. In a paternal way, Baum still referred to John White and me as "the boys"—though by the late 1950s I was pushing forty and John was nearly fifty. Baum certainly had a strong hand in protecting "the boys"— and discussing, examining, and hashing out our schedule and future plans. He was always well informed and totally supportive. Only once did we have a major disagreement with repercussions.

Jean Dalrymple wrote in her 1975 autobiography, *From the Last Row*, that I was Morton Baum's "special pet." But for a year or so beginning in fall 1958 I most definitely was not the teacher's pet. My fall from grace happened when I was planning the second American Season. Morton asked me whether *Show Boat* was included in the schedule. I said "No," and he reasoned with me, saying that he needed a "sure thing" for the box office because we were in financial trouble—and furthermore, was *Show Boat* not an important milestone in the development of Broadway? Since we already had *Show Boat* in our repertory, it was a logical thing. My instinct as well as my value judgment said we should not include *Show Boat* in this lineup; I felt it was too lightweight a property for the American Season, and that it would disturb the balance I was trying to achieve. Baum persevered, but I stuck to my guns, and *Show Boat* was not part of the spring '59 season.

Baum was furious; he was sure that my decision had resulted in a loss of income. To emphasize his disapproval, he named John White as my codirector of New York City Opera. We never spoke of the *Show Boat* incident again, and after a year or so, my relationship with Baum returned to its old pattern. (Sometime later, I asked Mac Lowry how he would have felt if I had included *Show Boat* as part of the second American Season. He confirmed my feeling that the Ford Foundation would not have been happy with *Show Boat*.)

For the second American Season, I followed the same formula as before (one world premiere, several New York premieres, and some revivals of operas that had already been seen), but enlarged the playing field from ten to twelve works—bringing back four of the operas from the first American Season (*Baby Doe, The Medium, Regina,* and *Susannah*) and adding eight new works to the repertory.

We opened with Menotti's *Maria Golovin,* which, while not on the same plane as *The Consul* or *The Saint of Bleecker Street,* was well crafted and displayed Gian Carlo's theatrical flair to good advantage. Richard Cross, who had played the role of the sensitive young blind man, Donato, in the opera's premiere at the Brussels World's Fair the previous year, reprised the role for us in his company debut. For the world premiere I selected *Six Characters in Search of an Author,* composer Hugo Weisgall and librettist Dennis Johnston's remarkable adaptation of Pirandello's play within a play (or, in our case, opera within an opera) that skewers the boundaries between illusion and reality.

I feel that Weisgall's best work—and *Six Characters* falls into that category—is in the same camp as Alban Berg's brilliant opera *Wozzeck.* Though we brought *Six Characters* back into the repertory the next year, and also took it on tour, I always felt that it should have had more of an afterlife. (The past few years have seen a resurgence of performances by regional companies and colleges, which is reassuring.) It really is an excellent piece.

Another eminently worthy work we brought into the repertory that season was Carlisle Floyd's *Wuthering Heights.* I spread the net and invited Delbert Mann, who had won an Academy Award in 1955 for his direction of *Marty,* to stage the production.

Del asked the cast members to jot down the "back stories" of their individual characters. David Atkinson, who was originally slated to play Heathcliff, took the assignment more seriously than the others and wrote volumes about Heathcliff's childhood. He was so busy construing Heathcliff's history that he neglected to learn the role; it was reassigned to John Reardon. Phyllis Curtin performed the role of Cathy; Jacqueline Moody was Isabella; Patricia Neway was Nelly, the maid (yet another wonderful role for her); and Frank Poretta was Edgar. I conducted *Wuthering Heights,* and still have a vivid recollection of a terrible thing that happened on opening night. During an "open scene change," the set was supposed to be transformed from indoors to outdoors as the performers, who began the scene inside the house, walked outside. The scenery (a partial turntable) moved in a contrary direction and it was a wonderful effect that carried the narrative forward. Unfortunately the stagehands didn't hear their call and the set did not move, which meant Heathcliff and the others had to stay inside the house and sing. The splendid effect was lost and we played the rest of the act on the wrong set. Everybody seemed to lose their concentration, and *Wuthering*

Heights failed to receive the strong reviews and positive word-of-mouth that it deserved. (Dire mishaps like this can truly affect the outcome and audience reception of an opera. Another equally traumatic opening night occurred in 1965, when Marguerite Willauer lost her voice at the premiere of Ned Rorem's *Miss Julie.*)

Street Scene turned out to be the runaway hit of the second American Season. Kurt Weill's music and Langston Hughes's libretto perfectly captured the essence of Elmer Rice's play about New York tenement life on a steamy summer day, and our large ensemble cast (anchored by Elisabeth Carron and William Chapman as the unhappily married couple Anna and Frank Maurrant) was beautifully directed by Herbert Machiz, who had been recommended to me by Lotte Lenya.

Among the other works performed that season, honorable mention went to Robert Ward's first opera, *He Who Gets Slapped*, a parable set in a circus and based on a play by Andreyev. The work, with a libretto by Bernard Stambler and direction by Michael Pollock (one of our company's character tenors), was a *succès d'estime*—colorful and lively, with interesting music.

In October 1959 the Ford Foundation announced a new initiative to foster American opera: an unprecedented donation of $950,000 to be used by four companies—the Metropolitan Opera, Lyric Opera of Chicago, San Francisco Opera, and New York City Opera—for the commission and production of eighteen new American operas. This funding was a true validation of our company's efforts to shine the spotlight on American composers. Not surprisingly, New York City Opera commissioned the majority of these operas—eleven works between 1961 and 1971, including Robert Ward's *The Crucible* (which was awarded a Pulitzer Prize and recorded with its original brilliant cast led by Chester Ludgin and Frances Bible); Abraham Ellstein's *The Golem* (Ludgin was truly frightening in the title role of this opera, though the work was in sore need of editing, which the composer would not agree to do until after the first-night reviews. Alas, by then it was too late); Douglas Moore's *Wings of the Dove*; Lee Hoiby's *Natalia Petrovna*, in which one Anthony J. Rudel—my seven-year-old son, following in the footsteps of his older sisters Joan and Madeleine, who had appeared in City Opera productions (along with many other children, including the future composer Adam Guettel and the aspiring young actress Bonnie Bedelia; we had a fabulous children's chorus director named Mildred Hohner who truly inspired her young charges)—made his company debut in the role of Kolia, for which he demanded a real contract!; Weisgall's *Nine Rivers* (one of the legendary failures of opera history—which suffered in part from the composer's weakness for over-orchestration); Rorem's *Miss Julie*; Moross's *Gentleman, Be Seated!*, an opera in the form of a minstrel show; Floyd's *The Passion of Jonathan Wade* (which I was very fond of); Jack Beeson's *Lizzie Borden* (which had a triumphant premiere, with Brenda Lewis in the title role, and has been revived numerous times over the years); and Giannini's *Servant of Two Masters* (which lacked the verve of his *Taming of the Shrew*).

Not all commissioning talks led to a happy conclusion. One commissioned opera that did not come to fruition was *The Ice Age*, with music by William Flanagan Jr. and a libretto by Edward Albee. The work was left unfinished at the time of Flanagan's death in 1969.

There were also a couple of renowned composers who turned down my invitations to write an opera. Duke Ellington asked me to visit with him between sets at the Rainbow Room—where he showed me some of *Queenie Pie*. It was not far enough along to be produced; too much work still needed to be done. And Ornette Coleman showed me an outline for an opera at his apartment in the Village. But nothing came of it. I also talked with George Crumb, but he wasn't ready to embark on an opera.

In addition, my efforts to produce *Candide* came to nil; Leonard Bernstein told me that he'd like City Opera to perform the work, as long as Lillian Hellman would make some changes to the book. Lillian, too, said she was in favor of a New York City Opera production of *Candide*—if Lenny Bernstein would make some changes to his music. They each said, "Julius, you decide this. We'll abide by your decision." But when I asked for this in writing, they both declined and the production didn't happen. It would be another decade and a half before *Candide* arrived at New York City Opera— with a book by Hugh Wheeler. Hellman had her book pulled from circulation, and I've heard that it's actually in her will that her version never again be licensed for performance.

The impact of the Ford Foundation's generosity was tremendous—and for once, classical composers were accorded the respect and financial rewards they deserved. Douglas Moore received $30,000 to work on *The Wings of the Dove*, which enabled him to take a leave of absence from his teaching duties at Columbia University.

Our third and final American Season, in 1960, included only two weeks of New York performances—this time paid for by City Center—followed by a five-week road tour to nineteen American cities. The four operas performed on the tour were *Susannah*, *The Ballad of Baby Doe*, *Six Characters in Search of an Author*, and *Street Scene*. The lone new production that season, performed at City Center but not on the tour, was Blitzstein's *The Cradle Will Rock*. Though it was an agitprop piece about the rise of unionism in this country, I had no complaints from Morton Baum or any of the other board members. It was the first time *Cradle* was given a full staging—with its original orchestration rather than a lone piano for accompaniment. I invited Broadway's Lehman Engel to conduct it, and our cast was a canny mix of City Opera members and Broadway actors, including Tammy Grimes, David Atkinson, Jack Harrold, Joshua Hecht, Chandler Cowles, and Nancy Dussault.

Before our final American Season and tour came to an end, I had come up with another idea that I hoped would appeal to Mac Lowry. I took my cue from Rolf Liebermann, the director of the Hamburg Opera, who would occasionally schedule a week of twentieth-century operas. But I wanted to do something on a much larger scale—five weeks of twentieth-century European and American works. Once again I went to Mac to outline my plan: "We don't want to present the American creative output in a hothouse, carefully nurtured but protected from any competition. I want them to be performed against Poulenc, Prokofiev, Shostakovich, Egk, and Von Einem."

Mac liked the idea, and in 1964 the Ford Foundation granted City Opera $250,000 to help us produce two five-week Twentieth Century seasons. Five weeks of contemporary works? Once again we were ridiculed and told that nobody would come. Once again we proved the doomsayers wrong. (Prior to the '64 Twentieth Century Season, underwritten by the Ford Foundation, I had tried out my plan during our three-week spring '63 season, opening with the East Coast premiere of Britten's *A Midsummer Night's Dream* and continuing with reprises of operas already in our repertory (*Love for Three Oranges*, *Baby Doe, Susannah*, and *Street Scene* plus a double bill of *Carmina Burana* and *Oedipus Rex*). The cast of *Midsummer Night's Dream* featured the young mezzo Tatiana Troyanos in her company debut as Hippolyta. We also witnessed a bit of real-life magic as love bloomed between our Bottom, Spiro Malas, and our Hermia, Marlena Kleinman, who have now been happily married for nearly fifty years. Britten managed to find just the right tone throughout the opera—whether he was writing for the children, the Mechanicals, the young lovers, or the gods—and Bill Ball's direction of the opera within the opera was hilarious, yet staged with exquisite taste.

The first Twentieth Century Season was spring 1965 and included the world premiere of Jack Beeson's *Lizzie Borden* with Brenda Lewis, Ellen Faull, and Herbert Beattie, all of whom were phenomenal. We also presented a trio of works that were new to our repertory: Shostakovich's *Katerina Ismailova* (directed by Frank Corsaro), Menotti's *The Saint of Bleecker Street*, and Weill's *The Threepenny Opera*. Lenya did not approve of our casting of Kurt Kasznar as Mack the Knife in *Threepenny*, and subsequently she would not come to see the production. As it turns out, Lenya was right: Kasznar did not have enough machismo for the role.

In the fall of 1965—our last season at the Mecca Temple on Fifty-Fifth Street—we opened with another contemporary work, Prokofiev's *The Flaming Angel*. Our cast was headed by Eileen Schauler (who had made her debut in spring 1965 in the title role of *Katerina Ismailova*) and the young Sherrill Milnes (who had made his debut the previous year as Valentin in *Faust*); and Frank Corsaro provided the rousing direction. The packed audience included George Balanchine and Igor Stravinsky sitting in the first row of the orchestra, looking over my shoulder as I conducted. After intermission, as I was about to give the downbeat to begin the second act, I felt a small tap on my shoulder. I looked up, and a little old lady in a coat with a fur collar was standing there in the first row of the orchestra. "Excuse me, I'm Mrs. Rockefeller and I just want to thank you," she said. Martha Baird Rockefeller had underwritten the production.

She was just one of several generous donors who paid for productions in the 1960s and 1970s. Other benefactors included Mary Flagler Cary, Fan Fox and Leslie R. Samuels, Ralph and Patricia Corbett, and Gert von Gontard. Also, Larry Deutsch and Lloyd Rigler were incredibly generous, underwriting our annual tours to Los Angeles and paying for our recording of *Giulio Cesare*.

There was one new production of a very important twentieth-century work that came my way by a roll of the dice. In the summer of 1961, I was engaged to conduct the American stage premiere of Britten's *The Turn of the Screw* at the Cambridge Music Festival in Massachusetts. It was a marvelous production staged by Allen Fletcher (with a highly effective set designed by Jac Venza, who went on to become executive producer of the long-running *Great Performances* series on PBS), and a superb cast including Patricia Neway as the Governess, Richard Cassilly as a spine-chilling Quint, and a boy named Bruce Zahariades who scared the living daylights out of all of us (even offstage) as Miles. The reviews were good, but at the end of the week's run an announcement was made that the Festival had gone bankrupt. "Give me the scenery in lieu of my fee," I told them. They did. We brought the production to City Opera the following spring (with most of the Cambridge cast), and have revived it several times over the years.

Our company performed brilliantly. Morale was high—even the stagehands and supers were proud of our achievements—and attendance was at least as good as expected.

The American seasons, followed by the seasons of twentieth-century operas, accomplished what I hoped. The works represented were of varying quality, but all of them kept the audience interested. My contention is that even if some of these works were not truly great, they were honest efforts, and our patrons hardly ever went away disappointed. Our seasons of new and unusual fare paved the way for regional companies to begin to explore twentieth-century American works.

I continued to put my money where my mouth was, producing thirty-five American operas during my twenty-two years as director of New York City Opera.

8

INTERMEZZO

The Company Way

In 1958 and '59 we rode the crest of the wave. Our spring seasons were devoted to American operas, and the fall seasons consisted of our standard repertory plus unfamiliar works like Richard Strauss's *Die schweigsame Frau* and Britten's *The Rape of Lucretia.*

Our success was due to the superb singing actors who were the backbone of New York City Opera. We were a repertory company, not a star company. We never used a prompter—it was simply a matter of belief that the audience and performers onstage must not be disturbed by the sound of someone "feeding lines." People worked their way up by proving themselves and sometimes with a little bit of luck in their favor. For example, in fall 1957, bass Herbert Beattie debuted in the small role of Baron Douphol in *Traviata* (one of those "talent test" roles); three weeks later—when both the scheduled singer and his cover were ill—Beattie astonished us all as Osmin in *The Abduction from the Seraglio*, singing in English (having had less than 24 hours to learn the translation) and switching to the original German for his arias.

No one balked at playing a leading role one night and a supporting part the next. In fall 1957, Norman Treigle performed Blitch in *Susannah* and Mephistopheles in *Faust*—but also Colline in *Bohéme* and Banquo in *Macbeth.* Seven years later, in fall 1964, Treigle opened the season with his first Boris Godunov and closed it with his mesmerizing Don Giovanni. In-between, he played the First Nazarene in *Salome.* He embodied our working philosophy: There are no small roles, only small performers.

We were all on a first-name basis. I was "Julius"—never "Maestro Rudel" (even the stagehands called me by my first name)—and the collegial "family feeling" was always present, whether in the dusty hallways and rehearsal rooms at City Center or at Francine's, our little hole-in-the-wall hangout— and of course onstage during performances.

Not everything was a success, of course. Some works disappointed us in reaction or in execution, but the critical community was never nasty or snide, always giving serious reaction to the work at hand and reasons why it had not succeeded. Britten's *The Rape of Lucretia* had very low attendance, but nevertheless it was considered a success because it was really meant for an intimate theater and we made it work in the large City Center auditorium. We always needed to have new productions, and Britten's work was (and still is) a great love of mine. Our budget permitted us to do *The Rape of Lucretia*—the orchestra was small, there was no chorus in the usual sense of the word (Britten and his librettist opted instead for a pair of narrators, performed in our production by David Lloyd and Brenda Lewis), and the set was minimal. The costume budget, also, was small—and would have been even smaller if I hadn't raised a ruckus. Fran Bible, who played Lucretia, wore an inexpensive form-fitting nightgown and our Tarquinius, Bill Chapman, came onstage at a rehearsal wearing nothing more than a white bikini-type loin cloth. There were some "oohs" and "ahs" from our staff. "To hell with our costume budget. He can't go out there naked!" I called out to our designer, Andreas Nomikos. By opening night, Bill's attire was less skimpy.

Werner Egk's *The Inspector General*, based on the play by Gogol, was musically well prepared and brilliantly performed by a large cast, but even with Bill Ball's direction (which brought out the story's humor—he invented hilarious situations where no one else had) and with Egk himself conducting the performances, it was not embraced by the audience.

On October 8, 1959, we entered a whole new era when we unveiled our production of *Così fan tutte*. Mozart's opera about romantic relationships—a comedy with cynical, Sondheimesque undertones—is a marvelous showcase for six performers highly attuned to each other. Thus it was a most logical choice for our strong ensemble. What a cast we had—Phyllis Curtin, Frances Bible, John Reardon, John Alexander, Judith Raskin (in her company debut), and James Pease—and what pride we took in our production! At rehearsals everything fell into place. We all felt the same way about the music; it simply "slipped off our tongues."

Bill Ball's production was simple, stylish *and* stylized—just a gazebo and occasional furniture on a stage that was raked in the middle. I had given Bill and our designer Robert Fletcher an impossibly small budget of $2,500 for scenery and costumes. Somehow they met it, with great ingenuity and wonderfully creative touches. In the final scene, the young military officers Ferrando and Guglielmo shed their outrageous "Albanian" attire and return as their normal selves. In his haste to change his costume, Ferrando (John Alexander) failed to remove half of his Albanian mustache. During a pause in the music, Guglielmo (John Reardon) fleetly and casually pulled it off his friend's upper lip as if it were the most normal thing in the world.

Howard Taubman in the *New York Times* called our *Così* "the overwhelming accomplishment of the season. . . . Under Julius Rudel's direction, it caught the Mozartean essence. It rejoiced, fairly sparkled, in radiant spirits."

Taubman went on to say that New York City Opera was making an "artistic contribution of tremendous value" to the entire nation: "One has seldom found an ensemble that sang with such community of feeling and taste as did this City Center group. . . . That is the strength of this company. It has an unmatched esprit de corps. At its best it does its work with irresistible ardor. If it had done nothing else, this *Così fan tutte* would entitle the company to continuity. . . . Its existence is salutary for New York, the country and opera."

Our *Così* drew large audiences and international notices; one manager even proposed taking it to the Salzburg Festival (a nice dream that never came to pass).

We performed *Così* in English—as had become our tradition with Mozart—in a splendid translation by Ruth and Thomas Martin. In those days there were no supertitles, so it was up to us to make the storyline as clear as possible to the audience.

That was just one part of our responsibility to our ticketholders. Throughout my tenure I fought the dangers of performances becoming routine. It was a particular gripe of mine. I would rail against "merely correct" performances, exhorting everyone to "Keep it fresh!" and reminding them, "For you it may be the hundredth performance, but for someone in the audience it will be the first—and we must give them an unforgettable experience."

As a boy in Vienna I loved Leopold Stokowski; his recordings, along with those of Toscanini, were ear-openers for me. In 1944 Stokie conducted the newly formed New York City Symphony in a season of exciting concerts at City Center (before turning the reins over to Lenny Bernstein), and when I became the director of City Opera, I wanted to get him involved with our company. In 1959 I had the good fortune to interest him in appearing with us. John Butler and I had talked about producing a staged version of *Carmina Burana*. It seemed a logical thing to ask Stokie to conduct it, but we needed a piece to pair it with. *Oedipus Rex* was such a monumental contrast that I thought we could effectively perform the two works in an evening. When I presented the idea to Stokie, he said yes immediately. "And as far as money is concerned, my fee is either $2,500 or nothing—and since you evidently can't pay, it's nothing!"

He donated his services to us (he would not accept so much as taxi fare), as he had previously done in 1944 when he founded the City Center symphony. When I told the orchestra that Stokie was coming in to conduct them, they were scared stiff. He had a reputation for being nasty. But with us he was like a lamb—so kind and polite to the musicians. There was only one moment where things could have gone wrong. It happened during a rehearsal when Stokie and the director, Christopher West, had a difference of opinion. Stokowski from the pit said something to West, who was onstage. Christopher—a very good director, erudite and well prepared—misinterpreted what had been said and got a bit huffy and said to Stokie, "Would *you* like to stage this?"

Stokie replied, "No, you're the stage director."

To which West coolly responded, "I thought so," and the tension was broken. There was such politeness in the whole exchange yet there was steel behind it. Fortunately it ended amiably.

The double bill, which opened our fall 1959 season, proved electrifying. Reri Grist was the soprano in the Orff work and Richard Cassilly was a noble Oedipus in the Stravinsky. "Taken together *Oedipus* and *Carmina Burana* represent a kind of musical theater too seldom presented hereabouts and practically never on the level projected by Stokowski. No one with a broad interest in the subject should pass it by," wrote Irving Kolodin in the *Saturday Review.* Not all the reviews were equally as enthusiastic as Kolodin's—one critic attacked *Carmina Burana* (featuring the dancers Carmen de Lavallade and Glen Tetley) as "bedmanship on the hoof"—but every performance was sold out.

Stokowski's presence was such a thrill for our company that, to thank him, Rita and I invited him to a potluck one night at our apartment. Stokie, usually a very private person, accepted and was pleased. We alerted our son, Tony, who at the time was two years old, to be on his best behavior because a very famous guest was coming for dinner. As it turned out he and the legendary conductor became fast friends—talking most of the night and playing with an erector set. They were still going strong at midnight when Stokie left. It was both beautiful and sad to see this old, lonely man connecting with our son. Stokie had just gone through a custody battle over his two sons with his ex-wife, Gloria Vanderbilt.

For the following fall season, 1960, we offered Stokie another double bill for opening night: Monteverdi's *Orfeo* and Dallapiccola's *Il prigioniero.* Again he was flattered to be asked; he had enjoyed working with our company. What especially intrigued me was the juxtaposition of one of the earliest operas with one of the newest. There was a three-and-a-half century gap between the two works. *Il prigioniero*—short (barely one thousand bars) and potent, with a chilling twist—was a huge success for Treigle and Cassilly. The French baritone Gerard Souzay was our Orfeo (opposite Judy Raskin's Euridice). Though his métier was art songs, I knew that Souzay wanted to try his hand at opera. We offered him the role, to which he brought his characteristic elegance and sense of style.

What very few people know is that another international star—the most famous diva of them all—once offered her services to City Opera. One spring morning in 1961 I was having a cup of coffee and was about to head down to City Center when I got a phone call. It was a lady who claimed to be "Mrs. Callas." After talking to her for a little while (and suddenly recalling the luxurious white yacht that was docked at the Seventy-Ninth Street Boat Basin, the "Christina," which belonged, of course, to Aristotle Onassis), I realized that she was indeed Maria Callas. She asked, "Would you like to have me sing in your theater?" I was floored: "It would be a great honor!" We made a date to meet and discuss this further, but when the day neared for our meeting, I received another breakfast call, this time from someone else: "Mrs. Callas is unable to come and must change the meeting." I never heard from her again. Clearly she had used me as bait for Rudolf Bing and the Met.

While moving our company into new waters, I continued to embrace the past. Mezzo Regina Resnik and I had crossed paths many times over the years, and she would always remind me that (as a soprano) she had sung Micaela and Frasquita in *Carmen* with City Opera during our first two seasons in 1944. In 1958 I said to her: "You haven't sung Carmen at the Met. Would you like to do one with us, for old time's sake?" Regina graciously agreed, and returned to City Opera for one performance of *Carmen* in October 1958. Vocally ideal for the role, she really understood the text and made the most of it. Though she was not to return to our company again until 1990 (during Christopher Keene's directorship) to play Mme. Armfeldt in Sondheim's *A Little Night Music*, Regina has always maintained a strong identification with New York City Opera.

During our fall 1959 season, we kept the lighter side of things going with Gilbert and Sullivan's *The Mikado*, directed by Dorothy Raedler with all the proper D'Oyly Carte touches in Donald Oenslager's Kabuki set. The cast included George Gaynes, Frank Porretta, Norman Kelley, Herb Beattie, Nancy Dussault, and Claramae Turner.

Our repertory kept expanding in all directions and the company thrived on the diversity. We had become "the very model of a modern major opera company."

9

POLITICS AND ACOUSTICS

The Move to Lincoln Center

Both the Met and the New York Philharmonic needed new homes. Carnegie Hall, where the Philharmonic performed, was scheduled to be torn down in 1960 and replaced with a parking lot (until Isaac Stern came to the rescue and saved the famous hall from the wrecking ball). The "Old Met" on Broadway and Thirty-Ninth Street was a most unattractive red-brick building with cramped backstage facilities and no offstage space. I shall never forget my first encounter with the Met shortly after my arrival in this country. One day, when I had arranged to meet a friend at the corner of Thirty-Ninth Street and Seventh Avenue, I saw an ugly building—a brewery perhaps?—and then noticed posters announcing upcoming operas. I looked more closely and realized I was looking at the rear part of the famous Metropolitan Opera House.

When the Lincoln Center project first evolved in the mid-1950s, we at City Center didn't pay much attention to it even as it got larger and larger (with the announced additions of a repertory theater, the Juilliard School, and a theater for ballet, operetta, and musical comedy). We felt smug and a bit condescending—proud of the fact that City Center was after all the grandfather of all performing arts complexes. Our attitude was, "Been there, done that." Since we already had our own cultural center on Fifty-Fifth Street—complete with opera, ballet, musical theater, drama (and even, for a time, a symphony orchestra directed first by Stokowski and then by Lenny Bernstein)—we were not concerned with Lincoln Center, which was snootily referred to as the new "cultural supermarket."

We were a bit curious when, in June 1959, Mayor Wagner, while addressing a Lions Club convention at Madison Square Garden, apparently let slip that Lincoln Center would be "the home of the Metropolitan Opera, the Philharmonic Society, and the City Center."

The "ballet house" was to be known officially as the New York State Theater (since a major portion of its funding was to come from New York State) and would open as part of the 1964 World's Fair. Lincoln Center needed a dance company, and Balanchine's New York City Ballet would fit the bill quite nicely. In our frequent meetings, Baum kept assuring me that even if the ballet were to move, New York City Opera would remain on Fifty-Fifth Street.

William Schuman, distinguished American composer and president of Lincoln Center, sensed the danger of going elitist—and advocated strongly for a first-rate opera company with popular ticket prices. The most likely candidate, of course, was New York City Opera. This didn't sit at all well with Met general manager Rudolf Bing, who was quite vociferous in letting it be known to the Lincoln Center board and the world at large that he did not wish to have a second company around. The feeling was mutual—I had not the slightest desire to play second fiddle to the Met. (For once, Bing and I were in full agreement about something!) Morton Baum reiterated to John White and me, "Don't even think about it—you won't have to go there. You'll stay in the Mecca Temple and be happy."

Initially it was decided that the State Theater would be a home only for New York City Ballet and for a musical theater company under the leadership of Richard Rodgers. But by 1963 it became clear that Lincoln Center wanted New York City Opera to be part of the new complex on Broadway between Sixty-Second and Sixty-Sixth streets.

Up to that time, the relationship between Bing and me had been like that of the poor and the rich cousin. He was polite and correct to me during the early years of my directorship; when he heard that my five-year-old son Tony loved Mozart, Bing offered us his box for a performance of *The Magic Flute.* Now, however, our relationship had changed. The poor cousin was not supposed to move next door.

The very idea of New York City Opera moving to Lincoln Center was as upsetting and disturbing for me as it was for Bing, and I was certain that if we moved to Lincoln Center the Met would insist on having approval rights over our repertory. I simply would not accept the "big guy" getting to call the shots over the "little guy." Our company had been gaining a reputation for adventurousness, and I was not about to let Rudolf Bing dictate to me what operas I could or could not do. If I wanted to mount a production of *Meistersinger* (and I did), I did not want to have to get permission from Bing to do so.

In addition, I knew our expenses would rise dramatically if we moved to Lincoln Center. We'd need a larger orchestra and more choristers, and we'd also be required to have more stagehands. Plus, our productions would have to be adjusted to fit the new stage—and some would have to be totally redesigned. Unlike the New York Philharmonic and the Metropolitan Opera, City Center did not have a large budget and endowment funds. The City of New York took care of our utilities on Fifty-Fifth Street, including our heating bills, and Newbold Morris and Morton Baum had managed to work out a deal with the city allowing us to pay only a dollar a year to lease the building.

We had good and loyal audiences. But ticket sales are never enough. We were constantly on the edge of bankruptcy, yet somehow Baum managed to keep us afloat. How could we possibly come up with the money for the huge Lincoln Center heating and air conditioning bills and other running expenses that would total about $1 million annually? Right from the start, there were critics who rather haughtily asked members of our City Center board, "Can you *afford* to come here?" And there were some members of the Lincoln Center board of directors who claimed that City Opera was "too much of a shoestring operation to be given major responsibility in Lincoln Center," according to an article in the *New York Times*.

Relying on Baum's reassurances, I tried to push the ever-present notion of a move to Lincoln Center from my mind, and instead concentrated on my latest Ford Foundation project, the "Twentieth Century Season" of international operas scheduled for spring '65.

Meanwhile, City Ballet's director Lincoln Kirstein worked with the architect Philip Johnson to make certain the New York State Theater would be perfect for Balanchine and his dancers. As New York City Ballet made plans for its spring 1964 move to the State Theater, it became known in the press that serious conversations were going on between Bill Schuman and Morris and Baum. Apparently the talks became quite heated, I later found out, as Baum waged a bloody battle for total independence; at one meeting Schuman and Baum very nearly came to blows. Among the issues at stake: Baum wanted City Center to be guaranteed the right to control the State Theater every week of the year, including the periods when City Ballet and Richard Rodgers's Music Theater were dark. Lincoln Center management, on the other hand, wanted the right to book the building as they saw fit, that is, to bring in outside attractions during the "dark" ten weeks of the year— and to charge prices for these events that were much above our City Center $5.50 top price. (Low-priced tickets to high-quality performances were part and parcel of City Center's raison d'être.)

By 1964 Mac Lowry and I—with the help of a marketing wizard named Danny Newman—had finally persuaded Morton Baum to let us sell subscriptions for the opera. Danny later wrote the book on the importance of subscription series for arts organizations. I first met him in the late 1940s when he was the local press representative for New York City Opera's annual visits to Chicago. Danny was a natural: affable, gregarious, enthusiastic, and extremely helpful—a little ball of energy.

Danny also worked as a consultant to the Ford Foundation; his passion was saving cultural institutions from death due to a lack of steady income. The solution, of course, was to sell tickets through subscription. Morton

Baum, who had long opposed the concept of subscriptions (claiming they limited our flexibility), feared incurring Mac Lowry's anger and finally listened to Danny. In 1964 we embarked on our first subscription drive—and Baum quickly became a convert when he saw the money that poured in ahead of each season.

On April 23, 1964, the New York State Theater opened with a nationally televised performance by the New York City Ballet. During intermission, the CBS newsman Robert Trout spoke to George Balanchine, Lincoln Kirstein, New York City Ballet star Jacques d'Amboise, and Richard Rodgers. The conversation was all very upbeat, in praise of the new theater. The fact that I had not been invited to participate in the "panel discussion" confirmed and reassured me that City Opera was not moving to the State Theater. Or so I hoped.

Before Lincoln Center opened, no one ever spoke of acoustics. But from the moment that Philharmonic Hall (since renamed Avery Fisher Hall) was inaugurated in September 1962 with a gala concert by Leonard Bernstein and the New York Philharmonic, it seemed that no one—from inveterate concertgoers to cab drivers who would never set foot in a concert hall—could speak of anything *but* acoustics. The opening program featured Vaughan Williams's *Serenade to Music* and the first movement of Mahler's Eighth Symphony. I was in the audience and was shocked to hear that during the musical climaxes, the chorus voices sounded distorted and out of balance. In addition, there was a discernible echo, with the low instruments sounding weak and distant. The acoustics at Philharmonic Hall were compared to those at Carnegie Hall and were found wanting. The blame for the sound of the new hall fell on acoustician Leo Beranek. All sorts of rumors were circulating. One anecdote that made the rounds was told to me by Erich Leinsdorf himself. (He and I had become friends over the years.) When he was rehearsing the Boston Symphony for a Philharmonic Hall concert as part of the opening week's activities, Leinsdorf shouted at one point, during a sound check: "Mr. Beranek, can you hear the celli?" No answer. Leinsdorf asked the question again: "Mr. Beranek, can you hear the celli?" Finally a little voice said, "What is celli?" Leinsdorf turned to the orchestra and said, "Now we know everything."

Unlike Philharmonic Hall, the New York State Theater was planned as a "ballet and operetta theater." Word was that Balanchine told the architect Philip Johnson he "didn't want to hear the pitter-patter of dancers' feet" during a performance. Balanchine's wish was Johnson's command. The architect, working in tandem with an unknown (to me) acoustician from Copenhagen named Dr. Wilhelm Lassen Jordan, built the theater so that reverberations from the stage were deadened. In designing a stage that would muffle the sounds of the dancers' toe shoes, they did a major disservice to the singers and actors who would also perform there. (Richard Rodgers, who was going to use amplification anyway, didn't seem to care.) When the State Theater was still in the construction stage, Balanchine made the discovery that Johnson had designed the orchestra pit for only thirty-five musicians. But the ballet orchestra had approximately fifty-five musicians. The problem was corrected. (When we opened with Ginastera's *Don Rodrigo* in February 1966, the pit held eighty-five musicians.) In addition, Balanchine realized that Johnson had neglected to add trap doors to the stage. "We need trap doors for *The Nutcracker*," he ordered, and that error, too, was quickly corrected.

In May 1964, a month after the State Theater's inauguration, the Royal Shakespeare Company arrived for a three-week residency, performing *King Lear* and *The Comedy of Errors* in repertory.

The acoustic *Götterdämmerung* had arrived.

The famed RSC opened with Peter Brook's production of *King Lear* starring Paul Scofield. He was renowned for his crisp articulation, yet Scofield and his costars (Irene Worth, Alec McCowen, and Diana Rigg among them) could scarcely be heard by a majority of the audience members. In a story published in the *New York Times* on May 20, 1964—two days after *King Lear* opened—an angry Peter Brook called the acoustics in the State Theater "appalling," and went on to say that echoes in the theater either "blurred" or "scrambled" the dialogue.

In the same article, Philip Johnson was quoted as saying the State Theater "[was] never meant to be used for the spoken word, unless the sound is reinforced." The State Theater "has the perfect reverberation time for [instrumental] music, 1.7, which is not fitted for the human voice," Johnson said; to which Brook responded that it was irresponsible to invite a guest company "to play Shakespeare in a building that was not properly tested for dialogue." Brook was indignant that "neither the architect, Mr. Johnson, nor the acoustical expert, Wilhelm L. Jordan, had bothered to come to listen to the dialogue" on opening night.

I attended the first performance of the Royal Shakespeare Company and several of the subsequent performances. The acoustics were indeed a nightmare, with sibilant consonants hanging on the walls and ricocheting back to the audience. (The actors' words were also bouncing off the glass windows in the Viewing Room at the back of the main floor.) It was a complete disaster, forcing the RSC to use amplification for the remainder of its New York run.

In the summer of 1964, Richard Rodgers' Music Theater presented its first two productions: *The King and I*, with Risë Stevens, and *The Merry Widow*, with Patrice Munsel. Plenty of miking was used for both productions, and there were no complaints. (Amplification had been regularly used on Broadway for the past decade.)

One fine day early in 1965 Baum informed John White and me that the time had come for us to "take a look at the State Theater." The battle for independence had been won. Baum had gotten all the conditions necessary for our safety and protection, and City Opera was moving to Lincoln Center.

I made it clear that City Opera was not going to use any sort of amplification. "We can't possibly move to the State Theater unless I have a chance to try it out and see what—if anything—can be done or needs to be done acoustically," I said to Baum.

I already knew that Philip Johnson's acoustician, Wilhelm Jordan, was not going to be of *any* help. It was Jordan who had told me that it would be good for the sound if we built our scenery out of hardwood!

The State Theater was beautiful, but I was dismayed at all the flat walls and the absence of architectural elements, that is, those surface irregularities and statues and other adornments that are traditionally found on the walls and ceilings of the world's great opera houses. Such adornments are not just ornamental. They help break up sound.

In order to test the acoustics, I had to go to the Ford Foundation and beg for a special grant to enable us to do the test. Mac came through with $10,000, and I scheduled a day of acoustics testing in May 1965. We performed one act each of *Carmen*, *La bohème*, *Die Fledermaus*, and *The Marriage of Figaro*. (I chose the program with care, making certain we covered all possible combinations of performance: full orchestra, Mozart-size orchestra, harpsichord, recitatives, full-volume singing of operas in English, French, and Italian—and even dialogue.) The day of the test, we held a closed rehearsal in the morning and a performance for an invited audience in the afternoon. One of our guests was our friend Leopold Stokowski, who, at the age of 83, climbed around the theater throughout the rehearsal, listening to the music from every level of the house.

A few days later Stokie sent a letter with his "verdict" to Lincoln Center board chairman John D. Rockefeller III.

May 7, 1965

Dear Sir,

I have been deeply impressed by the beauty and well-planned sight lines for the audience in the New York State Theater, and will you permit me to make two suggestions?

One is that the sound of the instruments and singers is slightly over-brilliant because the upper partials are being reflected a little more strongly than the fundamental tones. This could be obviated by placing absorbent material on vertical surfaces [at] the opposite end of the enclosed space from the stage. I would suggest that this be done only a little at a time, until the true balance of fundamentals and overtones is found.

The other suggestion is that if reflecting surfaces were hung over the stage at the optimum angles, this fine theater could also be used as a concert hall, and thus be made a house for every kind of artistic entertainment. It would then be an all-purpose theater which is so desirable.

Sincerely,
Leopold Stokowski

No changes were made in the State Theater during the summer, when musicals were once again being performed by Richard Rodgers's company, but things came to a head in the fall, when the Metropolitan Opera National Company (the Met's new touring company, made up of young artists) was engaged for a two-week stint at the State Theater.

They opened on November 3, 1965, with Rossini's *La Cenerentola* (performed in English as *Cinderella*). The next morning music critic Harold C. Schonberg complained in the *New York Times* that only one out of ten words was intelligible. At the company's second performance, the singers' voices were amplified. Risë Stevens, codirector of the national company, claimed "only the tiniest bit" of enhancement was used for all remaining performances of *Cinderella* and *Susannah*. The amplification consisted of microphones along the footlights and on the bridge above the stage—with a sound engineer raising and lowering the volume as needed to adjust the voices in relation to the orchestra.

There was quite an outcry against the artificial enhancing of voices, including an article by Theodore Strongin in the *New York Times* on November 17, 1965, with the headline "Microphones Stir Opera Lovers' Ire." Strongin wrote, "Opera lovers who treasure the sound of the natural voice have taken exception to the use of electronic amplification by the Metropolitan Opera National Company in two productions at the New York State Theater."

I was certain of one thing: amplification—or indeed *any* practice of "enhancing"—would be totally unacceptable for New York City Opera.

We had completed our final season in the old Fifty-Fifth Street building on November 14, 1965, with a performance of *The Merry Widow* followed by a chorus of "Auld Lang Syne." The next day we moved to our new, cramped underground quarters at Lincoln Center; Richard Rodgers's Music Theater staff and the New York City Ballet had gotten first choice of the cushier administrative offices, and Dick Rodgers refused to relinquish any of his office space. Ironically, Rodgers's Music Theater lasted for only a few seasons, with just one really big money-maker: the 1966 revival of *Annie Get Your Gun* starring Ethel Merman, which subsequently transferred to Broadway. The City Center Light Opera was disbanded in 1968, since it no longer made money for us, and the Music Theater of Lincoln Center gave its final production in 1969. There was no more competition between the two "light" companies; both were dead.

I now needed to turn my full attention to the acoustic problems of the State Theater.

I asked my friend Christopher Jaffe, a highly regarded acoustical consultant, if he would come to the State Theater and test the acoustics; he agreed to do it as a personal favor to me. Armed with a "white noise machine," he took measurements throughout the theater, showing me how the sound changed not just from row to row but from *seat to seat*. He explained that because of the theater's various flat surfaces (including the floor of the orchestra section of the auditorium, which was uncarpeted, and the walls of the theater, which were straight), the music had a hollow sound akin to the sound you hear in a bathtub. Everything was bouncing around so much that even people sitting side by side were hearing different balances.

As soon as the Danish Ballet finished their four-week stint in the theater on December 19, we began to make the changes that had been recommended by Jaffe. These included adding a cyclorama, an acoustic panel, rugs on the floor of the auditorium, and acoustic elements under the balconies, and taking out the glass windows in the Listening Rooms.

Lo and behold, our changes did improve the sound in the theater. Though the acoustics at the State Theater were never the greatest, somehow we made them work to our advantage. Before our opening season, Gian Carlo Menotti said he refused to let his opera *The Consul* be produced there without amplification. I asked him to come and listen to a rehearsal. He did, and afterward agreed that the sound was good and allowed his work to be done without microphones.

At one of the final rehearsals for *Don Rodrigo* in early February 1966, the *New York Times* music critic Harold Schonberg, who was always suspicious, pointed to a decorative element on the set and said, "Is there a microphone hidden behind it?" At the intermission I said, "Come onstage, I'll take you there." I walked with him to the 'suspicious spot' and showed him that there was nothing there. In his opening-night review of *Don Rodrigo*, he gave thumbs up to the acoustics. So did Leighton Kerner in the *Village Voice* ("Three cheers!" was his pronouncement on the acoustics) and Alan Rich in the *New York Herald-Tribune*, who wrote, "A pilgrimage around the hall during a dress rehearsal revealed few inequities in balance, and the sound in the First Ring on opening night was excellent. Voices, even against the teeming Ginastera orchestration, were clear and thoroughly projected."

Irving Lowens, writing in the *Washington Evening Star*, ended his laudatory review by giving the conductor the last word: "Rudel said there was nothing wrong with the house, and his singers would need no amplification. To my mind, he made his point. Despite the gigantic orchestra, no one had trouble projecting (including the two children in the final scene) and the diction was so crystal clear that even though my knowledge of Spanish is rudimentary, I had no trouble following the text phonetically."

All these years later, the acoustics at Lincoln Center are still an issue (the State Theater was recently renovated and renamed the David Koch Theater). In July 2009 Chris Jaffe and I got together for lunch and recalled the early days of the State Theater. A few days later, I received this note from him.

July 17, 2009

Dear Julius,

It was great to touch base once again and recall the wonderful success you enjoyed when the City Opera moved into the New York State Theater.

Here are my recollections of the acoustical problems experienced by the Met Touring Company at the State and the solutions we implemented prior to the opening program of the City Opera.

The smooth slightly curved sidewalls of the Theater and the smooth curved rear glass walls behind the rings created distinct echoes and focusing problems for those seated in the lower and middle orchestra seating areas. At some locations there was a four-decibel difference between seats located side by side.

In addition the curvature of the proscenium side walls were shaped to throw sound back onto the stage rather than project it forward into the audience seating area. It is my understanding that this was done to reduce noise from toe shoes when the plans for the State were prepared. As you may recall, the initial program called for a Ballet Theater and it was not contemplated that opera would be performed in the space.

My analysis of the problem enabled me to come up with the following solutions: add sound diffusing panels to both the sidewalls and the rear walls of the rings in order to spread the sound more evenly; rebuild the proscenium walls to project the sound outward; build an acoustical cyclorama for outdoor operatic scenes that would give the stage directors more flexibility for movement when the singers were upstage.

Since the Ballet Company did not want any permanent changes made to the proscenium and stage areas, we designed a twenty foot high, hard, portable proscenium cover that projected sound to the audience and was put in place for the Opera's Seasons and removed when the Ballet performed. In addition a temporary cyclorama was designed and flown behind a scrim curtain for outdoor scenes.

These conditions prevailed while you headed up the company. When you left, it is my opinion that the powers that be at Lincoln Center as well as Philip Johnson, the original architect, were upset that the inexpensive non-architectural elements were defacing the purity of the space. Additional money was acquired and Johnson was given the okay to architecturally modify the Theater according to plans developed by Cyril Harris, another acoustical consultant. [This I gather happened during Paul Kellogg's leadership.]

The temporary material was removed and Harris designed a forestage canopy over the pit and enlarged the pit. The Ballet refused to have the proscenium modified architecturally as part of this renovation.

From then on, the opera acoustic environment continued to be criticized. At one point, a sophisticated electronic reflected energy system was installed, but that did not solve the basic problems.

Best regards,
Christopher Jaffe

Once our company had moved uptown to the State Theater, Lincoln Center had its popular-priced residents and everyone was happy. Well, almost everyone. Rudolf Bing was less than happy, but he couldn't do anything about it; he could not stop us. He still felt that Lincoln Center didn't need a second opera company.

The Met opened in its new home in September 1966—seven months after New York City Opera opened in the State Theater. The morning of the Met opening, there was a Lincoln Center Council Meeting (where the heads of each division would meet for a discussion of mutual problems affecting everybody). I sent Bill Schuman a mock-congratulatory telegram—praising him for finally getting a second opera company at Lincoln Center. Everyone, even Rudolf Bing, had a good laugh!

One of my earliest photos, as a youngster in Vienna in the mid-1920s.

The Rudel family circa 1934. *Left to right:* my father, Jakob; younger brother, Ludwig ("Lud"), mother, Josephine ("Pepi"); and yours truly.

Man about town: here I am at the age of sixteen at a neighborhood park near my home in Vienna—uncharacteristically wearing a hat.

Our City Center board chairman Newbold Morris, *right*, and finance chairman Morton Baum, *left*—the *patres familias* of New York City Opera—along with Hon. Francis J. Bloustein, a longtime City Center supporter.

In the late 1940s, when I was the director of the Third Street Music School Settlement (in addition to my duties at New York City Opera), conducting a rehearsal of the student orchestra.

Carlisle Floyd's *Susannah*, which Erich Leinsdorf brought into the New York City Opera repertory in September 1956 during his single season as general director, starred Phyllis Curtin and Norman Treigle. Eugene Cook / Courtesy of New York City Opera.

In 1953 I made my Lewisohn Stadium debut, conducting two singers I had cheered years before from the Fourth Ring of the Vienna Staatsoper: Jarmila Novotna and Charles Kullman.

In 1956 I (*far right*) returned to Vienna for the first time since the war to conduct *Kiss Me, Kate* at the invitation of my childhood friend Marcel Prawy (*center*). The cast, *from left to right*, included Fred Liewehr, Olive Moorefield, Hubert Dilworth, and Brenda Lewis.

April 23, 1958: The crowning touch of our first American Season was the world premiere of *The Good Soldier Schweik* (with Norman Kelley, *center*, in the title role), by the wildly talented thirty-five-year-old composer Robert Kurka, who had died of leukemia just four months earlier. Courtesy of New York City Opera.

Of the fifteen world premieres produced during my tenure as general director, the two that received the most acclaim were Jack Beeson's *Lizzie Borden* (1965) and Robert Ward's *The Crucible*, which had its premiere on October 26, 1961. Pictured in act 4 of *The Crucible* are, *from left*, Eunice Alberts, Norman Kelley, Norman Treigle, and (*far right*) Chester Ludgin in the leading role of John Proctor. Courtesy of New York City Opera.

I'm surveying the scene as (*from left*) Prince Rainier, Princess Grace, and Jean Dalrymple await the next event at the Brussels World's Fair in the summer of 1958, where I conducted *Susannah* and *Carousel.*

Our 1959 production of *Così fan tutte*, simply and stylishly directed by Bill Ball, was a showcase for all six performers: *back row,* James Pease and Judith Raskin in her company debut, and *front row, from left to right,* Frances Bible, John Reardon, John Alexander, and Phyllis Curtin. Charles Rossi / Courtesy of New York City Opera.

Posing on the promenade of the New York State Theater shortly before we opened our first season at Lincoln Center in 1966. In the background is company member Donna Jeffrey. Courtesy of New York City Opera.

The North American premiere of Ginastera's *Don Rodrigo*, starring the young Plácido Domingo, was the first opera New York City Opera performed at its new home at Lincoln Center on February 22, 1966. Pictured here in the coronation scene are, *far left*, Malcolm Smith and Spiro Malas; *center*, Domingo; and *far right*, Jeannine Crader. © Beth Bergman, 1967, 2011, New York.

© BETH BERGMAN 1967, 2011

Longtime City Opera music administrator Felix Popper, *left*, and technical director Hans Sondheimer onstage with me before our new production of *Der Rosenkavalier* (directed by Otto Erhardt and designed by Donald Oenslager) in February 1967, with Elisabeth Grümmer in her company debut as the Marschallin. © Beth Bergman, 1967, 2011, New York.

I assumed the music directorship of the Caramoor Festival in 1964 and for the next fourteen summers presided over many memorable evenings of music making, including the US premiere of Britten's *Curlew River* in 1966. Here I am conducting, with my nine-year old son, Tony—dressed as an acolyte—assisting with page-turning and register changes on the Positive organ.

© BETH BERGMAN 1968, 2011

Handel's *Giulio Cesare*, starring Norman Treigle as Caesar and Beverly Sills as Cleopatra, had its company premiere on September 27, 1966—and forever changed the course of New York City Opera. © Beth Bergman, 1968, 2011, New York.

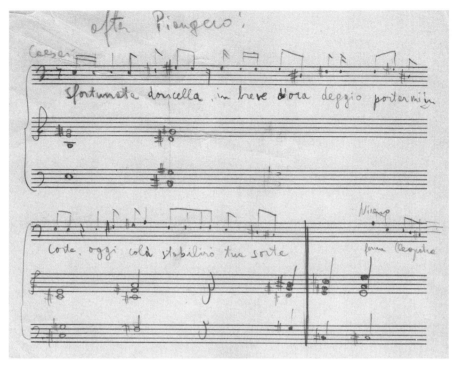

Partial page of my version of Handel's *Giulio Cesare*, which, because of all the changes I made, I copyrighted in 1967. It remained in the City Opera repertory for nearly two decades. © Julius Rudel, 1967.

Kennedy Center chairman Roger Stevens was the fighting spirit behind the arts center on the Potomac. Here he and I examine the progress of the Kennedy Center during its construction.

My dear friend Kay Shouse and I share some rare downtime on her lobster boat in Blue Hill, Maine. Shouse gave the land and the money to build Wolf Trap, the only national park dedicated to the performing arts, and cajoled me into becoming Wolf Trap's first music director in 1971.

© BETH BERGMAN 1967, 2011

Our beautiful new Beni Montresor production of *The Magic Flute* premiered in October 1966. Here, in the fall 1967 revival, are (*from left to right*) Michele Molese, Veronica Tyler, and Georg Schnapka. © Beth Bergman, 1967, 2011, New York.

Director Frank Corsaro, a mainstay of our company, was renowned for his naturalistic productions that allowed us to look into the characters' hearts and souls. © Beth Bergman, 1967, 2011, New York.

COPYRIGHT C BETH BERGMAN 1969/2007

The other director whose work embodied our company's signature style in the sixties and seventies was Tito Capobianco, who dazzled audiences with his elegant productions. © Beth Bergman, 1969, 2011, New York.

At a New York City Opera rehearsal of Ginastera's *Bomarzo* (production devised and directed by Capobianco) in March 1969. © Jack Mitchell.

© BETH BERGMAN 1969, 2011

Norman Treigle commanding the stage in the title role of *Mefistofele*, directed by Capobianco. You simply could not take your eyes off him, even when someone else was singing. © Beth Bergman, 1969, 2011, New York.

© BETH BERGMAN 1970, 2011

The Makropoulos Affair, with Maralin Niska in her spellbinding performance as the 337-year-old femme fatale Emilia Marty (a.k.a. Elina Makropoulos). The Corsaro production made stunning use of Ronald Chase's projected film images. © Beth Bergman, 1970, 2011, New York.

COPYRIGHT © BETH BERGMAN 1970, 2002

Beverly Sills and I collaborating on *Roberto Devereux* in 1970. Throughout our long collaboration, we brought out the best in each other artistically. © Beth Bergman, 1970, 2011, New York.

In 1973 I offered Rudolf Bing—who had retired the previous year as general manager of the Metropolitan Opera—a role in our forthcoming production of Hans Werner Henze's *The Young Lord*. Although he was initially not in favor of New York City Opera's move to Lincoln Center, over the years we ended up becoming friends. © Beth Bergman, 1973, 2011, New York.

© BETH BERGMAN 1974, 2011

Corsaro's 1970 production of *Pelléas et Mélisande* was a revelation. He directed it not as a dreamy bit of French Impressionism but as a real story about real people. Here, in the 1974 revival, are Patricia Brooks as Mélisande and Michael Devlin as Golaud. © Beth Bergman, 1974, 2011, New York.

On October 7, 1978, I made my Metropolitan Opera debut conducting *Werther*. Featured with me in the curtain call photo are, *from left to right*, Dominic Cossa, Betsy Norden, Elena Obraztsova, and Plácido Domingo. © James Heffernan / Metropolitan Opera.

Catherine Malfitano and Samuel Ramey were delectable together as Susanna and Figaro in our 1977 John Copley production of *The Marriage of Figaro.* © Beth Bergman, 1977, 2011, New York.

John White, managing director of City Opera and my colleague since the earliest days of the company, at a dress rehearsal in 1974. © Beth Bergman, 1974, 2011, New York.

© BETH BERGMAN 1975, 2011

Johanna Meier and John Alexander as Eva and Walther in our 1975 John Cox production of *Die Meistersinger*. © Beth Bergman, 1975, 2011, New York.

With my wonderful wife, Rita—my champion and my toughest critic—at home on the Upper West Side of Manhattan in the 1970s.

On my seventy-fifth birthday on March 6, 1996, it was business as usual; I conducted *Madama Butterfly* (with former City Opera company members Diana Soviero and Richard Leech) at the Met. At the party afterward I was joined by my children, *from left*, Joan, Madeleine, and Tony. Photo by Henry Grossman.

10

TINTINNABULATION

Don Rodrigo and a Young Star Named Domingo

When Plácido Domingo walked onstage for his audition in the fall of 1964, I remember thinking, "If he sounds anything like he looks, we have got ourselves a winner." These were my exact thoughts as I observed the young man with the unlikely name "Peaceful Sunday" who was getting ready to audition for me. I was not disappointed. He not only sounded marvelous, but he sang with such musicality that I immediately asked him about his background. I found out that he was also a fine pianist and had in fact wanted to become a conductor. (Was I relieved that he hadn't done that—at least not yet!)

Of course we signed him immediately.

At the time of his audition we were in the midst of making detailed plans for the company's move to our new and glamorous quarters at the New York State Theater at Lincoln Center. When Baum and Schuman had finally settled their differences and our move to Lincoln Center was assured, I realized that the second of our two Twentieth Century seasons funded by the Ford Foundation would be our first season in the new house, and I decided to make the most of it. The first contemporary season in spring '65 had gone well (capped by the world premiere of Jack Beeson's *Lizzie Borden* and our first performances of Shostakovich's *Katerina Ismailova* and Weill's *Threepenny Opera*, plus works by Gershwin, Moore, Britten, Menotti, Puccini, Stravinsky, Orff, and Floyd), and I figured public curiosity would help fill the house at Lincoln Center.

I envisioned a rather spectacular first season in our new home—five weeks and thirty-four performances of works by Prokofiev, Stravinsky, Orff, Poulenc, Von Einem, Shostakovich, Moore, Gershwin, Menotti, Weill, and Richard Strauss. For opening night we would present the US premiere of *Don Rodrigo*, by the Argentinean composer Alberto Ginastera.

Maestro Ginastera had attended our production of *Katerina Ismailova* in March 1965, and—impressed with what he saw—asked if I would be interested in producing his opera *Don Rodrigo*, which had premiered at the Teatro Colón in Buenos Aires the previous July.

The score had been brought to me by Stuart Pope, the president of Boosey and Hawkes (Ginastera's publisher). I got very excited when I saw it—a large-scale work with pageantry (as well as some engaging intimate love scenes) and literally hundreds of participants onstage and off including no less than eighteen French horns and twelve trumpets, partly deployed backstage and throughout the auditorium. I was quite impressed with Ginastera's musical personality; his formalism so wonderfully covered the emotional aspects of the piece. It seemed to me like a modern *Aida*. I couldn't imagine a more ideal work to conduct for our opening. I also couldn't imagine translating the opera into English, since the poetry of *Don Rodrigo* (libretto by Alejandro Casona) was almost impossible to translate. We would perform the work in Spanish, as it was written.

That's when Domingo, who was born in Madrid, came forward.

I was convinced he was the man for whom the title role—the last Visigoth king of eighth-century Spain—had been written. I immediately assigned this difficult part to Plácido over the strong objections of some of my staff, especially John White, who—worried about Domingo's youth (he was twenty-four at the time), his lack of experience, and his "too lyrical voice"—tried to persuade me to engage another singer named Giovanni Gibin, an adequate but uninspiring Brazilian tenor who had appeared with the company a few seasons earlier. I felt reassured when I watched Plácido make his company debut as Pinkerton in *Madama Butterfly* in October 1965.

The opening night of *Don Rodrigo*—February 22, 1966—was a huge triumph. The opera was performed in Spanish, and there was praise for all: the composer, the production team, and of course for Plácido and his fellow cast members, Jeannine Crader, David Clatworthy, and Spiro Malas. Daniel Webster of the *Philadelphia Inquirer* wrote that the tenor "sang the searing part strongly" and that "his voice combined power and warmth and the clarity crucial to the success of the role."

Domingo's personal achievement was just one dazzling facet of the evening, which began with a pre-curtain speech by Mayor John Lindsay and ended with a gala black tie party given by our Opera Guild. The most thrilling "podium moments" for me were the Hunt Interlude (with what seemed like every freelance horn and trumpet player in the tri-state region) and the chimes at the end of the opera—the Miracle of the Bells. Our company had established its right to life at Lincoln Center.

Opera News editor Frank Merkling paid *Don Rodrigo* the highest compliment of all: "The production was a triumph; its unity and discipline made one think of Bayreuth. Ming Cho Lee's sets and Theoni Aldredge's costumes, beautifully lighted, bore out the music's stamp of impassioned austerity, and Tito Capobianco's direction in general succeeded in convincing one that Visigoth rule in Spain must have ended like this—not with a whimper but a bang."

The orchestra, chorus, and I were also rhapsodically reviewed, and my only regret is that we never got to record *Don Rodrigo*. Because of the exceedingly large forces involved, several companies that wanted to record it shied away when they calculated the cost.

Don Rodrigo catapulted Domingo into immediate world recognition and the Met and other international companies came calling; but he remained with us, on and off, for the next nine years. As a follow-up to his Don Rodrigo— and for a total change of pace—Plácido portrayed Alfredo in Frank Corsaro's new production of *La traviata*, which premiered in fall 1966. He *was* a vulnerable, naïve, and ardent young man. I particularly remember the last act duet, "Parigi, o cara," which he sang while cradling Violetta in his arms like a baby. Happily, Patricia Brooks, who was an amazing Violetta, was rather petite and did not weigh much, and he carried her throughout that duet.

Many roles and styles followed for the tenor, and he performed them all impeccably, so it seemed like a natural progression when I invited Plácido to make his New York conducting debut with New York City Opera in fall 1973. The opera was *Traviata*, and once again Pat Brooks was singing Violetta, but Domingo was more nervous about this debut than he had been about his singing debut. (It goes without saying that the singers who were going to perform under his baton were also quite nervous, particularly the tenor Roger Patterson.) No one needed to have worried—it turned out to be a lovely performance. Plácido was so happy with the respect and cooperation the orchestra showed him that he sent them a case of champagne.

When he had already become a world star, Domingo would still do some performances for me whenever possible, and always at the preposterously low fees for which New York City Opera was infamous. I particularly remember a performance of *Carmen* that he sang with our company in the early seventies during our Los Angeles tour. Six hours before curtain, the tenor took ill. I couldn't think of anyone to replace him, and then all of a sudden it occurred to me that Plácido was in San Francisco rehearsing with the opera. I gave him a call, and as fate would have it he had just finished rehearsing for the day. When he heard about our situation, he agreed to fly to Los Angeles if I could get Kurt Herbert Adler's permission. Adler, the longtime general director of the San Francisco Opera, said yes. (He also behaved like a mensch a few years later, when he heard of my resignation from the City Opera directorship and immediately called to invite me to guest conduct *Pelléas et Mélisande* in San Francisco.) Domingo hopped on a plane, arrived in the nick of time, and of course gave a splendid performance. Nobody could have guessed that he had not known his partners prior to his stepping onto the stage.

With Plácido, it is always great fun; his musicianship is so natural that we could always make spontaneous music together. This was particularly important when we were recording, because of the danger of segmentized and repeated "takes" that tend to work against the architecture and natural flow of an opera. In this regard I feel quite happy with our *Mefistofele* recording (with Domingo, Montserrat Caballe, and the late Norman Treigle in his trademark title role).

Plácido's warmth and generosity toward his "alma mater" and me personally were evidenced in two separate instances. Beverly Sills's farewell performance on the New York City Opera stage in October 1980 was the occasion for a Gala Benefit evening that I had agreed to conduct. Plácido had already done two strenuous recording sessions that very day, yet he appeared and gave a rendition of "Grenada" that brought down the house. I also invited Plácido to sing a benefit concert for the orchestra pension fund at the Buffalo Philharmonic shortly after I became its Music Director in 1979. He sang a long and demanding program, topping it off with several encores. After the concert he donated a substantial portion of his fee to the orchestra.

Throughout the years, the odd coincidences of musical life have continued to entwine our careers. My conducting debut at the Met on October 7, 1978, was with Plácido as Werther, and two years later we opened the San Francisco Opera season together with *Samson et Dalila*. The first day of rehearsals, Shirley Verrett and I found out that Plácido was detained by an urgent family emergency and would be delayed. At first we took the news in stride, but after Domingo had missed an entire week of rehearsals, Shirley Verrett was very angry and was about to leave town. When he finally arrived, he brought her a bouquet of roses and apologized so humbly, profoundly, and charmingly that he melted her heart. She forgave him and so, of course, did I. We had a wonderful run of performances, and fortunately one of them was televised.

I made my debut with Lyric Opera of Chicago in 1982 with Plácido as Cavaradossi, and conducted Domingo and Martina Arroyo in *Forza del destino* at the Paris Opera. Our 1985 performance of *Andrea Chenier* at Covent Garden (with Anna Tomowa-Sintow and Giorgio Zancanaro) was preserved in a telecast. We also recorded an album of all-Viennese songs that show Domingo's versatility, and another album of early Puccini arias, *The Unknown Puccini*, which we did very intimately—just Domingo and I (accompanying him on the piano) in a small studio in New York, with Justino Díaz dropping by for a duet.

Most recently, in 2008, Plácido turned the tables and invited me to conduct *Carmen* at the Washington National Opera, where he was the general director. During intermission he came to my dressing room; we had a reunion and happily reminisced about the early days at City Opera.

11

A SUMMER IDYLL

The Magic of Caramoor

Some forty miles north of New York in the town of Katonah lies an estate of 117 acres on which Walter and Lucie Bigelow Rosen built Caramoor, one of the earliest and most distinguished summer music venues in the US. The festival began in 1945—an offspring of the private musicales that had taken place in the Rosen mansion for more than a decade.

Mr. Rosen, an investment banker and avid art collector, died in 1951. Mrs. Rosen, an aristocratic beauty with long flowing red hair, was a virtuoso on that most exotic of instruments, the theremin—a wooden box with two metal rods that is played by waving the hands through a magnetic field (and sounds a bit like a singing saw). She continued, until her death in 1968, to preside over the summer concerts with grace and charm.

The main building is in the Spanish style and has a cloistered courtyard; chamber music and solo recitals take place there. All other concerts are given in the Venetian Theater on a stage built around a set of Greek and Roman marble columns that were collected by a fifteenth-century Venetian nobleman (and imported from Italy by Walter Rosen). The theater, which seats 1,500, opened in 1958 with Marian Anderson singing Gluck's *Orfeo* for the first and only time in her storied career.

In 1961 Caramoor's executive director Michael Sweeley and the festival's publicist Audrey Michaels approached me on behalf of Mrs. Rosen, inquiring if I would be interested in taking over the music directorship of the Caramoor Festival. The beauty and enchantment of the surroundings coupled with Mrs. Rosen's wish—"to have more things at Caramoor . . . things that people cannot get elsewhere"—were very appealing indeed. Though I was already committed to conducting at Menotti's Spoleto Festival in Italy in 1962 and 1963, I assumed the music directorship of Caramoor beginning with the 1964 season, and happily held that post for the next fourteen summers. Mrs. Rosen and I got along famously. I discussed with her all of the works I wanted to perform, and she was always in agreement.

My first concert in 1964, a double bill of the Bruckner *Te Deum* and Rossini's *Stabat Mater*, introduced many in the audience to newcomer Tatiana Troyanos and included the City Opera stars Norman Treigle, Arlene Saunders, and John Alexander.

Later we performed Orff's *Catulli Carmina* (featuring the glorious dancers Carmen de Lavallade and Robert Powell) with John Butler's highly erotic choreography. After the dress rehearsal, Mrs. Rosen asked John, Michael Sweeley, and me to come to her quarters for a conference. (She would often retire to her bed—the result of a car accident a decade earlier that had greatly impaired her ability to walk.) A regal vision in a Victorian nightgown, she gently pleaded with John to tone down a few of the more explicitly sexual moments. "Westchester is not yet ready for what you want to do," said Mrs. Rosen. This was the only time that she ever felt a need to ask for changes in the staging. John honored her request and excised some of the more over-the-top moments.

There were so many memorable concerts: Purcell's *Dido and Aeneas* with Maureen Forrester and Benita Valente; Monteverdi's *L'incoronazione di Poppea* (with Cesare Valletti in his operatic farewell and Judith Raskin); *Medea* with Maralin Niska; *Idomeneo* with George Shirley; Debussy's *L'enfant prodigue;* and Cavalli's *L'Ormindo* with Catherine Malfitano, Dominic Cossa, and Neil Rosenshein, just to name a few. Our lighter fare included *The Gypsy Baron* with Johanna Meier and *Countess Maritza* with Mary Costa. Among the contemporary operas was Marvin David Levy's *Escorial.*

With the expansion of the festival, it became beneficial for me to live on the grounds (to my greatest delight!) during the season. Mrs. Rosen ordered an old barn to be converted into an apartment for me. Indulging me, she even let me design my residence. My kids would often come up to visit Rita and me, and would stay a few nights.

The big events were always on Saturdays, preceded by what we jokingly referred to as "undress rehearsals." I would rehearse in a bathing suit, and the moment the rehearsal was finished—at exactly 4:25 p.m., because of union rules—I hurried to one of the neighbors' pools to get a little swimming in before dinner and the show.

I have fond memories of our late-night ritual after the concerts, when the audience and friends of the artists had left and we were alone. Just Mrs. Rosen, Michael Sweeley, Audrey Michaels, Rita, and I, and occasionally one or two of the soloists who were staying overnight; we would sit in the courtyard with a few candles lit and have a glass of wine and chat. It was a relaxed, magical time.

In studying Mahler, I had come across his first big work—*Das klagende Lied* (The mournful songs). It is written for large orchestra, soloists, chorus, and an offstage band. I very much wanted to do it at Caramoor, and Mrs. Rosen was willing, even though it was going to be expensive. We positioned the twenty-five-member woodwind band in a concealed tennis pavilion several hundred yards from the Venetian Theater. To compensate for the lag in sound at such a distance, the band had to play a beat and a half ahead of the orchestra. We worked it out with a closed-circuit television. My assistant Charles Wendelken-Wilson was standing with the band, and when it came to the point where they played, he would anticipate *my* beat and cue them accordingly. The music emanating from the tennis pavilion provided a startling and marvelous effect for the audience (although one officious usher, upon hearing the band, thought that it was music coming from one of the neighboring estates giving a party and began running toward the source of the noise!).

When I learned that Britten was writing an allegory for performance in churches, I immediately secured the first United States performance rights. Mrs. Rosen, an Anglophile, was happy to have work by this esteemed British composer performed at Caramoor.

Curlew River is a wonderful combination of art forms: part religious parable and part Japanese Noh play. It is performed by twenty monks—some of them singers and the others instrumentalists. It arrived at Caramoor in July 1966. All of the performers (myself included) entered the cloisters walking through the columns and chanting the plainsong until we arrived at our position. We were dressed in simple monk's robes, and my son Tony, age nine at the time and dressed as an Acolyte, assisted me with page-turning and register changes (since I was using a copy of an old and relatively large Positive organ). To stage this highly unusual work we engaged Bliss Hebert. I was certain that his half-stylized, half-realism approach would be just right. Andrea Velis was simply shattering as the Mad Woman. The small cast was quite perfect and the audience was deeply moved. Britten led the way. The next year we added his *The Burning Fiery Furnace*, and in 1968 we concluded the trilogy with *The Prodigal Son*.

A few years later I encountered Benjamin Britten in Venice, where I was conducting *Turandot*. We both were staying at the Grand Hotel. He was working on his opera *Death in Venice*. One day we met in passing and exchanged a few pleasantries. I asked him directly about *Death in Venice*, which I hoped to produce at New York City Opera. He was aware of my success with his music but was not forthcoming. When *Death in Venice* was given its American premiere at the Met in 1974, I was angry and very disappointed, but now I understood the brevity of our conversation.

12

GIULIO CESARE AND THE SILLS PHENOMENON

Ifirst met Beverly Sills in 1953. At twenty-four she was already a seasoned pro, having been featured as a child soprano on the Major Bowes radio program. She had made her operatic debut at seventeen as Frasquita in *Carmen* at Philadelphia Civic Opera. Her preliminary audition at City Center was for John White and me. Beverly had a winning personality and a gorgeous voice—and I immediately arranged a second audition, this time onstage, for our general director Maestro Joseph Rosenstock. Once again she sang beautifully, but Rosenstock couldn't make up his mind about her—not about her voice but her height. (Beverly was 5 feet 9 inches tall, but Rosenstock could not have been much more than 5 feet 2 inches.) Also, she seemed a bit self-conscious, as if she were watching herself sing—as do many young artists when they first start performing. At those early auditions Beverly seemed to be almost amused at herself, as though she were thinking, "What am I doing here? What foolishness this is!" Of course the dramatically gifted performers, like Sills, quickly learn how to work through this self-deprecating hurdle and emerge victorious.

Over the next two years Beverly had to audition for Rosenstock four more times. At her fifth audition she said something rather cute and a bit impertinent to him about her height. Amazingly enough, Rosenstock's face did not get its customary shade of red—he liked her humor. Sills was engaged, and right from the start, she was a valuable member of our company. She produced a clear and pure sound, and had impeccable intonation, superb musicianship, great flexibility, a natural wit, and the ebullient personality that earned her the childhood nickname, "Bubbles." Her sense of humor complemented my own (we both laughed at the same things), and her can-do attitude was much appreciated by her colleagues. Very early on, Beverly and my wife Rita became close friends. They were both of Russian Jewish lineage, both born and bred in New York City—Beverly in Brooklyn and Rita in the Bronx. In addition, they were bright, amusing, and outgoing—and similar enough in appearance that they could have been sisters. I can still hear the peals of laughter when they got together for a shopping spree at Loehmann's (a bargain store) or when we all traveled together when Beverly and I performed in Israel or made recordings in London. (We'd joke about our "London kibbutz.")

I was in the pit when Beverly made her City Opera debut as Rosalinda in *Die Fledermaus* on October 29, 1955. She looked gorgeous in a dress her mother had made for her, acted with commitment and high spirits, and proved she had the right stuff vocally—capping it all off by holding on to the high D at the end of the "Czardas." The following week she sang the relatively small role of Oxana in Tchaikovsky's *The Golden Slippers*—a bland rarity that did not excite a soul and disappeared immediately.

Beverly traveled with the company on our postseason tour in November 1955 with major stops in Boston, Detroit, and Cleveland. It was in Cleveland that she met Peter Greenough at a party at the Press Club. Peter was a very wealthy man, a Boston Brahmin whose family owned the *Cleveland Plain Dealer*, where he worked as an associate editor. He was tall and handsome, but also brash and impudent. When he met Beverly, he was going through a rather nasty divorce with his first wife, with whom he had three daughters. A year later, when the divorce was finalized, he and Beverly were married.

When I was planning my first season as director, I assigned Beverly the title role in Lehar's *The Merry Widow*. I knew she would be a "natural" and I cast Robert Rounseville as Danilo. We put together a splendid production team consisting of the director Glenn Jordan, the designer George Jenkins, and our choreographer Robert Joffrey and told them to improvise out of existing stock and lots of drapes—and they came up with a winner. Franz Allers conducted, taking time off from conducting *My Fair Lady* on Broadway. Sills was superlative in the title role, a part she was to return to over the years. (Twenty years later, we recorded highlights from *The Merry Widow*—in a pleasing English translation by the Broadway lyricist Sheldon Harnick—which won Beverly, me, and the entire company a Grammy Award.)

That season I also scheduled Beverly to sing Violetta in *La traviata*—her first Violetta with our company—conducted by Arturo Basile, the rising young star from the "old-school Italian" tradition.

For opening night of the spring 1958 season (the first "All-American Season"), I had chosen a work that would show our company in its best possible light: Douglas Moore's *The Ballad of Baby Doe*. The opera, based on the life of real-life "silver baron" Horace Tabor, who left his wife for the young beauty Elizabeth ("Baby") Doe, had received a lot of positive attention two years earlier at its world premiere at Colorado's Central City Opera. We were able to acquire from Central City the atmospheric scenery of Donald Oenslager, who adjusted the set to fit our stage. The very fine staging was by Vladimir Rosing, a Russian tenor-turned-director who was steeped in the tenets of the Moscow Art Theatre but also at home in America. Val was very good in bringing out the best of everybody's characterizations.

Moore expected Dolores Wilson, who had created the title role in Central City and done it well, to play it again. But the moment I saw the score, I knew it was ideal for Beverly. She had originally expressed interest in playing Baby Doe in the world premiere, but had been told by the conductor Emerson Buckley that Moore was looking for a "more petite woman." I totally disagreed; I knew that her height was irrelevant (especially since Horace was to be played by the tall, handsome baritone Walter Cassel) and that the role would be perfect for her. I sent her two of Baby's arias and asked her to look at them. She protested, but I wouldn't take no for an answer. My trick worked. She saw the music and fell in love with it. Now I had to convince Moore and Buckley that she was the best choice—and I was sure that if they heard her, they would be convinced. Her husband, Peter, in cahoots with me, planned a trip to New York for his birthday and got tickets for a Broadway show. He suggested casually to Beverly, "As long as we're going to be in New York anyway, why don't you sing for Douglas Moore, just for the satisfaction?"

Beverly arrived at City Center wearing a large white mink hat and high heels, and rather charmingly announced to Douglas, "This is how big I am before I sing, and I'm going to be just as big when I finish." Douglas, one of the kindest and most polite men I've ever met, quickly walked to the stage and said, "Miss Sills, you look just fine to me."

She began "The Willow Song." Douglas Moore gasped when she started to sing—her voice was so ethereal and pure. Emerson Buckley's fingers started to twitch and he rushed down to the footlights and gently guided her through the music.

Well, we had our Baby.

Walter Cassel, who had created the part of Horace Tabor in Central City and really "lived the part," repeated his role for us. Martha Lipton, who had sung with City Opera during our very first season, also recreated her Central City role as Tabor's long-suffering first wife, Augusta. The role was later taken over by Frances Bible and became one of her signature parts with the company.

The opening night went exceedingly well—with superb performances by all three of our leading players and indeed by our entire ensemble.

Beverly's transformation of Baby's character from a frivolous gold digger to a woman in love was deeply touching—and of course she nailed every one of her five arias. There were audible sobs from the audience during the final scene, when Walter Cassel's Horace—now a broken man and dying—sang to Sills, "You were always the real thing, Baby." There was also a bit of extra suspense for those of us in the wings as Baby Doe sang her final aria of eternal love for him—"Always Through the Changing" (nicknamed the "Leadville Liebestod"). The opera ends with her alone on stage, singing her way through time as the figure of Horace gradually disappears and snow begins to fall gently. At the dress rehearsal, as Beverly sang the aria, she walked backward as she had been instructed to do but couldn't find the assigned spot for which the lighting had been set—a tiny stool where she was supposed to sit down. On opening night, no one would have known from Beverly's completely in-the-moment rendition of the aria that conductor Buckley (a very savvy man of the theater), while continuing to conduct was actually directing her to slowly edge her way backward until he gave her the sign to sit down on that small stool. There she sat, singing, as snow swirled around her and the audience dissolved in tears. As she floated the final note on the words "ever young," the opera ended. Simply. Perfectly.

To give focus and bring attention to the second American Season in 1959, I wanted to present a world premiere (following on the heels of *The Good Soldier Schweik* in 1958). I chose *Six Characters in Search of an Author*, Hugo Weisgall's adaptation of Pirandello's play. I cast Beverly in the role of the troupe's ditzy Coloratura Soprano—who has a very funny aria in which she admits that she doesn't understand what (or why!) she's singing but nonetheless wants to be given plenty of high notes. Howard Taubman praised Beverly's delightful portrayal and the "striking agility" of her coloratura flights of fancy. Truth be told, Beverly couldn't stand the role. A great deal of her dislike had to do with a run-in she had experienced with the opera's conductor, Sylvan Levin. Beverly, who at the time was six months pregnant with her first child, had been placed by director Bill Ball high on a ladder. "After the rest, do I take a ritard?" she asked Levin from her high perch. "Don't talk to me while I'm speaking to someone else," he responded gruffly. "I'll go you one better," said Beverly, climbing down from the ladder. "I won't sing while you're conducting." She started to walk out of the theater and John White and I ran after her, using all of our combined powers of persuasion to get her back. This was one of our very few backstage eruptions. For the most part, we were a very amiable company.

Our spring 1959 season ended in May. The following month Beverly returned to New York to record *The Ballad of Baby Doe*, and then went back to Cleveland, where her daughter Meredith ("Muffy") was born in August 1959. Beverly was on maternity leave during our fall season.

Except for two performances of *Baby Doe* and one of *Six Characters* in the spring of 1960, she didn't return to us again until the spring of 1962 (for another two performances of *Baby Doe*). By then Beverly had moved from Cleveland to Boston, where she had given birth to her second child, Peter Jr. ("Bucky") in 1961. Shortly thereafter Muffy, at two, was diagnosed with a profound hearing loss—and less than six weeks later, Bucky was found to be severely mentally disabled.

For nearly a year after Bucky's birth she withdrew from the world, quite literally, staying at home in Boston and refusing to come to New York to see her mother or for her weekly singing lessons with her longtime voice teacher, Estelle Liebling. We all tried to do whatever we could to lift her from her depression. Her manager, Ludwig Lustig, who was very devoted to her, was invaluable to me during that time. I would trust him to tell me when I could send her a note or phone her. I would attempt to be funny—inviting her back to the company and offering her either of two roles in *Boris Godunov*—"Boris *or* Godunov"—or *any* role she wanted to play in *Billy Budd* (an opera with an all-male cast). When all else failed, I gently but firmly reminded her that she had a contract to fulfill. In addition, Peter gave her fifty-two round-trip plane tickets from Boston to New York so she could resume her weekly voice lessons with Estelle Liebling.

Beverly somehow managed to pull herself out of her depression and returned to City Opera in the fall of 1962 to portray Milly Theale in two performances of Douglas Moore's *The Wings of the Dove*, in which she sang an especially lovely aria, "When All Is Still and Fair." Moore had written the opera, which had premiered the previous year as part of the Ford Commissioning Program, with Sills in mind for the leading role, but Beverly had pulled out of the rehearsals after Bucky was born. Though it was a matter of only months until the opening night, we were lucky to find someone to replace her; Dorothy Coulter took on the role for the opera's premiere. The lukewarm reception this work received (there were even a few boos from the avant-garde contingent that disapproved of Moore's old-fashioned music) was one of my biggest disappointments. I thought it was a well-written and interesting opera, but clearly the audience had a different response.

During our fall 1962 season, Beverly assayed the title role in a single performance of Charpentier's *Louise*, an opera that she loved (and which she and I subsequently performed and recorded together in 1977).

When Beverly returned to us, she seemed the same—and yet inevitably different. On the surface she was her old ebullient self. But those of us who were close to her noticed something deeper, something richer in her performances. She had found a new solace in her singing. Her audiences and fans had no idea what trials she was up against at home, and those of us who knew kept quiet. She *needed* to sing; she needed the escape that performing could offer. As Beverly was later to say, "I'm not a happy woman. How could I be, with all that's happened to me? But I'm a cheerful woman. Work has kept me going."

New Challenges, New Roles

While City Opera played out its final years at the old Mecca Temple, Beverly took on new roles, including Donna Anna in *Don Giovanni*, with Norman Treigle as the Don and the inimitable Donald Gramm as his sidekick Leporello. Beverly and Norman were incredibly attuned to each other. As I stood on the podium for those performances during our fall 1964 season,

I was thrilled at how true their portrayals were; when they both emerged from Donna Anna's rooms, there was such intensity! As I gave those slashing downbeats, it seemed that Treigle's Don was actually going to rape Donna Anna—or if she found the dagger, she would kill him. In August 1965 we took our production to Stanford University in Palo Alto, at the school's invitation, for a mini Mozart festival that included two other Mozart operas in excellent English translations by Thomas and Ruth Martin: *The Marriage of Figaro* and *The Abduction from the Seraglio*, in which Beverly played Constanza. Bill Ball's searing production of *Don Giovanni* (updated to the era of Goya) with Sills, Treigle, Herbert Beattie, and Eileen Schauler, was a phenomenal success.*Years later, when I was conducting *Pelléas* at the San Francisco Opera, West Coast opera lovers were still coming up to me and talking about those earlier Palo Alto performances.

In 1964 the Argentinean director Tito Capobianco, who was then running the Cincinnati Zoo Opera, invited Beverly Sills and Norman Treigle to Cincinnati to perform in Offenbach's *The Tales of Hoffmann*, with Beverly playing the three heroines opposite Treigle's four villains. *Hoffmann* was ecstatically received in Cincinnati—Sills's trills competed with the zoo seals' squeals, and the seals were squelched—and Norman and Beverly persuaded me to bring the production to New York for our fall 1965 season. Tito, whose brilliant staging this was, loaned us the sets and costumes and directed the production. Michele Molese played the role of the poet Hoffmann. It was an exciting production with a highly dramatic ending. At the conclusion of Antonia's scene, Treigle would suddenly jump up from behind me in the orchestra pit and start to conduct the last bars. It was such an effective *coup de théâtre* that I permitted Tito to do away with the Epilogue and end the opera at this point for this particular production. (Strangely, in 1972 when we mounted a totally new Capobianco production of *Tales of Hoffmann* for Sills, Molese, and Treigle, it was not as effective as the earlier borrowed shoestring production.)

Beverly grew very close to Capobianco and his wife, the choreographer Elena ("Gigi") Denda, and Tito became her director of choice. I have no doubt that the Capobiancos were immensely helpful to her in achieving greater depth in her portrayals—especially the "British queens" operas.

In fall 1966 the Met and New York City Opera opened within eleven days of each other. The Met premiered Barber's *Antony and Cleopatra*, and our City Opera opening on September 27 was the first production by either company of a Handel opera, *Giulio Cesare* (*Julius Caesar*). Rudolf Bing claimed that I had chosen the opera to spite him and to show that George Frideric Handel was a better composer than Samuel Barber, but in fact, I mounted *Giulio Cesare* for Norman Treigle. I can still recall going with Rita to the opening night of *Antony and Cleopatra* at the Met as guests of Mr. Bing. It was quite a crowd, filled with VIPs, and as we walked across Lincoln Center Plaza to the

Met, I heard cheers. Glancing up at the terrace on the promenade of the State Theater, I saw the whole cast of *Giulio Cesare*, apparently on a rehearsal break, cheering our arrival. Then the Met onlookers recognized me and joined in the applause. (I have to confess that now, as then, when I go to Lincoln Center and look out and see thousands of people going here and there, and the air is filled with anticipation, I still get a thrill.)

Sometime in 1964 Norman and I had been sitting at the piano, and Norman said he wanted to show me what he could do with coloratura. He sang a Handel aria—coloratura fireworks and all—and I was astonished at how fabulous it sounded. That's when the idea of *Giulio Cesare* began to take shape.

"There hasn't been a Baroque work done in a long time. Let's see if we can assemble a cast," I said. We evidently already had our Caesar. When I told Morton Baum what I was contemplating, he said, "You'll lose your shirt!" I convinced him it was time for a Baroque piece. When the tickets went on sale and lots of people bought them, he was happy to reverse his opinion.

I invited the Canadian contralto Maureen Forrester to join the cast in the role of Cornelia. As her son Sextus, we had our own Beverly Wolff. Originally I talked to Phyllis Curtin, a mainstay of our company from 1953 to 1960, about the role of Cleopatra. Though she had joined the Met in 1961, Phyllis had returned to City Opera in 1962 for the world premiere of Carlisle Floyd's *Passion of Jonathan Wade* (a work containing some outstanding music) and in 1964 for *Salome.*

Phyllis's management and John White, my prime negotiator, hit various roadblocks in the early negotiations. Phyllis's husband Gene Cook joined the negotiations, and ultimately I entered them as well. I've learned over the years that, with *very* few exceptions, it's a mistake for spouses or any relatives to act as managers. Gene claimed that since Phyllis was a Met artist, she was entitled to a higher fee than our top compensation. There were other picayune things, but finally we seemed to agree on all terms. Then Gene told me that Phyllis would actually not be available for the last two performances. I remember where we were when I learned this news—it was a cold day late in November 1965, and we were talking on a bench in Riverside Park, where I was watching my eight-year-old son Tony. (Not that I usually go into the park to negotiate, but this was at the time when we had just moved into our new offices at the State Theater, and because our offices were underground and had no windows, I thought it would be nice to get a breath of fresh air.) Gene and I ended the meeting with things still up in the air.

Meanwhile Sills had gotten hold of a score for *Giulio Cesare*. She fell in love with the music, and told Ludwig Lustig she wanted to do the role. When John White and I met with Lustig in the fall of 1965 to talk about roles his artists would do for us the following year, we offered Beverly Donna Anna in *Don Giovanni*, Constanza in *Abduction from the Seraglio*, the three roles in *Hoffmann*, and the Queen of the Night in our new production of *The Magic*

Flute. Lustig agreed, and then said, "Miss Sills has a wish. She wants to be considered for Cleopatra." On hearing that, I whistled to myself "Greedy girl" (there's an aria in Blitzstein's opera *Regina* by that title); she has all these lovely roles and she wants more. I told Lustig the role had already been assigned to Phyllis, and that was the end of that—until some weeks later, when Beverly asked to see me and told me directly how much she would like to do the role. I reiterated that I had promised it to Phyllis. Beverly made a big deal out of the fact that Phyllis was "no longer a member of the company" (which wasn't actually true, since Phyllis had returned for *Jonathan Wade* and *Salome*) and that Cleopatra should in fact go to a current City Opera soprano—herself. I agreed to "think on it."

A few days later—by now it was early December—Beverly asked if she could "invite herself" to my home for breakfast—she would bring the bagels. The next morning she dropped by my apartment. Of course both of us knew the real purpose of this friendly breakfast meeting. Over bagels and coffee, Beverly told me again that she would be ideal for the role. In a jokey, half-serious way, she mentioned that her husband had offered to rent Carnegie Hall for her, and wouldn't it be "exciting" if she were to sing some of Cleopatra's arias? It was all good-natured, with smiles and laughter. Breakfast ended with both of us maintaining our respective positions. Over the years Beverly turned the story of this quite amiable breakfast encounter into a showdown in which she presented me with an ultimatum: "My husband intends to hire Carnegie Hall for me to do a New York recital—and I assure you, when I sing at Carnegie Hall, my program will contain five of Cleopatra's arias—and you're going to look sick."

Beverly didn't actually say that. I was her boss, and though she was a valued member of the company, she was not yet a star and would never have said something that brazen to me while angling to get a role assigned to someone else.

Still, from that moment forward, the power dynamics of our personal relationship were changed.

After my frustrating "park conference" with Phyllis's husband a few weeks earlier, I asked myself what I had to lose if I gave the role of Cleopatra to Sills. What was I fighting? Phyllis couldn't do the last two performances anyway. The negotiations couldn't just continue indefinitely.

I asked John White to write a letter to Phyllis's agent terminating our negotiations, then telephoned Sills directly and asked if she was still interested in the role. "And how!" she said.

John White apparently did not send a letter but instead phoned Phyllis's agent, Carl Dahlgren. I have recently come across a typewritten letter to me from Gene Cook dated December 15, 1965. In it he wrote that Carl Dahlgren had "earmarked" but not actually booked the engagements in California and Hawaii that would have kept Phyllis from doing the final two performances of *Giulio Cesare*, but that "John White had phoned and said that the whole question was academic because the City Opera had now engaged Beverly Sills." Gene concluded by writing, "Not that it matters, for in all this murk—from Fifty-Fifth Street and from Fifty-Seventh Street—one plain fact emerges. In the future, I would like to suggest that negotiating be done by the friends, strain or no strain, instead of by the negotiators. Because my recollection of the way things were left when we went to Europe was that Phyllis was going to come into the house to try the acoustics and to learn at first hand what they really are." Gene also handwrote a postscript, in which he said that he never received the letter about the role going to Beverly. (Naturally he hadn't, since it had not been written.) All these years later I still regret how things were handled with Phyllis. She is a marvelous, intelligent performer—and this incident put a rift in our friendship that has taken a long time to heal.

What happened when Sills sang Cleopatra was totally unexpected.

The role was perfect for her in every way. Beverly had a ball with the appogiaturas and coloraturas and cadenzas and everything else I gave her to do, and she skillfully handled both the pathos and the humor of the role. After more than a decade of faithful service she became, literally "overnight," a superstar.

From day one Beverly and I had a special and unusual artistic relationship—free and easy. We could always talk things out—convince one another of a particular point of view—and throughout our long collaboration we brought out the best in each other artistically. We were "in sync" at all times; she used to say that I could "pre-guess" her by five seconds, which meant that I was never surprised by anything she sang. When things went wrong onstage, she would rebound quickly. Once, when she inadvertently skipped a few bars and hit a high A too soon, I held up my hand. She knew immediately what the problem was, and held the note until I lowered my hand eight bars later.

The score of *Giulio Cesare* has forty numbers, most of those in the so-called ABA form, and all beautiful. A complete performance takes more than four hours. Capobianco, who was directing, and I agreed that some editing was essential. And so we reluctantly cut several numbers. To aid the dramatic flow, we repositioned some numbers and made a few other minor changes.

Would I do such extensive cutting and pasting of a Handel opera today? Probably not. But in 1966 it seemed the right thing to do, and years later our choices were vindicated when the musicologist and Baroque specialist Robert Donington told me that the City Opera production of *Giulio Cesare* had been a pivotal moment in the reconstitution of Handel. (My editing was not limited to one composer; in 1991, I "tightened" Dvorak's opera *Rusalka* for Renée Fleming in Houston, and there were no complaints.)

As much as possible, I did want to present a historically correct performance, so I asked the cast—all of them superior musicians—to invent their
own ornamentation, as was Baroque custom. This was not an easy task for
modern performers. They were more familiar with Donizetti than with
Handel, whose music required a quite different sound. Imagine my chagrin
when their inventions were full of anachronistic touches! Ultimately I wrote
all of the cadenzas myself, trying to match them to the singer's strengths and
abilities. (Because of all the changes, I copyrighted my version of the score
in 1967. It remained in the City Opera repertory for nearly two decades.)

Beverly was leaving town for the summer and going to her home on Martha's Vineyard. She invited Rita and me to visit for a few weeks. After breakfast I would sequester myself and work on the musical embellishments and
ornamentations. An hour or so later Beverly would join me and we would
try them. She'd toss them off—roulades, trills, runs, leaps—and dare me to
make them even more difficult. We'd urge each other on to ever greater
feats. She trilled the birds out of the trees and seemed to silence the pound-
ing of the surf. The sound wafting through those crystal mornings is still in
my ears.

Beverly originally intended to model her character on Elizabeth Taylor's
Cleopatra. But Tito Capobianco had other things in mind for her.

He wanted the opera to be a combination of Baroque opera and French
ballet harking back to Handel's time. He asked Ming Cho Lee to design
a "broken Baroque" look with partial arches, balustrades, and staircases to
give the impression of an ancient Egypt in ruins. The singers were given stylized balletic movements (choreographed by Gigi Denda) that were unlike
anything they had ever done before. The production was a combination of
burlesque and baroque grandeur right on the edge of bad taste and kitsch;
but to Tito's credit, it never went over the brink, and was quite effective.

In the weeks leading up to the premiere, the attention in New York's artistic circles was focused on the inauguration of the Met's brand-new house.
The little interest that came our way went to Maureen Forrester; shortly
before our opening night, *Time* magazine published a feature article on her.
I can still recall a rehearsal break in the canteen where some of the cast
members—the two Beverlys, Norman, Spiro Malas, and Dominic Cossa—
were sitting around and talking. Sills bemoaned the fact that Maureen was
getting all the attention. "I don't understand it. I get all this fan mail. Something's not right," she said; to which I responded, "Well, Maureen has a
press agent." Without missing a beat, Beverly said, "Then I will have a press
agent." "So will I," said Norman. "I will, too," Spiro chimed in.

Sills was true to her word. Within a few days she had signed on with one of the finest publicists around, Edgar Vincent—who, as it happened, was also my representative. Her husband, Peter, agreed to pay for several months of Edgar's services. It was one of the best career moves—some have said *the* best move—Beverly ever made. For me it eventually proved to be problematic.

Though I knew that musically our cast was first-rate, I had no idea how the audience would react to the production. On opening night, the State Theater was packed. Among the audience members were a number of critics from the international press who had come for the Met's opening and stayed on for ours. There was an air of anticipation in the auditorium that seemed more pronounced than usual. I walked briskly to the podium trying to pretend it was business as usual, but I knew damn well that everyone was wondering if we could match the success we had experienced seven months earlier with *Don Rodrigo*.

I needn't have worried. Norman was every inch the aristocratic ruler and Maureen was superb. (She and Beverly Wolff delivered a melting, moving duet at the end of act 1, "Son nata a lagrimar.") But it was Sills's night from start to finish; she was positively scintillating and nailed every one of the arias. I had an inkling at the end of the first act that we were a hit, but since I'm superstitious by nature, I didn't let my emotions get the better of me. By the time Beverly sang "Piangerò," I could feel everyone in the house collectively holding their breath during her stunning pianissimos. The applause at the end of that aria—and later, at the end of the opera—seemed to go on forever.

The next day the reviews were ecstatic. Alan Rich of the New York *World Journal Tribune* praised the "beautiful, intelligent and wholly admirable production" and Sills's sublime delivery of "some ferocious coloratura writing." He called her "the Cleopatra of anyone's dreams." Treigle, however, did not fare quite as well in Rich's review: "He lacks the total agility for one of the most taxing roles ever conceived, but sings out with great strength and purity." Harold Schonberg in the *New York Times* raved about the production and singled out both Sills and Forrester, but though he complimented Treigle's "intelligent, splendid" acting, he was critical of his singing: "He does not have the vocal equipment for the part, not when it comes to the coloratura, which he either slurred or barked." I couldn't have disagreed more. I had actually planned the opera as a vehicle for him, and we had both thought it would result in a breakthrough for him. Yet it did not work out that way, and from the moment that *Giulio Cesare* opened, there was a tremendous change in Treigle's personality. He was angry.

Sills had become a star overnight, and Edgar Vincent saw to it that feature articles about her appeared in every major newspaper and magazine. Beverly was a "natural" celebrity; she gravitated toward the media, and the media reciprocated gladly. With her outgoing personality and highly quotable quips, she quickly became the darling of the press. Norman was not so inclined—he was a private kind of guy who hated "working the press."

Before long people were lining up en masse at the State Theater box office, asking for tickets to "the Beverly Sills opera," and opera companies around the world were extending open invitations to her. Our ensemble company was turning into a star company, with Beverly as the big draw.

Norman was understandably bitter at Beverly's success but tried to control his true feelings. The two, after all, shared the same manager, Ludwig Lustig, and were as close as could be; Norman often referred to Beverly as "my little sister." Since he couldn't turn his anger on his adored spiritual sibling, he turned it on me. He became cold and standoffish—and our comfortable friendship of more than a decade ground to an end.

His feelings toward me became apparent to everyone in November 1967, during our company's first annual tour to Los Angeles. Larry Deutsch, who with his partner Lloyd Rigler underwrote the trip, remarked that he found it odd that all the artists were given solo bows but that I was not, and he asked me to take a solo bow after *Giulio Cesare.* That night, when Norman went out for his curtain call, he grabbed my hand as he passed me in the wings and said, "If you take a solo bow, you can sing the next performance yourself." I was stunned. I've never seen such hatred in anyone's eyes. I skipped the bow and walked back to my dressing room.

Of course the report of this incident spread like wildfire and—although Norman did apologize for his irrational and shocking behavior—our relationship was totally changed. I had always considered Treigle to be one of the world's great basses, on a level with Pinza and Chaliapin—but when his reviews turned out to be so negative he actually spoke of ending his stage career and becoming a teacher at one of the vocal conservatories.

(Fortunately Treigle's performance was preserved for the ages. Larry and Lloyd gave us $10,000 to make an RCA recording of *Giulio Cesare.* In April 1967 we assembled the cast and orchestra in Webster Hall on East Eleventh Street in New York, and recorded everything on the first take, since there was no money for retakes. We stopped briefly only once; the pigeons on the roof were making such a god-awful racket that we had to chase them away.)

In an effort to lift Norman's spirits I tried to find an opera exclusively for him (Carlisle Floyd was writing *Of Mice and Men,* with Treigle in mind for the role of George; unfortunately, the libretto was weak and needed to be reworked, and it was not to have its world premiere until several years later in Seattle—with Julian Patrick as George), but in the meantime, in the fall of 1967 I reunited our *Giulio Cesare* team—the Capobiancos, Ming Cho Lee, and Beverly and Norman—for Rimsky-Korsakov's delightful *Le coq d'or,* based on a Russian fairy tale by Pushkin. Strangely enough, the rehearsal period for *Coq d'or* was productive and lots of fun. On the surface it was like old times.

Le coq d'or was a real crowd-pleaser—a showcase for our company's shining couple, who were both outrageously funny, topped off with Beverly's hilariously seductive belly dance. It was a real tongue-in-cheek follow-up to *Julius Caesar*—and this time the two stars shared equally in the kudos.

The time had come to introduce Beverly's Manon to our audience. Our spring 1968 season included a new production of Massenet's *Manon*, directed by Tito and designed by Marsha Louis Eck in the style of Fragonard. I conducted, and it was a work that was to become a calling card for both Beverly and me. (We recorded it with the New Philharmonia Orchestra in 1970 for Westminster Records with Nicolai Gedda as Des Grieux, Gabriel Bacquier as Comte des Grieux, and Gérard Souzay as Lescaut.) Beverly brought resplendent vocal artistry to the title role and convincingly embodied the many different moods and sides of the character: the charming awkwardness of the country girl in the first scene, the sensuality, the glittering egotism, the sweet sorrow. I always thought that Michele Molese, her Des Grieux at City Opera, was a much underestimated tenor. He was altogether effective in the role—albeit lacking the finesse that Sills brought to her part.

Beverly was enamored of the bel canto repertory Maria Callas had specialized in, and began to look for works that could show off both her singing and acting skills. In a postcard from St. Thomas, Virgin Islands, dated January 29, 1968, she wrote (beginning with the nickname she had given me):

> Chulyus dollink—I am looking through 6 or 7 Rossini and Donizetti operas to give you some alternatives to *Puritani*—like *La Donna del Lago, Linda di Chamounix, Maria di Rohan, Lucrezia Borgia*. Meanwhile think Bel Canto. You'll hear from me some more. B xo

Bel canto was put on hold for a few months while we tackled a mainstay of the French repertory: Gounod's *Faust*. Frank Corsaro directed our new production in the fall of 1968, with Molese in the title role and Beverly and Norman as Marguerite and Méphistophélès. Frank viewed *Faust* not as an old warhorse but as a Gothic romantic opera that needed to be taken out of mothballs. (Frank and I certainly agreed on that!) Beverly, on the first day of rehearsal, quipped, "Just tell me, which side do I wear my pigtail on?" to which Corsaro responded, "Surprise! Surprise! Surprise!" and then proceeded to give her a much more complex "take" on the character of Marguerite.

There were inspired touches throughout, beginning with the opening scene, in which Faust tries to find the secret of life by experimenting on cadavers. Frank made Méphistophélès one of the corpses. To see Norman rising from the dead, dressed in Victorian devil's garb, was truly frightening.

Everything was within bounds until we arrived at the final scene, the dungeon, and Corsaro revealed that he was going to show Marguerite's execution—albeit only in silhouette. I said, "You're over the top. I won't allow it."

But both Frank and Beverly pleaded to at least let them try it once, and I reluctantly agreed.

Frank said, "If you really don't like it, after the first performance I will restage it." Famous last words—after the first performance the damage was done. The critics had a field day. Opera audiences have memories like elephants, and for the past four decades that ending has been much maligned (even by people who never actually saw it).

In the beginning of 1969, there was an emergency release request for Beverly to go to La Scala to sub for a pregnant Renata Scotto. It meant we had to find another Queen of Shemakha for *Le coq d'or*—Patricia Wise, who did a lovely job.

Sills's La Scala debut, on April 11, 1969, was as Pamira in Rossini's *The Siege of Corinth*. Thomas Schippers conducted, and the cast included Justino Díaz and Marilyn Horne. *Corinth*, filled with coloratura fireworks, was perfect for Beverly. The notoriously capricious La Scala audiences loved her, and *Newsweek* published a cover story on Sills a few weeks later. *The Siege of Corinth* was also the opera in which Beverly made her Met debut in 1975. Marilyn Horne did not sing in the Met production. Apparently there had been friction between the two women at La Scala that remained unresolved. When I wanted to invite Marilyn to do a role for us at City Opera in the mid-1970s, Beverly threatened to walk out, claiming our company "would become a star company and lose its character." When Sills became director of the company, she promptly engaged Victoria de los Ángeles and Grace Bumbry without worrying about loss of character.

In June 1969 Sills and I (and a fine cast including Léopold Simoneau and the versatile Elaine Bonazzi) collaborated on a semistaged production of Handel's *Semele* at the Caramoor Festival. Roland Gagnon, Beverly's trusted vocal coach since 1962, wrote the excellent ornamentation for her *Semele* arias. The Caramoor performance occurred at the height of our collaboration, when Beverly was at the pinnacle of her artistry and her voice was still fresh. I've always regretted that we were not able to bring *Semele* to City Opera—though after Caramoor we were able to do an additional performance of it at the Waterloo Festival in New Jersey. (In attendance was the legendary Maria Jeritza, who lived nearby—whom I had first seen onstage when I was a toddler.) I am also sorry that *Ariodante*, which I conducted during the opening week of the Kennedy Center in 1971 with a terrific cast including Beverly, Tatiana Troyanos, Veronica Tyler, and Donald Gramm, never made its way to New York.

We scheduled City Opera's first production of *Lucia di Lammermoor* starring Beverly for our fall 1969 season, to be directed by Tito and designed by Marsha Louis Eck. Since I was going to be busy rehearsing Boito's *Mefistofele*, which opened a few weeks ahead of *Lucia* (and scored a tremendous personal

triumph for Treigle, who was positively spellbinding in the leading role, and a
box office hit for the company) and more importantly, since *Lucia* was not a
work I particularly liked (I once referred to it as "a Scotch *shmatte*"), I turned
over the conducting duties to our staff conductor Charles Wendelken-Wilson.
Beverly and Tito opted to do an uncut *Lucia*, and she chalked up another victory. The "mad scene" was both poignant and exquisitely sung; Beverly had
turned the *shmatte* into fine embroidered lace.

(Three and a half decades later, I changed my opinion of *Lucia di Lammermoor*. In 2003 Plácido Domingo invited me to conduct it at the Los Angeles Opera. When I learned that Anna Netrebko was to be the star, that gave
me the push to take a good, hard look at the opera. I had seen Netrebko in
War and Peace, and was struck by the purity of her sound. Upon reexamining
the Donizetti opera, I found a lot of wonderful music. There's some note-
gnashing, for sure, but there's also some great musical drama, including
the very last scene, which was lustrously sung in Los Angeles by the Spanish
tenor José Bros. Too bad so many people rush out after Lucia's mad scene
and miss out on Edgardo's final lament!)

It was late in 1969 that Beverly entered a whole new realm of superstar-
dom. After La Scala and the *Newsweek* cover story, she made the first of many
appearances on Johnny Carson's *Tonight Show*. Beverly was a perfect guest—
funny and always ready to tell a backstage story—and she would perform a
selection or two (usually lighter "pops" fare that everyone would enjoy). She
put a human face on an art form that was inaccessible to many Americans,
and there is no telling how many people attended their first opera because
of her influence.

Beverly embraced it all—her newfound fame and her role as a spokes-
person (for the arts and for the March of Dimes)—with her characteristic
exuberance. As Spiro Malas, who performed with her frequently, tells it:
"We'd go out and sing and she'd show me a $5,000 check; then she'd show
me a $7,000 check; then one for $10,000. I said, 'Beverly, don't show me
anything else,' and she said, 'And to think I was doing the same thing ten
years ago.' It was not so much gloating as it was a sort of rhetorical question, 'Can you believe that Bubbles Silverman from Brooklyn is being paid
this much to sing?'"

By 1969 Roland Gagnon and Tito Capobianco persuaded Beverly to
tackle some of the more challenging bel canto roles, beginning with Donzet-
ti's *Roberto Devereux*, about the aging Queen Elizabeth I. Her voice teacher,
Estelle Liebling, warned her not to take on such a taxing role but Sills—
who had just turned forty—had no qualms. The production (directed by
Tito, designed by Ming Cho Lee, and conducted by me) opened during
our fall 1970 season, and the critics were all over themselves with superlatives—with the exception of Harold Schonberg in the *New York Times*, who
complimented the "handsome" production and Capobianco's "smooth and

intelligent" direction but was critical of Beverly's voice: "She sounded shrill and nervous, and was constantly having pitch trouble."

Nonetheless, tickets for all performances sold out immediately, and Roland Gagnon suggested to Beverly that she perform the title roles in two other Donizetti operas about British sovereigns, *Anna Bolena* and *Maria Stuarda*. When she proposed the idea to me, I answered with the only possible response: "Yes!" By this time Beverly was such a huge draw that her fans would flock to City Opera for *anything* she performed. In addition, Ming Cho Lee's set design could be made to work for all three operas with the addition of a few supplementary elements, thus making the whole *trittico* a cost-effective undertaking as well. Most everyone agreed that the "Three Queens" was Beverly's crowning achievement as a singing actress, though the repertory most definitely took a toll on her voice. The only one of the three I did not conduct was *Maria Stuarda*, which opened in spring 1972. (Again, I handed it to Charlie Wilson. I conducted fewer performances at City Opera that season because of my duties as music director of the newly opened Kennedy Center in Washington.) The role of Mary Stuart turned out to be Sills's least favorite of the Three Queens; that opera has the least interesting music of the three.

We postponed *Anna Bolena* for a year to mount a new production of *The Tales of Hoffmann* for Sills, Molese, and Treigle in October 1972; the Offenbach opera was again directed by Capobianco but was not an improvement on the brilliant previous production. Sadly, it was the last work Norman was to perform with New York City Opera at Lincoln Center. Though he continued to perform in the US (and he and I exchanged letters and had a few phone conversations in 1974 about his possibly rejoining New York City Opera), he was severely traumatized by his unsuccessful Covent Garden debut in the fall of 1974 (in Gounod's *Faust*) and died in February 1975 at the age of 47. There is still speculation as to whether or not he took his own life. What is not in dispute is that our company had lost its most mesmerizing male performer.

In the fall of 1973, our musicians' contract negotiations had not gone well (the orchestra wanted more weeks of guaranteed income) and there was a company strike for four weeks. *Anna Bolena* was scheduled to open on October 3, 1973, but was in danger of being derailed before its heroine was beheaded. Amazingly, this was one strike that actually worked to our advantage. We were scheduled to open three new productions that season: *Bolena*, *A Village Romeo and Juliet* (a dreamy rarity by Frederick Delius in a mixed media production by Frank Corsaro), and *Ariadne auf Naxos*, which was being directed by Sarah Caldwell. Sarah, true to form, was way behind in finishing the staging of *Ariadne*. (That, coupled with the fact that she continually changed her mind about how a particular scene would be played, was driving us all a bit batty; Dominic Cossa, who played the role of Harlequin, still tells stories of props that swiftly came and went during rehearsals, from a skateboard to a beach ball.) Even though the singers were officially supporting the striking musicians, we were still able to get together a bit on the side with the soloists. When the strike ended after four weeks, the *Ariadne* was at last fully staged. We had to rearrange our entire schedule because we had already missed the opening dates of two of our new productions, but we rather boldly scheduled three premieres within a four-day period, starting with *Anna Bolena* on October 3. Amazingly, all three productions clicked with the critics and the public. As William Bender wrote in *Time*, "Soprano Sills earned her right to sing [Anna Bolena] by her performance. And with such adventurous programming, the company more than earned a warm welcome back."

We were back on top, and immediately after the fall season ended, we were bound for Los Angeles, where Beverly took on another new role.

13

THE KENNEDY CENTER

From Concept to Opening

Prior to 1971 it was almost an embarrassment for a diplomat to be stationed in Washington. It was unforgiveable that the capital of the richest nation in the world did not possess adequate performance space for opera and concerts. Concerts were given in Constitution Hall (the meeting place of the Daughters of the American Revolution) and opera at the Lisner Auditorium of George Washington University—and our artistic community would blushingly apologize for DC's lack of a symphony hall and an opera house.

Happily, the apologies ended in 1971 with the opening of two spectacular showplaces for the performing arts: Kennedy Center and Wolf Trap.

The idea for an arts center in Washington was first broached during the Eisenhower administration, but there was lack of agreement about the budget, the location, and the mission of the center. In 1961 President Kennedy appointed the real estate tycoon and Broadway producer Roger L. Stevens to the chairmanship of the projected National Cultural Center and told him "to make it a reality." Congress, after some oppositional posturing from the usual suspects who objected to public funding for this "Pleasure Palace on the Potomac," authorized $23 million for the building, with the remainder to come from private contributions. The architect Edward Durrell Stone was engaged to design the stately edifice in the neighborhood known as Foggy Bottom on the banks of the Potomac River.

Following the national tragedy of President Kennedy's assassination, the cultural center became a memorial to him and was officially named the John F. Kennedy Center for the Performing Arts. The groundbreaking took place in Washington on December 2, 1964. President Johnson was photographed with a gold-plated shovel, and Senator-elect Robert F. Kennedy recalled his brother's belief "that America is judged as every civilization is judged—in large measure by the quality of its artistic achievement" and not by its wars.

Just as Morton Baum was the fulcrum of New York's City Center, Roger Stevens was the fighting spirit behind the Kennedy Center. He somehow managed to deal with the congressional naysayers and provocateurs who wanted to change the location and mission (one congressman went so far as to suggest that it should be "a multipurpose hall that can also be used for sporting events") and to raise a good part of the $30.6 million in private financing that was ultimately needed for the construction of the Kennedy Center.

The extraordinary Stevens, whose Broadway credits included such hits as *West Side Story* and *A Man for All Seasons*, was an idealist and a dreamer who loved to read, especially Shakespeare and Shaw. He had spent some time in the school of hard knocks—his original plans to attend Harvard had been thwarted when his father lost his fortune during the Depression—but Roger was determined to be successful, starting out at a Detroit real estate firm, where he quickly advanced before moving on to New York. In 1951 he led a group of investors who bought the Empire State Building for the then-astronomical sum of $50 million.

In 1965 I was one of several artists invited by a committee of the Kennedy Center board to share our thoughts and ideas about the center—what its mission should be as well as potential directors and programming. We were directed to a room at New York's Plaza Hotel, where we met individually with the committee. My conversation lasted thirty minutes and I was thanked for my contribution and that was that—or so I thought.

One of the committee members who interviewed me that day was Catherine Filene Shouse, known to her friends as Kay. Born in Boston in 1896, she was the heiress to a retailing fortune (her grandfather, William Filene, was the founder of the department-store chain Filene's). After earning a master's degree in education at Harvard, she opted for a career in public service and philanthropy. In 1930 she purchased Wolf Trap Farm in Vienna, Virginia—fifteen miles west of Washington—as a bucolic retreat for her family. A lifelong fan of the arts, in the late 1940s Kay joined the board of the National Symphony Orchestra; it was she who came up with the idea of organizing and sponsoring a series of concerts to supplement the salaries of the NSO musicians. In 1959 President Eisenhower appointed her to the first board of the National Cultural Center; over the next two decades she was reappointed by Presidents Kennedy and Nixon.

When I first met Kay in March 1960, she was hosting a reception at her house in Georgetown for our New York City Opera American Tour. We brought three operas to Washington that spring: *Susannah, Baby Doe,* and *Six Characters in Search of an Author*—and we performed, of course, in Lisner Auditorium. Kay and I took an immediate liking to each other. She had a sharp sense of humor and was feisty—as demanding of herself as she was of others. When she visited New York, she would often stay with my wife and me. Kay and Rita were very close except when the conversation turned to politics. (Rita, a diehard liberal, very early on referred to Richard Nixon as "that crook," much to Kay's chagrin.)

Kay considered it her mission to bring the arts to everyone, and in 1966 she did something quite amazing and totally unprecedented: she donated one hundred acres of her Virginia farmland and $2.3 million of her own money to the US Government to build Wolf Trap Farm Park—the first national park for the performing arts. Her gift was made official by an Act of Congress and the money was used to build the 3,500-seat theater (with outdoor seating for an additional 3,000 on the lawn) known as the Filene Center, which was designed by John MacFadyen and Edward Knowles and opened in July 1971, two months before the opening of the Kennedy Center. (In the early 1980s, in yet another magnanimous gesture, Kay donated additional land and money to construct "The Barns"—Wolf Trap's indoor year-round theater and reception hall.)

Late in the summer of '67, Kay invited Rita and me to spend a week at her summer home in the picturesque coastal town of Blue Hill, Maine. Nearly every night at sunset we would go out on her ancient lobster boat (affectionately known as "Tugboat Annie") for a cocktail cruise. One evening, returning from one of our twilight excursions, I was surprised to find Roger Stevens waiting at Kay's house. He, too, had a summer home in Blue Hill, and ostensibly had come to pay his respects to Kay. Roger asked me to go for a walk with him. Then, while we were strolling in Kay's garden, he informed me that the board of the Kennedy Center had decided to offer me the position of Artistic Director. Would I be interested?

I was stunned.

Roger did not expect an immediate answer. He told me to think about it over the next few weeks. I did just that, and sought the advice of a number of friends. Eugene Ormandy said, "Take it! Take it!" and also implied that it might be time for me to leave New York City Opera. Stokowski, on the other hand, counseled caution: "This is a new thing that will have to be made from scratch." Of course I also informed Baum of the flattering offer but assured him that I had no intention of leaving my New York City Opera post, where I was very happy.

My dilemma became known to the public on October 31, 1967, when it was reported in the *New York Times* that William McCormick Blair Jr., the former Ambassador to the Philippines and a friend of the Kennedy family, had been offered the post of General Director of the Kennedy Center and I had been offered the position of Artistic Director. Blair accepted without hesitation; I asked for additional time to make my decision.

What, exactly, would I do at the Kennedy Center? With the National Symphony in the expert hands of Antal Dorati and the Washington Opera Society not quite active enough, would I have to stop being a musician and become a fulltime administrator? After several nights of self-questioning, I finally decided to decline the artistic directorship of the Kennedy Center and wrote Roger Stevens a letter to that effect on January 10, 1968. But

Roger wouldn't take no for an answer. A few days later I received an invitation to lunch with Jacqueline Kennedy at her Fifth Avenue apartment. The small guest list consisted of Roger Stevens, Arthur Schlesinger (undoubtedly to give historical gravitas to the enterprise!), and me.

Mrs. Kennedy (who later that year was to marry Aristotle Onassis) was gracious and charming. During the course of our meal she appealed to me to rethink my decision and managed to convince me that I was "the only person" for the job. At the end of the meal I gave her the only possible answer, "Yes," agreeing to serve part-time as the center's "music advisor" (rather than full-time artistic director) with the understanding that I would also require someone of stature to act as my administrator. And of course I made it clear that I would be staying in New York and keeping my other posts. "Whatever you'd like," said Mrs. Kennedy sweetly.

My appointment was announced on January 31, 1968. When Roger called to discuss my contract, I told him I couldn't possibly accept a salary. "This is my way of paying back the country that welcomed me thirty years ago," I said. For the first three years I did indeed work "pro bono," but when the Kennedy Center opened—by which time I had accepted the title of "music director," the board requested that I accept a salary.

The person I had in mind to be my administrator was George London. A beloved singer and the first American to tackle the role of Boris Godunov at the Bolshoi Opera in Russia, he was internationally admired and spoke several languages. His singing career had been abruptly curtailed in 1967 because of a paralyzed vocal cord, and I thought the Kennedy Center job would be a perfect fit for him. I knew he would have the right stature—plus the respect of the music community. He enthusiastically accepted.

George and I came up with the idea of inviting our foremost singers and instrumentalists to appear in a series of special recitals and orchestra concerts at Kennedy Center and asking them to donate the money from ticket sales to the center. These "Founding Artists," as they were called—among them Gina Bachauer (who gave a recital during the opening two-week celebration in September '71), and Plácido Domingo and Birgit Nilsson, both of whose benefit concerts I conducted—were presented with miniature marble models of the Kennedy Center, each engraved with an inscription of thanks.

In addition we devised a plan to have the most important opera companies of the world bring some of their best productions to our opera house, to put the Kennedy Center on the world map. George London began negotiating with companies including the Berlin Opera, La Scala, the Paris Opera, and the Bolshoi.

I wanted to create certain music festivals (which did indeed happen, most notably the "New and Old" festival featuring music from the eighteenth and twentieth centuries), but my ultimate plan was to create a national conservatory, much as Dvořák had wanted to do in Washington in the 1890s. I recall standing with Roger Stevens and looking at the Old Naval Hospital building, and telling him I'd love to turn it into a Conservatory that would be open to students from across the United States: "Each state would be represented, and students would be tapped by their Congressmen. It would be a point of pride—a long range plan." Alas it never happened, in Dvořák's time or in mine.

The three main theaters within the Kennedy Center are the Eisenhower, which seats 1,163; the Opera House, which seats 2,200; and the Concert Hall, which seats 2,400. (In addition to these main theaters, there are also some smaller venues, along with a rooftop promenade.) The man in charge of sound was Cyril M. Harris, the acoustics engineer who had also been responsible for the Metropolitan Opera House at Lincoln Center. I brought New York City Opera's technical director Hans Sondheimer to Washington with me many times between 1968 and 1971. All the guiding lights were in place, and we were able to anticipate and avoid some of the mistakes that had been made at Lincoln Center. My multiple connections facilitated our "test performance" of *La traviata* in the Opera House during the first week of August 1971, using a combination of Washington and New York forces—New York City Opera was performing *Traviata* at Wolf Trap that week—and giving us the opportunity to try-out the Opera House and iron out the few remaining "kinks in the system." The invited audience was made up of Kennedy Center and Wolf Trap workers and their families, many of them seeing their first opera, and all of them enthusiastically applauding our two Violettas (who alternated in the different acts; I wanted to see how two different sopranos sounded in the new opera house). The results were most satisfactory: The acoustics of the Opera House (along with the other auditoriums at Kennedy Center) have been much praised by performers and audiences. My friend Richard Kidwell, who in 1971 was the fresh-faced new manager of the Kennedy Center Opera House (and who today remains in the exact same position), recently reminded me that the *Traviata* test run was the first music ever heard at the Kennedy Center.

It came time to plan the opening programming. I felt strongly that the first week's performances should include a ballet, a symphony concert, and a chamber music recital with all-American performers. The most difficult programming would be for the Opera House.

It had previously been announced that Leonard Bernstein was to write a work that would be performed on the official opening night of the center; although Lenny had received the Kennedy Center commission in 1966, at the time of my appointment in 1968, he had not yet decided what kind of piece he wanted to write. In addition, the Washington Opera Society had commissioned a new opera by Alberto Ginastera: *Beatrix Cenci*. With two brand-new twentieth-century works already scheduled, I felt we needed a connection to the past and decided on the beautiful Handel opera *Ariodante*, which we cast entirely with American singers led by Beverly Sills, Tatiana Troyanos, and Veronica Tyler. (*Ariodante* was a Kennedy Center production, approved by the board and paid for by the center itself. A few years later New York City Opera would coproduce two operas with the Kennedy Center, *Salome* and *Idomeneo*—the latter turned out to be one of the highlights of our Kennedy Center Mozart Festival.)

So I was planning a two-hundred-year-old opera that none of the participants had ever heard, let alone performed, plus two not-yet-written works, all to be produced in a theater not yet built. Roger Stevens—steady as ever—supported this bold, or as some called it, "just plain insane" plan. He never waivered, and his confidence made the whole process possible.

In those days, whenever I ran into Lenny Bernstein I would casually ask, "What are we doing?"

"I have no idea," he would respond. I didn't push the issue, but as the months flew by my question became ever more urgent. One Sunday morning in late 1969 Lenny called me on the phone. "CHEW-lee-us," he said, drawing out the first syllable as he liked to do, "If you have time, would you come over? I want to show you something."

I immediately went to his apartment, and he showed me some parts of what would become the *Mass*. "What do you think?" he asked.

My response was swift: "It's great! A brilliant idea! By all means let's go with it."

What I saw and heard that day as Lenny played and sang for me in his inimitable gravelly voice was a musical hybrid, an immediately accessible work that would "speak" to the world (although I was a little bit concerned with his "Mahlerian sections"—he wanted so much to be taken seriously as a composer, not a "songwriter").

The next two years were among the busiest and certainly the happiest ones of my career, as I embarked on the "Three Queens" trilogy and the Corsaro production of *Pelléas and Mélisande* at New York City Opera, commuting back and forth between New York and Washington. In the midst of running New York City Opera, along with Caramoor in the summers, and readying the Kennedy Center for its opening, I took time out to guest at the Cincinnati May Festival in 1971 and 1972 (among the highlights there was a first-rate performance of Rossini's *Stabat Mater* with Leontyne Price, Susanne Marsee, John Alexander, and Robert Hale) in gratitude to the Corbetts for helping me with *Mefistofele* at City Opera. In addition Kay Shouse had bullied me into the music directorship of Wolf Trap. (I pleaded "lack of time," and she countered with "If you want something done, ask a busy man.") So it was that on July 1, 1971, I mounted the podium at Wolf Trap to lead the National Symphony Orchestra in the Prologue to *Mefistofele* with Norman Treigle, and the MacDowell Second Piano Concerto with Van Cliburn. The first-night gala crowd—including President Nixon—had to contend with the sound of airplanes flying overhead on flight patterns to Dulles Airport. (We were prepared for everything, but nobody had thought of that.) At the following night's concert no noise was heard; such was Washington's love for Kay Shouse that someone in a position of authority had seen to it that planes did not land on certain Dulles runways during the performance. ("Kay's having them shot down over Maryland," my wife quipped.) As a tribute to me and to Beverly Sills, who was to perform at Wolf Trap several times over the next few years (she and I collaborated on *Traviata* and *Roberto Devereux* there, both of which were telecast), Kay had the two star dressing rooms named after us.

I've always been able to make practical use of every moment on a plane or train, studying scores and preparing notes for my colleagues. During this hectic time, our efficient City Opera secretary Bobbie Edles arranged my schedule down to the split second so that somehow I managed to get everything done (thirty-two minutes for one rehearsal, forty-five minutes for another, eighteen minutes for lunch, five minutes for a call to New York) as we prepared for the official opening night of Kennedy Center—a gala performance on September 8, 1971, of Leonard Bernstein's *Mass: A Theatre Piece for Singers, Players, and Dancers*, with staging by Gordon Davidson (the director of the Mark Taper Forum in Los Angeles), choreography by Alvin Ailey, and a cast of some two hundred including a blues band, a rock band, a street chorus, and a children's chorus. *Mass* was conducted by Maurice Peress, and Alan Titus, soon to become a valuable member of New York City Opera, was chosen to play the central role of the Celebrant. The work was based on the traditional Roman Catholic Mass, with liturgical passages sung in Latin and additional texts in English by Bernstein and young Stephen Schwartz, who had written the songs for the rock musical *Godspell* (and was working on a new show called *Pippin*).

In a *New York Times* article ("Rudel Logs a Hectic Day in Kennedy Center Roles") published on August 30, 1971, Howard Taubman asked me about my schedule between September 10 and 14. "On the 10th I conduct the premiere of *Cenci*. On the 11th I rehearse Handel's *Ariodante* all day. On the 12th I conduct Handel in the morning, a matinee of *Cenci* and a pre–dress rehearsal of *Ariodante* in the evening. On the 13th I rehearse the recitatives of *Ariodante* in the morning, [with] a full dress rehearsal in the afternoon and a public performance of *Cenci* in the evening. On the 14th I fly to New York to attend the dress rehearsal of [New York City Opera's] new production of Benjamin Britten's *Albert Herring* and [after giving notes to the cast] fly back to conduct the premiere of *Ariodante* in Washington in the evening."

I didn't bother to tell Mr. Taubman of a potential disaster two weeks earlier. Everything was in full swing and nearing completion when suddenly Schuyler Chapin—Lenny's representative and a good friend of mine— informed Roger and me that the *Mass* was not going to be ready.

"It needs more rehearsal time and space," Schuyler said.

I asked Roger to call a production meeting, which is how we all came to be together on a steamy summer afternoon in August, sitting deadlocked on Roger's back porch in Georgetown with his wife, Christine, graciously dispensing lemonade. Schuyler maintained that he and Bernstein felt they didn't have adequate rehearsal space, and he suggested that one of the other gala events in the Opera House (i.e., *Ariodante* or *Beatrix Cenci*) should be canceled. I pointed out what an embarrassment that would be, adding that I was certain "the problem could be solved by transforming some of the Kennedy Center's public areas into temporary rehearsal spaces."

"Can you guarantee the results?" Roger asked.

I sipped my lemonade and swallowed hard before responding. "Yes."

"Then we go ahead as planned," said Roger simply.

And we did—rehearsing everywhere throughout the center, even in the Grand Foyer, a 630-feet-long corridor and de facto lobby for the Concert Hall, Opera House, and the Eisenhower Theater (at the center of which stands the Robert Berks bronze bust of President Kennedy). As it turned out, the acoustics in the Foyer were more than acceptable, which gave me the idea of having the Mozart Serenades performed there during our Mozart Festival in 1974.

The initial preview performance of Bernstein's *Mass* was on Labor Day, September 6, with 2,200 members of the general public and even a few celebrities (including Danny Kaye) in attendance. The audience reaction was very positive and Lenny's eyes were filled with tears. There was a second preview on September 7—again, with enthusiastic audience response.

The opening on September 8 was attended by "everyone who was anyone" except for Jacqueline Kennedy Onassis, who had declined for security reasons. (President Nixon declined to attend, giving some sort of excuse but in reality staying away because the FBI's J. Edgar Hoover had warned him that the Bernstein work would no doubt contain antiwar messages.) The Kennedy family was represented by Senator Edward Kennedy and his wife Joan, and family matriarch Rose. The audience response was again terrific, but the following day the critics weighed in. While Paul Hume of the *Washington Post* was highly enthusiastic ("A shattering experience. . . . The central message of *Mass* and its crucial challenge is the place and function of religion in a world of violence"), many more of the critics were not so kind; some even called it "pretentious." Lenny was hurt and angry. I tried to discreetly guide him away from self-pity, pointing out how much the public loved it.

The Concert Hall opened on September 9 with President Nixon attending a program by the National Symphony Orchestra. Conductor Antal Dorati chose an array of works that showed off the acoustical properties of the hall: Beethoven's *"Consecration of the House"* Overture; Mozart's Violin Concerto in G Major (K. 216) with Isaac Stern; William Schuman's "A Free Song," with bass Simon Estes; and Stravinsky's *Rite of Spring*. The National Symphony Orchestra rose to the challenge.

Additional performances during the opening week included the local premiere of Alvin Ailey's ballet *The River*, with music by Duke Ellington (his only ballet score), in a performance by the American Ballet Theater in the Opera House; and a chamber concert by Eugene Istomin, Isaac Stern, and Leonard Rose in the Concert Hall (which confirmed that the hall's acoustics were also good for small groups). There was also a pops concert by the Fifth Dimension.

On Friday, September 10, the Washington Opera Society presented the world premiere of their commissioned opera: Alberto Ginastera's *Beatrix Cenci*. I had worked with the composer on the world premiere of his previous opera, *Bomarzo*, and knew that he was sometimes late in delivering finished scenes. But this time Ginastera literally brought me the final score pages the day of the dress rehearsal. Luckily the production, directed by Gerald Freedman (with sets by John Conklin and costumes by Theoni Aldredge), was well rehearsed, and Arlene Saunders and Justino Díaz, our two brilliant leads in this Gothic tale of incestuous rape and murderous revenge, were unfazed by the delay. It was a weird and wonderful opera—part Grand Guignol and part "total imagination."

The following day, Harold Schonberg of the *New York Times* awarded measured praise to Ginastera's newest work (ultimately conceding "the opera undeniably is theatrically effective") and strong praise to the singers and even me ("Rudel, who had introduced the previous Ginastera operas to the United States, conducted. His work was what it always is—confident, powerful, musical, the guiding force in a very difficult work"). But when it came to the acoustics, Schonberg was positively rhapsodic. "Cyril Harris, the center's acoustician, has created an acoustic ambience that is rich, colorful and exceptionally clear. From any point in the house, a singer's pianissimo can be heard clearly without the least loss of quality. The effect is startling. Such super-fidelity is the province of only a few opera houses in the world—Vienna, perhaps, or Munich. . . . A great acoustic installation, a powerful opera—Kennedy Center has come of age on the third night of its existence."

All the performances during the opening weeks of Kennedy Center went without a hitch. But there was almost a catastrophe.

On September 14, the day of the premiere of *Ariodante*, I needed to be back in New York for the dress rehearsal of City Opera's first production of *Albert Herring*. (I wasn't conducting the Britten opera, but I always attend final rehearsals.) I flew to New York first thing in the morning and booked a four o'clock return flight. After the *Herring* dress rehearsal I returned to La Guardia and boarded the plane; the crew was getting ready for take-off when someone discovered a "small problem" with the cabin lights. An announcement was made that they would fix the problem and then we'd take off. To make a long story short, we didn't leave La Guardia until seven o'clock and *Ariodante* was scheduled to begin at eight. This is when I almost lost it. I thought of switching planes, but was strongly advised against it. My thoughts at that point were not very pretty.

The plane arrived in Washington at 7:45 p.m. Luckily Washington National Airport is directly across the Potomac River from the Kennedy Center. There was a police escort waiting, and my wife was in the car with my tails. During the ride there, I changed clothes—and the performance began at 8:12.

Capobianco directed the elegant production and Ming Cho Lee designed a stunning red-and-gold Baroque Opera curtain. The chorus sat in the side boxes, watching the stage action or participating in the presentation—and our cast, including Sills, Troyanos, Tyler, Donald Gramm, and newcomer Philip Booth, all performed gloriously.

While I was conducting Handel, the country singer Merle Haggard was playing to a full house next door in the Concert Hall.

The Kennedy Center had officially opened.

14

GLORY DAYS

As part of the twenty-fifth anniversary celebration of New York City Opera in 1969, Larry Deutsch and Lloyd Rigler honored me by establishing the Julius Rudel Award for Young Conductors. The award provided an invaluable education for the winner, who would learn how to run an opera house by serving as an apprentice in all administrative and artistic matters of the company, under the supervision of my staff and me. The first recipient of the award was Christopher Keene from Berkeley, California, a self-assured young man who had made his conducting debut the previous year at Menotti's Spoleto Festival. (Our choice turned out to be a good one; Christopher later became General Director of New York City Opera.) When he arrived at City Opera, he was immediately put to work on *Mefistofele*, which was then in final rehearsals.

The late 1960s and early 1970s were truly the golden age of New York City Opera. What a strong company we had! In addition to Sills and Treigle and Domingo (who continued to return to us when he could, though his international career was burgeoning), we had talent in-depth to boast: Pat Brooks, Frances Bible, Maralin Niska, Patricia Craig, Johanna Meier, Carol Neblett, Susanne Marsee, Dominic Cossa, Spiro Malas, Michele Molese, Enrico Di Giuseppe, Michael Devlin, Richard Fredricks, Gianna Rolandi, Diana Soviero, and Veronica Tyler, among others, and later in the 1970s, Carol Vaness. More and more frequently the Met called on our singers. John Alexander and Louis Quilico, who had been with City Opera since the mid-1950s, and Dominic Cossa, who joined us in the 1960s, continued to appear with us regularly while singing at the Met. Others, like Tatiana Troyanos, Willard White, Arlene Saunders, and Karan Armstrong, graced our stage all too briefly before establishing their careers in Europe. José Carreras also made his debut with City Opera during this era—as Pinkerton in *Madama Butterfly*, on March 15, 1972—and sang with us for the next three years.

The dictionary defines *comprimario* as "a singer of a secondary role in an opera." To my mind the strength of a good repertory company is the quality of its comprimarios—performers who can do one day a peasant, the next day a student or a nobleman; one day an elegant partygoer, the next day a rag picker. We were blessed with wonderfully versatile performers such as Ruth Kobart (who also appeared on Broadway, but left New York in 1966 to join Bill Ball at the American Conservatory Theater in San Francisco; she was an extraordinary actress who gave us a wide variety of portrayals), Nico Castel, Jack Harrold, James Billings, John Lankston, and Muriel Costa-Greenspon—all fine singers as well as distinguished actors.

One thing remained the same as it was in our earliest days: anyone could audition for us. That's how we discovered Samuel Ramey, who made his debut with City Opera in the spring of 1973 as Zuniga in *Carmen* (our traditional "tryout role" for basses) and later put his imprint on Mefistofele after Treigle's early death. Our staff kept their eyes open for new talent, which is how Catherine Malfitano first came to our attention. I was so impressed with her 1973 performance as Annina in *The Saint of Bleecker Street* at Wolf Trap that I engaged her to make her City Opera debut the following year as Mimi in *La bohème*. Ramey and Malfitano were delectable together as Susanna and Figaro in our new John Copley production of *The Marriage of Figaro* in 1977.

I am proud to say that prejudice—racial or otherwise—did not exist at New York City Opera. Much to Halasz's immense credit, black singers, including Camilla Williams, Lawrence Winters, Betty Allen, Adele Addison, Shirley Verrett, and George Shirley had sung with our company from our earliest days, and the black conductor Everett Lee was on our staff in the mid-fifties; so it came as a bit of a surprise to me when our March 1965 revival of *Porgy and Bess* sparked a controversy. When I had first brought the Gershwin opera into our repertory three years earlier, we had encountered no problems, but now the cultural and political climate had changed. The 1964 Civil Rights Act prohibited discrimination based on race or color, and in March '65 there developed a real catch-22. The Congress of Racial Equality declared it racist that African American singers were given only "black parts" to perform. They wanted African American singers to have access to a broader repertory, and tried to prevent black performers from auditioning for our production of *Porgy and Bess* (they seemed to have no knowledge of our company's history of casting black singers in a variety of roles). Then, when we had no other option but to hire white singers for the chorus, the American Guild of Musical Artists protested, claiming we were depriving black singers of employment. It was a no-win situation. We ultimately used a mixed-race chorus in *Porgy and Bess*, and there were no protests.

There was, however, another incident the following year. In October 1966, after the premiere of our beautiful new Beni Montresor production of *The Magic Flute*, I received a letter from an angry subscriber who objected to the casting of Veronica Tyler as Pamina. "How dare you have a mixed race couple?" the patron asked. I wrote a terse reply: "I chose the best available singer for the role. Besides, we have no idea who Pamina's mother, the Queen of the Night, cohabited with."

Following the extraordinary successful premiere of *Don Rodrigo*, it was evident that Ginastera would have no difficulty getting a commission. And indeed Hobart Spaulding, president of the Opera Society of Washington, commissioned the next two works: *Bomarzo* and *Beatrix Cenci*, the latter for a Kennedy Center opening-week premiere. *Bomarzo* was slated to receive its premiere at Lisner Auditorium in DC, after which the Teatro Colón in Buenos Aires intended to give the South American premiere for its native son Ginastera. And I planned to give the New York premiere. We had carefully selected our cast and signed them for all three venues. During rehearsals it became clear that *Bomarzo*—an opera of "sex, violence, and hallucination" (as the composer himself described it) about a hunchbacked duke who was twisted in mind as well as body was, if anything, even more masterful than *Don Rodrigo*. Indeed the premiere was a triumph for Salvador Novoa, who led a distinguished cast in Capobianco's superb staging. We even recorded the opera for the CBS label. During rehearsals I had made a number of modifications to the score, including tempo changes and dynamic alterations. After the opening, as we were preparing for the recording, Ginastera asked me to come to his hotel with my score. Now I'm in for it, I said to myself. When I arrived at his suite, he met me with pencil in hand. "Maestro, please give me all the changes you made. I want to copy them into my score," he said.

The Washington premiere took place on May 20, 1967. The Buenos Aires opening was scheduled for late July, so toward the end of June I flew to Argentina to start orchestra and chorus rehearsals. Rita accompanied me. For her this was to be a working vacation; she had scheduled a number of meetings and conferences with colleagues in her field (neuropsychology, specifically brain function in developmentally learning-disabled children). The flight to Buenos Aires was long. Near its end Rita said to me, "For once you don't have to worry. You know the singers. You know the directors. You know the music. So enjoy."

I just said, "Shush!"

When we landed I immediately saw Alberto looking rather distraught. He pulled us aside and said to me, "The opera has been banned," and told my disbelieving ears that the wife of Argentina's de facto president Juan Carlos Onganía, apparently a very religious woman, had been told that the opera was full of sex and violence and had asked her husband to forbid its performance. When his edict became known, it caused cries of outrage and

ridicule in the international music community. Mme. Onganía became a
laughingstock and the press had a field day, pointing out that operas are
generally full of sex and violence, with the possible exception of *Hansel and
Gretel*. (But even those kids burn the Witch at the end.) We sat around hoping that the world's reaction would encourage a reassessment of the edict,
but after nine days it was clear that we had lost. (We later learned that Mme.
Onganía also pulled the plug on the Argentine release of the Antonioni film
Blow-Up and banned a production of Pinter's *The Homecoming*.) We departed,
brokenhearted. I did not make my debut at Teatro Colón until 1991, when
I conducted *Tosca*, an opera filled with—you guessed it—sex and violence. I
never conducted *Bomarzo* in Argentina. The opera, by the way, had its triumphant New York City Opera premiere during our spring 1968 season, with
Salvador Novoa, Joanna Simon, and Claramae Turner reprising the roles
they had created in DC.

After *Giulio Cesare* made Beverly a megastar, I was determined to find an
opera that would provide a star turn for Norman.

   One day in 1967 Tito Capobianco came to me with a potentially exciting idea: an opera based on John Steinbeck's *Of Mice and Men*. When I
expressed interest he confessed that he had already talked with Treigle and
Carlisle Floyd and that they were both interested. The project appealed to
me because, in addition to providing a starring role for Norman, it would
give me the chance to cast the underappreciated Richard Cassilly in a sensational part. It would also give me the opportunity to commission Carlisle as
part of the Ford Foundation Commissioning Program.

   Tito wanted to write the libretto, and I was surprised that Carlisle, who up
to that point had always written his own libretti, had agreed to this. Once the
subject and scope of a commissioned opera had been agreed on, my usual
modus operandi was to leave the composer and librettist alone until they
came to me with their work completed—or with a problem unsolved. I don't
know what instinct made me ask Carlisle and Tito to show me something
from their work-in-progress, but in early 1968 I did just that. What I saw
upset me greatly. The flaw was mostly in the libretto, which lacked authenticity and skilled dialogue and hampered Carlisle's efforts. Still, I had to be
absolutely sure of my misgivings, so I asked some of our younger singers to
learn several sections of the opera under the guidance of the composer, and
arranged a reading for me and several of our senior staff members. Hearing
the excerpts confirmed my negative impression. It was clear we could not go
ahead with the plan for *Of Mice and Men*.

   Because I admired Carlisle and enjoyed his friendship, it was extremely
difficult for me to break the news to him. But I told him the truth, and

he graciously accepted my judgment. Happily, by the time the opera had its premiere in Seattle a few years later, with Carlisle's own libretto in a production by Frank Corsaro, it was a completely different and much stronger work.

Nevertheless, I still needed an opera for Treigle. Every now and then I would look at the score of Boito's *Mefistofele*. I knew that this practically unknown work would be ideal for Treigle. But I also knew I could not afford to mount what would surely turn out to be a very expensive production. I decided to appeal to my generous friends from Cincinnati, the Corbetts. I knew that they had been fond of Norman since the days of the Cincinnati Zoo Opera, and so I told Ralph and Pat the whole story. They came to the rescue with a check for $250,000 (our most expensive production of that time), and *Mefistofele* became one of our greatest hits. Treigle's performance as the devil was the stuff of legend. The incredible effect of that giant voice coming out of this thin man who sometimes slithered around like a snake and at other moments seemed larger than the set itself was simply astonishing. He personified evil—and was utterly mesmerizing. Even when he was standing perfectly still with his back to the audience, listening to another performer, all eyes were riveted on him.

The rehearsal period, which began in late summer 1969 for a September 21 opening, was a happy one, with Norman and me nearly regaining our former close friendship.

In the prologue, the score calls for "celestial fanfares" throughout the opera house. My intention was to surprise the audience and have some of the music come from behind them and above them—from the sides and from the balconies. The dress rehearsal was proceeding smoothly when suddenly there was a wrong brass entrance from the fifth ring. I stopped everything and yelled angrily, "Who's in charge over there? Who's in charge? Who gave that cue?"

A cunningly humble voice was heard from the front of the fifth balcony. "That was the winner of the Julius Rudel Award, maestro,"said Chris Keene, who had been assigned to the fifth ring with part of the brass choir there. Everyone—including me—burst out laughing. "Let's try Heaven again," I said. This time, all went well. In fact the premiere made such an impact that the audience kept applauding throughout the entire six-minute scene change between the prologue and act I.

I welcomed the occasional moment of comic relief because as our company grew, the stress levels rose—and there was less time for our customary bonhomie. Since the move to Lincoln Center, our seasons had grown substantially. In 1965, our final year on Fifty-Fifth Street, we had a five-week spring season and an eight-week fall season. By 1969 the seasons had expanded to nine weeks in the spring and ten in the fall—for a total of 143 performances, and two years later we were up to 156 performances in 20 weeks compared to the Met's 217 performances in 31 weeks. Each week-end, between Friday and Sunday, we did five different operas. We allotted ten hours per opera—three for setting up, four for performing, and three more for "breaking down" the sets afterward—which meant fifty hours of work between late Friday afternoon and Sunday night. Occasionally, when we first moved to Lincoln Center, our orchestra members were called upon to do six "services" in three days—a dress rehearsal Friday morning and per-formances Friday night, Saturday afternoon and evening, and Sunday after-noon and evening. ("We had such a spirit in those days," Ruth Hider, the former administrative director of New York City Opera, recently recollected. "No one balked at doing two performances in a single day.")

I demanded a lot from our company—and I admit that I could be auto-cratic and short-tempered. But ultimately we were all working toward the same goal, creating an experience together. There was always a give-and-take between the singers and me, and the audience could sense that we were a close, united group.

I've never been able to separate the music from the drama. By always being aware of what was physically happening onstage—not only in regard to scenery, props, and "stage business," but most importantly the emotional context of a scene—I could anticipate what might go wrong or when a singer might need a bit of additional help. Or not.

As Johanna Meier recently reminded me, there were occasionally times when the singers got off track musically and I would just let them figure it out for themselves rather than doing a lot of frantic arm waving and fin-ger pointing. "Somehow we always recovered quickly!" Johanna says of my tough-love tactic.

New York City Opera became renowned for its total theatrical approach to opera, something I continued to strive for throughout my tenure with our two house directors, Frank Corsaro and Tito Capobianco, and the other directors I brought into the company fold.

From the time I saw my first opera at the tender age of three, when I was mesmerized by Maria Jeritza's Carmen as she made her spectacular escape over a bridge at the end of the first act, I have never been able to sepa-rate the music from the drama. Opera for me is total theater: acting and directing, scenery and costume design, singing and orchestral playing are all essential to the experience.

Today's opera company managers like to boast about bringing theatri-cality to opera, but this concept is far from new. Wagner applied the term *Gesamtkunstwerk* (loosely translated as "a joint work of all the arts") to opera for the first time in his 1849 essay "Art and Revolution." I grew up in Vienna in an era when there was an extraordinary outburst of work in the Austrian-German theaters and opera houses. A number of Mahler's striking, spare productions were still in the repertory of the Vienna Staatsoper—and Max Reinhardt's theatrical spectacle of Goethe's *Faust* was presented in the old riding school that had been carved into the rock of the Mönchsberg, a mountain in the center of Salzburg. It was all visually spectacular. Reinhardt staged the prologue, which takes place in Heaven, on top of the mountain. I could look up and see paradise right there—a fantastic image (courtesy of Reinhardt and his designer Clemens Holzmeister) that has stayed with me all these years. I'm sure their ingenuity in no small way influenced my own artistic sensibilities and the resourcefulness ascribed to New York City Opera. The fantastic lighting effects in the prologue of Capobianco's production of *Mefistofele*—one of our signature works—were created by one of those mirrored balls that you find in cheap dance halls. It's amazing how a simple device can give you such a bang for your buck.

Over the years, many prominent directors have staged productions at New York City Opera. In the beginning Theodore Komisarjevsky was the most interesting of our directors. Born in Russia and renowned for his groundbreaking London productions of plays by Shakespeare and Chekhov, he was invited by Halasz to stage our company premiere of *Eugene Onegin* in 1946, followed by *Don Giovanni* and *Aida*, among others. I was a bit shocked the first time I observed "Komie" at work—during a rehearsal of *Don Giovanni*. He told the performers what he expected them to do, and then instructed the pianist to begin playing. While the singers went through their motions, Komisarjevsky turned his back on them and looked at his production notes. Not once did he so much as glance at the singers. It's not that he had distain for them; rather, he wanted to allow them to go through the initial mechanics, make their mistakes, and straighten out the problems by themselves without his presence making them uncomfortable. Once they had "routined" the staging, he would help them fine-tune their performances.

Aida (in 1948) was the perfect showcase for Komie's knowledge and mastery of the craft. Our cramped Fifty-Fifth Street theater had absolutely no side stage and no backstage areas—yet Komisarjevsky and our house designer Heinz Condell were resourceful enough to mount a magnificent "Triumphal March" in spite of our limited stage space. Since they couldn't "build back," they instead "built up" via ramps and steps, deploying the chorus on various levels. The Temple was practically choking with people. All the singers were lined up and facing the audience, and it was startlingly effective.

Komie knew the secret of design—he was able to break it down into almost "mathematical" components. In our theater we often used "neutral stuff"—stairs, ramps, returns, walls, and so on—that our designers could utilize as needed for each individual production so that we didn't have to totally rebuild every show from scratch.

In 1949, Komisarjevsky suffered a heart attack while the company was in the midst of rehearsals for Prokofiev's *The Love for Three Oranges*. A colleague of his, Vladimir Rosing, who was born in Russia and had begun his career as a tenor before turning to directing, was called in to pinch hit. Rosing—who in the early twenties had presented a season of opera at London's Aeolian Hall with Komisarjevsky and conductor Adrian Boult— had attended the world premiere of *Love for Three Oranges* in Chicago in 1921 and thought it had the potential to be a huge hit for New York City Opera. Indeed it was, and it has been revived frequently over the years. Its initial success was in no small part due to the fact that Komie plotted out the overall mechanics—the movements, the entrances, the actions— and Rosing worked individually with the performers and gave them their characterizations and lots of interesting "bits."

In a sense, Komie's indisposition was a fortuitous break for us, and the combination of his vision and Val Rosing's work with the singers made for a truly comic romp. Our production of the Prokofiev opera was such a success that it was featured in *Life* magazine.

Rosing always worked closely with the singers every step of the way— sometimes even dressing up like a chorister (always the performer!) and going onstage "to reinforce the sense of spontaneity," as he liked to say. He was to become a mainstay of our staff in the 1950s, going on to direct Donald Oenslager's colorful production of Moore's *The Ballad of Baby Doe* in 1958. Val made every member of the large cast a three-dimensional character, adding immensely to the authenticity and warm-bloodedness of the performance.

Another of our distinguished directors in the early years was Leopold Sachse, who had been the *intendant* of the Hamburg State Opera before the Nazis came to power. He was extraordinarily imaginative and knowledgeable but would occasionally get hung up on minutiae. When he was asked to direct our first *Rosenkavalier* in the fall of 1949, Sachse insisted upon having an hour of rehearsal time with the chorus, specifically "to tell them the story of the opera so they can react properly." In my capacity as music administrator, I had scheduled a special rehearsal with the chorus; lo and behold, when I walked into the rehearsal room at the end of the hour, Sachse was still talking about the first act. I was upset, especially since the chorus does not even sing in that act.

We never had the luxury of having our own supers travel with us when we went on tour (it would have been too costly). Our local presenters would get us some students from a local high school—and then we'd quickly give them their "marching orders" for each particular opera. One time Sachse came along on tour and personally instructed the supers in *Tosca*, explaining to them what to do and how to do it. We were running out of time before the performance, so he told them, "Look, you see that woman [indicating the soprano who was playing Tosca]. You follow her in the last act wherever she goes and don't let her out of your sight." At the end of the opera, of course,

Tosca jumped to her death—and all of the soldiers dutifully followed, one
after the other.

During Joseph Rosenstock's tenure as general director (1952–56), several
Broadway and Hollywood directors were engaged, including Otto Preminger, Robert Lewis, and Jerome Robbins. The noted Shakespearean director Margaret Webster, who directed Maurice Evans and José Ferrer in plays
by Shakespeare and Shaw for City Center's drama division, also staged four
operas for us: Walton's *Troilus and Cressida* (based on Chaucer; Walton himself came and conducted one of the orchestra rehearsals), Vittorio Giannini's *The Taming of the Shrew*, Verdi's *Macbeth*, and Richard Strauss's *The Silent
Woman*. Peggy Webster was a joy to work with, and the singers all loved her.
Her directions to the performers were always musical and to the point; she
encouraged them to think about the meaning of the words they were singing and "to keep one's ears open for the moments when neither word nor
action, but the music itself, is doing the work of drama." She always completed what needed to be done in the allotted rehearsal time.

The witches' cauldron scene in *Macbeth* was especially tricky to stage, since
Verdi increased Shakespeare's trio of witches tenfold—and the female chorus of thirty had to vanish in half a measure! (Mezzo Lou Rodgers remem-
bers Webster politely calling out to her: "Number Nine, would you hop on
your rock?") The director injected a bit of humor into rehearsals with the
creation of a "Witch of the Month Club" award for whoever best mastered
the difficult stage business. Her wit often saved the day. Once, when Peggy
was directing Zinka Milanov in a new production of *Aida* at the Met, Rudolf
Bing turned to her and said, "Miss Webster, can't you make her act?" Her
response: "Mr. Bing, la donna è immobile!"

Another director who came on board during the fifties was Otto Erhardt.
He had worked with Bruno Walter in Vienna and Salzburg before becoming stage director of the Teatro Colón in Buenos Aires in the 1930s. Erhardt
staged the runaway hit of the Rosenstock era, Rossini's *La Cenerentola* (fall
1953), a sparkling production with colorful designs by Rouben Ter-Arutunian (who modeled the set after a Victorian-era toy theater from Lincoln
Kirstein's private collection) and a flawless cast headed by Frances Bible.
Erhardt's high spirits were boundless. One day, during a dress rehearsal for
Falstaff, he got so caught up in his work that he absent-mindedly stepped
backward off the stage and fell into the pit, hitting a kettledrum and timpanist Elaine Jones in the process. Jones, who was pregnant at the time, joked
that if the baby were a boy she would name it "Otto Fall-staff Jones." Erhardt
was taken to the hospital and released later that day with only a sprained
ankle, in time for the opening.

When I became general director in 1957, I naturally reached out to stage
directors whose productions on and off Broadway I had much admired. Our
first American Season in 1958 included operas directed by Carmen Capalbo

and José Quintero. I also engaged Frank Corsaro for the first time during that initial American Season, when he graciously agreed to stage a new production of Floyd's *Susannah* for us, using just a few trees, a brook, a little bridge, and a small cabin. It was simplicity itself. This was City Opera's third production of Carlisle Floyd's opera in as many years—a situation unheard of in the opera world!

Circumstances forced me into this path. Erich Leinsdorf had brought the work into our repertory in fall 1956. One of the first things I did after being appointed director was to discard the dreadful turntable set that he and designer Leo Kerz had devised for their entire season—which meant we quickly had to make a new set for *Susannah*, scheduled to be performed the second night of the fall '57 season. It was the first "new" production of my tenure, yet I had no budget for it. I asked Marcella Cisney to direct the opera and our house designer, Andreas Nomikos, to design a new set. Unfortunately Nomikos—who was of Greek heritage—had absolutely no feel for Appalachia. He designed Susannah's cabin as a little white clapboard house with a picket fence. It looked more New Rochelle than New Hope Valley.

The following year, when we were invited to bring *Susannah* (along with the City Center Light Opera production of *Carousel*) to the 1958 Brussels World's Fair, I knew that we could not possibly take this "white picket fence" production. Frank Corsaro and I had several talks, and he and the designer Paul Sylbert came up with the idea of an extraordinarily good set that cost practically nothing. (I told Frank and Paul that the scenery had to be less than $1,000. They spent only $900 on a production that remained in our repertory for more than a decade.)

Herbert Machiz, who directed our production of *Street Scene* for our second American Season in 1959, had staged many of Tennessee Williams' plays and was recommended to me by Lotte Lenya. He worked beautifully with the performers and was not flummoxed by the music. Nor was John Houseman, who staged the original Broadway production of Douglas Moore's one-act opera *The Devil and Daniel Webster* in 1939 and, for our second American Season, directed our first production of this same work.

My way of mounting a new production was to rehearse the music in a particular scene, and then to let the stage director work with the performers. When the director was ready, he would run the scene for me, and we'd take it from there. It was a very constructive way of working. When I scheduled the world premiere of Hugo Weisgall's *Six Characters in Search of an Author* for our second American Season, I found William Ball, whose direction of an Off-Broadway production of Chekhov's *Ivanov* so impressed me with its operatic quality that I knew he would be perfect for the job.

He was all that and more. Ball's debut with our company was most auspicious. His direction was fluid and inventive—he helped the performers to "find their way" on their own, and made ingenious use of such unusual set elements as ladders and monkey bars. Bill could not read music, but he had incredible innate musicality; when he staged *The Inspector General* in 1960, the opera's composer Werner Egk (who conducted the City Opera premiere) told me that Ball knew the opera as well as he did.

Bill's production of *Don Giovanni* in fall 1963 was quite extraordinary, achieving the most stunning results with the simplest of means. For example, according to Mozart and Da Ponte's instructions, Donna Anna is to give her dazzling second act aria "Non mi dir" (Do not speak) in a nondescript "dark room." Bill moved the location to the graveyard, in front of her father's grave, thereby increasing the poignancy and emotional weight of the entire scene immensely.

Another image that I cannot forget from that same production: Treigle literally hanging from the Commendatore's hand (actually the extended hand of Ara Berberian, who was situated inside the larger-than-life statue designed by Robert Fletcher), unable to free himself after accepting the Commendatore's invitation.

The two directors who were to become most closely associated with New York City Opera in the sixties and seventies were Tito Capobianco and Frank Corsaro. They embodied the two aspects of what evolved into our company's signature style.

Simplistically speaking, Corsaro worked from the inside out and Capobianco worked from the outside in. Capobianco's near-balletic productions were planned down to the last detail in tandem with his wife, the choreographer Gigi Denda, while Corsaro's naturalistic productions were concerned with believable human behavior—giving us a look into the characters' interior lives. I remember vividly Corsaro's 1966 production of *La Traviata*: Pat Brooks—our Violetta—pauses for nearly a full minute at the end of act 1 while she recovers from the party she has just thrown (as the sounds of the departing guests fade away). She stands near the fireplace. Her maid Annina brings a shawl and places it around her shoulders while the servants tidy up and turn down the lights. This is all done in silence. Then she sits down and starts to think. Only then does she sing "È strano."

It is a beautiful, touching moment.

But it took much convincing to get the conductor Franco Patané to go along with Corsaro's plan. Patané, very much of the old school, couldn't understand why he had to wait; he thought Corsaro to be quite mad—until the audiences and critics went wild for the production. Frank jokes that after the success of *Traviata*, Patané would give him "ideas for pauses" for *Madama Butterfly*, telling Corsaro he could have twenty pauses if he wanted them!

(In a terribly sad twist of fate, Patané was killed in a car accident after a performance in Italy in May 1968. A few days later I received a telegram from Arturo Basile, who had conducted at City Opera during my first few seasons as general director, asking if he could help out by taking over the repertotry

Patané was scheduled to conduct for us during our upcoming fall season. I was delighted that Basile wanted to return to City Opera, and—since I was in Europe at the time, conducting *The Bartered Bride* in Stuttgart—I made a date to fly to Milan between performances to meet with Arturo. The meeting never took place. Basile died a few days later when his own car veered off the road and hit a tree. Ironically, on the plane ride to Milan I read a copy of the daily paper *Corriere della Sera*, which had a report of Basile's death. Imagine my bewilderment as I read this. They're crazy—they've got the wrong guy, I said to myself. Little did I know.)

Corsaro's production of *Pelléas et Mélisande* was also a revelation. He directed it not as a dreamy bit of French Impressionism but as a real story about real people. Clearly I felt the same way about the music.

Frank's use of a scrim in front of the stage gave everything (even the moments of violence) a kind of distant quality without disturbing the realism. Our production of *Pelléas* became an unlikely hit, drawing a large number of young people.

Alan Rich of *New York* magazine gave high praise: [This production] did away with the "wraithlike woodland sprite" and "restored a measure of bloodedness" to the Debussy opera, revealing "far more than a collection of pretty puddles of lavender sound."

Our November 9, 1971, performance of *Le coq d'or*—with Treigle and Sills, conducted by me—was carried live to cable-television subscribers in Manhattan. The driving force behind the telecast was John Goberman, who had been a cellist in the City Opera orchestra (and whose father, Max Goberman, had conducted *The Devil and Daniel Webster* for us in '59). To avoid complications with the unions, John agreed that the program would be a one-time-only telecast and that it would not be taped (which means, sad to say, that no official record of the telecast exists, although a rather grainy pirated version has made the rounds). Our company's first official television appearance, on the PBS series *Live from Lincoln Center*, of which John Goberman was (and remained until 2012) the executive producer, was *The Ballad of Baby Doe* on April 21, 1976. Though the television lighting was criticized for being a bit dark, it was an excellent performance of one of our hallmark productions, with Ruth Welting and Richard Fredricks as Baby Doe and Horace, and Fran Bible recreating her touching portrayal of the first Mrs. Tabor. It was conducted by Judith Somogi, our former rehearsal pianist, who became the first woman to conduct at City Opera in 1974.

When New York City Opera was firmly established at Lincoln Center, Rudolf Bing and I had a rather nice working relationship that included informational meetings about matters that affected our two companies and even the occasional lunch. Once he invited me to conduct a revival of *Die Fledermaus*, which I politely declined. But in 1973 I offered him—and he accepted—the role of Sir Edgar in our forthcoming production of Henze's *The Young Lord*. How could he refuse when I described Sir Edgar to him as "a distinguished looking, elegant, and witty man." (Silently witty; the part was mimed.) Sarah Caldwell directed and I conducted the production. On the first day of rehearsal Caldwell took Kenneth Riegel to the Central Park Zoo to observe the monkeys. The field trip was a success; Riegel was outstanding as the title character—an ape that Sir Edgar attempts to pass off as his nephew.

The close proximity of the two opera companies raised the possibility—nay, probability—of overlapping repertoire, but there were only three or four times I recall when both companies played the same opera and it caused no problem at all; both theaters were sold out.

Only once, during the 1974 spring season, did we have a real crisis on our hands. We had just given our premiere performances of Cherubini's *Medea* with Niska in splendid form when, on the morning of the third performance, Maralin phoned, sounding terrible, and informed me that she had a frightful cold and could not possibly sing that evening. That was just the beginning. I had no sooner hung up the telephone when the singer who was covering Niska called, alerting me that she was running a high fever and had swollen vocal cords.

With the leading lady and her cover both ill, there was no way we could do *Medea*. Luckily we were running a series of *Traviatas* at the same time, and after checking the availability and the willingness of the singers, we assembled a first-rate cast led by Pat Brooks, John Stewart, and Dom Cossa, and we did the unprecedented: we changed the opera of the evening to *Traviata*. When I went before the curtain to explain the situation, the audience was most sympathetic. The performance was excellent and everyone was happy.

However, the next scheduled performance of *Medea* was fast approaching, and Niska and her cover were still both unable to sing. To compound the problem, I got a telephone call from the Met informing me that Mme Caballe, who was to sing *I vespri siciliani* the following night, was ill and was canceling. The reason that this was of any interest at all to me was that—in an administrative snafu and an excess of "good neighborliness"—we had given permission for Miss Niska to cover Mme Caballe in the Met's *Vespri*. Of course this turned out to be a moot point, because Niska could sing neither *Medea* nor *Vespri* that day.

With all the sopranos ill, there was no one at either house to step in. Both *Medea* and *Vespri* are rarely performed, and few singers know the roles. So the Met changed their performance to *Bohème*, and we were about to go ahead with *Traviata* when we discovered that Miss Brooks was not available.

What to do? There was only one desperate move that seemed feasible. In this period Beverly Sills was doing a series of Elviras (in *I puritani*) and Anna Bolenas with us. Though she would be singing three big and demanding roles in four days (*Traviata* and *Puritani* on successive evenings!), and had never even seen our Corsaro production, which contained several unusual touches, I appealed to Beverly's "the-show-must-go-on" philosophy. She agreed to perform *La traviata* if I would conduct. Of course I immediately agreed, even though I had not conducted *Traviata* for some fifteen years.

I would not recommend it as a steady diet, but sometimes a totally improvised performance can genuinely "take off" if the performers are real artists and know what they're doing. This was just such an evening. The audience enjoyed the performance as much as Beverly and I did.

As far as I know, the situation of one singer causing two opera companies to have to change their programs has never again occurred.

Like Ado Annie in *Oklahoma!* I found it hard to say no to the many interesting offers that came my way. As a result, for a brief period in the early 1970s, I found myself holding five administrative posts simultaneously. In addition to my directorship at City Opera, I was music director of the new Kennedy Center, the Cincinnati May Festival, and the Caramoor Festival in Westchester County (forty miles north of Manhattan), and music director of the Wolf Trap Festival near Washington.

One important aspect of "spreading myself all over the place" was the cross-pollination of productions that it allowed. *The Coronation of Poppea* was performed at Caramoor before we brought it to City Opera. I conducted the world premieres of Ginastera's *Bomarzo* and *Beatrix Cenci* for the Washington Opera Society and their subsequent performances at New York City Opera. We also brought to New York City Opera the Washington Opera Society production of Delius's *A Village Romeo and Juliet*, staged by Corsaro and designed by Ronald Chase.

My Burgeoning International Career, or the Flights of the Concorde

It was during this time that my guest-conducting engagements in Europe really took off. Prior to this my overseas bookings had been sporadic but enjoyable: *Kiss Me, Kate* in Vienna in 1956; five recordings in Vienna in the late 1950s; and two seasons at Menotti's Festival of Two Worlds in Italy, in 1962 (where I conducted the opening night production of *Love for Three Oranges* with tenor Franco Bonisolli—a loose cannon to be sure) and '63.

In the sixties Rolf Liebermann (whom I had first met in April '56, when his opera *School for Wives* was performed at City Opera) had been after me to conduct at the Hamburg Staatsoper. I told him that I would gladly come "for a maximum of two weeks at a time," but he always replied, "No, if you come I want you there for at least half a year." Clearly my existing commitments would not allow that.

Eventually we were able to arrive at an agreement, and in May 1973 I made my debut in Hamburg conducting the final production of the "Liebermann Era," Richard Strauss's *Capriccio*, starring former City Opera singers Arlene Saunders, Tatiana Troyanos, and Jeanette Scovotti. Since Liebermann's last season in Hamburg overlapped with his first season as director of the Paris Opera, he also engaged me to conduct in Paris, where I was scheduled for several *Trovatores* and *Figaros*—taking over the Mozart from Solti, who had conducted the first performances of the brilliant Strehler production featuring Margaret Price as the Countess and Frederica von Stade as Cherubino. Strehler's take on the work was very poetic, very human, and very touching (with only one gimmicky, uncharacteristic moment, when Basilio and Antonio the gardener had to pee against a wall).

Riccardo Muti was originally signed to conduct *Trovatore*. He was scheduled for the first six performances, and the plan was that after I had got the first batch of *Capriccios* out of the way in Hamburg, I would fly back and forth between Hamburg and Paris to conduct the remainder of the run of *Trovatore*. But during rehearsals Muti withdrew from the Capobianco production. Liebermann then decided that Charles Mackerras (who was already in Paris) would lead the final rehearsals and the opening performances, and then he and I would split the remaining *Trovatores*.

On Sunday, May 20, 1973, just hours after conducting the final performance of *Mefistofele*, with Treigle (in what turned out to be his final appearance with our company) on City Opera's Washington tour, I flew from DC to Hamburg for my first *Capriccio* rehearsal. On Monday we started rehearsing *Capriccio*. Four days later Liebermann came to me and said, "You're going to have to start conducting the *Trovatores* in Paris earlier than we anticipated. Mackerras can't conduct the next performance."

Liebermann gave me the news on Friday. *Trovatore* was scheduled for Monday.

A piano rehearsal was hastily arranged for Saturday and I flew to Paris late in the day on Friday. But as it turned out (since no one had expected yet another change of conductors), none of the *Trovatore* cast was in town that weekend except for Shirley Verrett. She and I met and we had a lovely chat and then said, "See you Monday!" and that was that. Still, I felt fairly confident and didn't anticipate any problems. I had always enjoyed the thrill of walking into a new situation and giving a downbeat. Little did I know what was to transpire.

On Monday afternoon the chorus sent Liebermann an official remonstrance, saying they could not guarantee the quality of that night's performance because they had never met—let alone worked with—"the conductor Rudel." The orchestra members did exactly the same thing.

The music critic Martin Mayer, who quite by chance happened to be at the opera that night, subsequently reported on my debut in *The New Republic:* "Rudel, before mounting the podium made a gesture of going backstage and showing himself to the assemblage. Then he took his place, gave a firm but not unfriendly look to the men on his left, the same for the men on his right; the stick went firmly up and came firmly down; and it was a hell of a *Trovatore.* At the end, Rudel had to be summoned back for a second solo curtain call, because the men had stayed in the pit to applaud him, and he hadn't expected that."

I had an inkling that things were going well during the intermission, when a delegation from the orchestra and the chorus had come backstage and introduced themselves to me—and apologized for sending the memo.

Martin told me that he later said to Liebermann, "That was living dangerously!" Liebermann replied: "Not for me. Only for Rudel."

My eleventh-hour debut turned out to be the beginning of a beautiful friendship with the Paris Opera. Among other highlights, I conducted the glorious Kiri Te Kanawa in her first Fiordiligi in *Così fan tutte,* and in 1975 I became the first American to lead the premiere of an opera in that house when I conducted Verdi's *La forza del destino.* Liebermann spared no expense in hiring absolutely the best performers available: Arroyo, Cossotto, Domingo, Talvela, and Bacquier. *Forza* is one of those operas that has been much "worked on" over the years; Verdi himself was never quite satisfied with it. John Dexter's production was first-rate (physically stylized but still recognizable), and he and I were in complete agreement that the chorus should end the second act with the rousing "Rataplan"—a powerful and emotionally true moment.

Sadly, I was to work with John Dexter again in much less happy circumstances a decade and a half later, when I conducted the 1989 Broadway production of *The Threepenny Opera* starring Sting. John was even more acerbic than usual, ailing with the heart problems that were to take his life the following March.

15

JON VICKERS

The Third Time Was Not the Charm

In almost seven decades of conducting I have encountered many artists, many personalities, but only two who can be described as "impossible." One was the great New York City Opera bass-baritone Norman Treigle, the other, Jon Vickers. Jon and I first met in Philadelphia, where I had been engaged to conduct *Die Walküre* on January 4, 1963. In the Philadelphia Lyric Opera Company cast were Régine Crespin (Sieglinde), Andras Farago (Wotan), Mignon Dunn (Fricka), Anita Välkki (Brünnhilde), Richard Cross (Hunding), and Vickers (Siegmund). Rehearsals were to begin in December, but Vickers could arrive only in time for the dress rehearsal.

Eager to work with this stellar artist, I accepted this condition. Later, when Vickers's manager informed us that Jon could only be present for the actual performance, I accepted that, too. Having heard that Vickers could be difficult, I asked for a short meeting with him prior to the performance in which to discuss a few musical points. Even that never happened, because when I went to his dressing room, Jon was putting on makeup and did not feel like talking about *Walküre*, so we chatted about world politics and other mundane matters. As a matter of fact, the performance went exceedingly well and we were all extremely happy.

Our paths did not cross again for fifteen years. In April 1976 I received a telegram from Rolf Liebermann offering me Monteverdi's *L'incoronazione di Poppea* scheduled for Paris Opera in March and April 1978. Since the time overlapped with the New York City Opera spring season, I declined and thought that was the end of it.

But then I received a second telegram from Rolf listing the cast: Jon Vickers, Gwyneth Jones, Christa Ludwig, Richard Stilwell, Valerie Masterson, Jocelyne Taillon, Michel Sénéchal, and Nicolai Ghiaurov. The cable ended with six fatal words: "Hard to resist isn't it Julius?"

The temptation was indeed enormous, but I was scheduled for a new production of *The Merry Widow* with Sills and Titus at City Opera (in addition to my regular repertory, which included *Mefistofele* and *The Marriage of Figaro*) and was not about to give up one for the other. Was there any way to alternate rehearsals here and abroad? The challenge roused the former music administrator in me. Certainly I would have to divide my weeks between Paris and New York.

Luckily, at that time the Air France Concorde was making the transatlantic trip in three-and-a-half hours. Equally lucky was the fact that *Merry Widow* contained a lot of dialogue—and I was not needed when the cast was rehearsing "book scenes." Therefore I could spend half a week in New York and half a week in Paris (although not in the traditional sense of spending three days in Paris and four in New York—it was more like: Monday and Tuesday, Paris; Wednesday and Thursday, New York; Friday, Paris; Saturday and Sunday, New York).

The situation in Paris was somewhat complicated. Before the venerable director Günther Rennert could start rehearsals, I would have to have two full days of intensive music rehearsals with the entire cast. In addition, all of the soloists had to swear not to make any changes during my absences in New York. The singers agreed, and miracle of miracles, everyone kept their word. For the singers, this schedule was not too strenuous, but for me it eventually led to a crazy three-week period in which I made sixteen transatlantic crossings. Vickers made a couple of minuscule changes, more in the spirit of rebellion against my New York trips than for artistic reasons. But since his changes were inconsequential, I accepted them without argument.

And when Jon complained to Liebermann about my absences, he was quickly reminded of the promise he had voluntarily made. Evidently he had argued very strongly for accepting my conditions for the rehearsal period; he very much wanted me to conduct it.

One would not expect a Wagnerian tenor like Vickers to be able to handle early Baroque music, but Jon astonished us all at the very first rehearsal when he took his part of the duet with Michel Sénéchal (Lucano) at a clip more brilliant even than Sénéchal's as the other cast members looked on in astonished amusement. Altogether Vickers was a pleasure to work with—disciplined yet creative, and a good colleague.

Poppea was a real hit—Liebermann proudly referred to it on several occasions as "the jewel in his crown"—and was immediately scheduled for the next two seasons. Most of the cast members and I returned to Paris the following year and again in 1980. Fortunately one of the performances was filmed by French television. I recently saw a clip on the Internet of Gwyneth Jones and Jon Vickers performing the duet "Pur ti miro," which one YouTube viewer who had seen the production described as "unforgettable," going on to recall the "20 minutes of nonstop standing ovation after this moment of pure magic." I hope they someday reissue the entire performance on DVD.

After the 1980 run of *Poppea*, I lost touch with Vickers until 1983, when I received a phone call from him. This was no social call, and Jon came to the point immediately: Covent Garden wanted to mount a production of Handel's *Samson* for him. Would I be interested in conducting it, not only in London but also at Chicago Lyric Opera and ultimately at the Met? This was a most exciting offer, and I accepted the invitation with joy.

Before hanging up Jon said derisively, "But, none of that 'castrati stuff!'" He had been taught how to sing Handel "by none other than Sir Thomas Beecham himself." I pointed out that musicology had made some strides since that time. But I figured that this was one of Jon's grandiose statements, and that I could reason him out of that position.

Immediately at the start of rehearsals I realized that the situation was going to be difficult. To "arm myself with ammunition," I even spent days at the British Museum studying Handel manuscripts, but Jon was not to be moved; in fact he became more and more disagreeable—arguing about tempi, stopping rehearsals when another singer sang an appoggiatura. For some mysterious reason he vehemently objected to my conducting from the harpsichord; when I talked about authenticity he retorted, "Beecham was the last great man" when it came to Baroque practice. John Tooley, general director of the Royal Opera House, advised me to "give up this conceit." Fortunately the musicians in the Royal Opera House orchestra, steeped in the tradition of Handel, were of enormous help to me during this trying period.

It was too late to do anything about my playing the harpsichord in London. But even though I did not play the harpsichord in Chicago, the atmosphere did not improve. In fact it went from bad to worse, and I had begun to worry about the honesty of my interpretation. In one of the final run-throughs in front of the entire company, Jon stopped singing and shouted, "I can't teach you how to conduct!" and stomped offstage. I managed to conclude the rehearsal, then rushed to the office of Ardis Krainik, general director of Lyric Opera of Chicago, and offered my resignation, which Ardis did not accept. She called for a meeting in my dressing room, in which she made Jon apologize. Of course this meant that although the entire company had witnessed his insult, I was the only one who witnessed the apology.

Our relations from then on can best be described as "cool but correct." The Met performances of *Samson* were the last contact between us.

16

REVERSAL OF FORTUNE

City Opera had weathered a strike in the fall of 1973 and bounced back triumphantly with three new productions in four days: Donizetti's *Anna Bolena*, Richard Strauss's *Ariadne auf Naxos*, and Delius's *A Village Romeo and Juliet*. After the New York season ended with a high-spirited *Barbiere* on November 11, the company flew to Los Angeles for our seventh annual visit. (City Opera toured to Los Angeles sixteen times, from 1967 to 1982.) Our "Operatic Airlift," as I liked to call this operation, was a much-anticipated event where we presented the entire repertory of our just-concluded New York season with special emphasis on the new productions. This year, for the first time ever, we would reverse our own tradition and premiere a new production in Los Angeles, and then bring it to New York the following spring—Bellini's *I puritani*, starring Beverly Sills and Enrico Di Giuseppe. It was being paid for by our dear friends Lloyd Rigler and Lawrence Deutsch, who, as the movers and shakers behind the Los Angeles Music Center Opera Association, also paid the lion's share of the expenses for our visits to the City of Angels. Lloyd and Larry, who were partners in business and in life, had made their fortune on Adolph's Meat Tenderizer, which makes a cheap cut of meat more tender and tasty.

My friendship with Larry Deutsch went back nearly thirty years. He was Laszlo Halasz's administrative assistant at City Opera during our first few seasons, but he quit when Halasz refused to give him a raise of $5 a week. (Lucky me! If Halasz had given him the $5, Larry would have stayed on and never made his millions.)

After the dress rehearsal for *I puritani*, Beverly and her husband Peter Greenough joined Rita and me for dinner at Scandia (a Sunset Boulevard shrine to Scandinavian gastronomy that was famous for its veal with béarnaise sauce, asparagus, and crab legs). Our spirits were high because it seemed we had another hit on our hands. In addition to Beverly and Di Giuseppe—for whom top notes held no threats—the fine cast included Richard Fredricks and Samuel Ramey in the other leading roles. With Capobianco in charge of the staging, we had a very strong case to make. (*I puritani* opened on November 29 to unanimous raves, with even the hard-hitting *Los Angeles Times* critic Martin Bernheimer heaping praise on the production, which he called "one of the supreme triumphs of [Sills's] spectacular career.")

During our meal, we talked about the future. Beverly, who was forty-four at the time, confided that she planned to stop singing at fifty ("and no end-less farewell tours," she said, with a laugh). She also mentioned that she had received a phone call from Cyril Magnin of the San Francisco Opera board asking whether she would be interested in becoming the director of San Francisco Opera ("not now, of course, but several years from now").

"Isn't that silly?" I said. "Why not think about something closer to home?"

"What do you mean?" she replied, with an innocent smile.

"Why San Francisco?" I inquired. "Why not New York City Opera—your home?"

Beverly said she would indeed be interested—but only if I would stay on as an advisor or codirector.

"Sure. Why not?" I responded joyfully, with a touch of relief. By this time I was combining my duties at City Opera with my obligations as music director of the Kennedy Center and the Caramoor Festival, as well as conducting in some of the major opera houses of Europe. I enjoyed this freedom, and could do with a little less responsibility at City Opera.

Unfortunately things did not unfold quite as planned.

In the 1970s financial support for the arts seemed to be drying up, and—unlike the government-subsidized theaters of Europe—we were still very much dependent on private and corporate donations. In spite of our artistic successes, we continued to struggle from season to season. The lack of leadership on our board was becoming more and more of a problem—and more and more I found myself in the position of fundraiser.

In the earliest days of our company, our City Center board chairman Newbold Morris and finance committee chairman Morton Baum were the *patres familias* of New York City Opera, concerned with our budget and taking care of us. During the first few years, whenever there was a monetary crisis, Morris—the scion of an old-money family with longtime roots in New York—would look to his patrician friends for money. And on two separate occasions—when things were really dire—an impassioned Baum had eloquently addressed our audiences between acts, asking for donations.

Morton Baum was single-handedly responsible for keeping City Center going during its first quarter-century of existence. To give some idea of the staggering work load he took on—balancing his unpaid duties at City Center with his "day job" as a highly successful tax lawyer—the *New York Times Magazine* wrote in a 1965 profile of Baum ("He Calls the Tunes at the City Center") that he "set the budgets, acted on them, negotiated with every Mayor since La Guardia for extensions of the Center's lease, for physical improvements to the theater and approval of the price scale. He pushed legislation through Albany to eliminate the city's rent and to exempt the Center from local admission taxes [such as the entertainment tax]." The *New York Times* article then went on to quote Newbold Morris, "There is no one to replace Morton Baum."

When Morris died of cancer at the age of sixty-four on March 30, 1966, Baum succeeded him as chairman of the board; it was a job he had been fulfilling in everything but name for a long time anyway. But two years later—on February 7, 1968—Baum himself died of a heart attack. He was only sixty-two, and his death left us devastated. Though he had successfully fought the good fight to get New York City Opera and New York City Ballet safely ensconced in the State Theater—with City Center winning the struggle against Lincoln Center over control of our operations at the theater—there's not a doubt in my mind that the continued pressures of our existence played a role in his death. During the months leading up to his fatal coronary, he seemed unusually tense and preoccupied.

No words can express the loss that all of us who were part of City Center felt upon Baum's death.

As I wrote in my eulogy:

> Morton Baum is dead. I have read it, written it, said it, and heard it, but these four words still fail to elicit a sense of reality. I am not ready to face the void, for I feel that I have been orphaned. The man who fathered the idea which shaped so much of my life had, in the course of time, become a father to me.
>
> Here was no indifferent progenitor, for with that germinal act, there arose a sense of responsibility, of pride, and of destiny that hard facts and harsher reality ever failed to shake. This was no comradely father, no contemporary pal but a pre-Freudian, biblical patriarch who moved heaven and earth and parted seas, courted friends, and made great enemies that his offspring might survive. He was stern, always demanding, and although one would cry out "It's impossible!" he always evoked more from us than we thought we had it in us to give. He shaped a dream, that benevolent tyrant, but he earned our love and deep respect by letting us glimpse through his eyes his limitless horizons.
>
> It was almost twenty-five years ago that I first met him. I had only five years before fled a maddened Europe and was just beginning to find myself in the musical world. Incredibly, my luck had taken me headlong into a grand plan to bring the best in culture to the people. There was no cynicism in this, no "bread and circuses" for the masses. It was a revelation to see dedicated, practical men wanting, without political motivation, to do something for that mysterious entity known as "the people." Nor was there condescension in this, for Morton Baum had the deep conviction that poor people had all the capacity of the rich, if not the money, to enjoy the better things of life. He set out to prove this and in doing so provided us with the finest audience I have ever known or could have wished for. Two theaters filled with people every night are his living monument. What temple ever built, what pyramid ordered into being by a wonderful pharaoh can equal the living monument Morton Baum created, but for which he gave his life?

There are many men with artistic convictions, there are many builders of monuments, but few of them are artists themselves. Morton Baum was an artist. It is not only that he could read a score, play the piano, or sing operatic roles; he had the discerning eye, discriminating ear, and the unfettered soul of the artist. He was a thorough realist, but in an uncanny way Morton Baum's reality was vaster than anyone else's. He did not "play it safe" for himself, but never risked our existence. He could see what was beyond the vision of others and then take the most practical steps, make the most mundane gestures to grasp what had only a short time before appeared to be beyond reach. There is no truer artist than the man who can make real or tangible what others have never fully envisioned. It was with this gift and not with his financial wizardry that he created the most unique climate for other artists. It was a climate churning with creative challenge, not one tempered by affluence.

These years we spent together, Morton Baum, John White and I were rich ones, filled with terrors and hopes, anxieties and laughter, nadirs and crests. The three of us were riding a crest on February 6, but until the moment he left us, Morton Baum was searching, from that lovely vantage point, for the next peak to conquer. He never let up, not out of need for personal accomplishment, but because there was so much to do, more than most of us could even imagine. Without him, that soaring crest has ebbed for John and me.

Like the austere father he was, Morton Baum was sparing in his praise, but John and I knew how he exulted in the cheers of the crowds, in the mounting success, in the increasing recognition we achieved. We didn't need to hear praise or words of affection from his lips. We read it in the way he always referred to us as "the boys" when he spoke of us to others. Just recently I heard it in his voice when, looking at me, he remarked to John, "The boy is becoming so gray." He acknowledged the passage of the years, my graying hair, my growing children, but to him I could never grow old. And to me he can never be dead.

Baum had one failing. He was unable to delegate authority. He did everything himself, and never trained a successor. After his death, no one could even begin to fill his shoes.

Some of us wondered whether Lincoln Center, sensing our vulnerability, would once again try to seize the reins of the State Theater. But they behaved absolutely correctly, trying to help in the search for a leader with money—or with access to money. Meanwhile, a few changes were immediately enacted. Ernest S. Heller, an art gallery owner and a member of the City Center board of directors, was selected as the temporary chairman of the executive committee, and Mayor Lindsay, in his role as president of City Center, appointed a most unlikely individual as chairman of the board: Richard Clurman, chief of correspondents at Time-Life. Clurman was a very good writer and editor who knew next to nothing about the arts. (He once joked that perhaps he had gotten the chairmanship because his uncle was the famous theater director and critic Harold Clurman.) At his first meeting with George Balanchine, Clurman proudly announced that he had been to the ballet only once in his life. I suspected he had been to the opera even less frequently.

Within six months, a young man named Norman Singer—who had been the program director for the Hunter College concert series—was brought in as executive director of City Center. He stayed for six years and left no particular imprint.

For the first few years after Baum's death, the board, still in search of strong leadership, left me and New York City Ballet's Lincoln Kirstein alone—and our companies did fine work artistically. We were running on momentum and money from the Ford Foundation, from Larry Deutsch and Lloyd Rigler, and from the other foundations and big-hearted individuals who stepped up to underwrite our productions: The Mary Flagler Cary Charitable Trust, Fan Fox and Leslie R. Samuels, Ralph and Patricia Corbett, Jean Tennyson, and Gert von Gontard.

Frantic attempts were made by John Mazzola, the managing director (and, from 1977 to 1982, the president) of Lincoln Center, to find a "savior" for our company who would provide able leadership and money.

New Inititives

In 1974 the Ford Foundation gave the City Center of Music and Drama a forward-looking grant—$6.3 million, to be spread over seven years. It was a "matching grant" that required City Center to raise a total of $8.6 million from other private sources. The grant came with a set of conditions that would completely change the governance of both New York City Opera and New York City Ballet. The main stipulation was that the City Center of Music and Drama would separate the assets of City Opera and City Ballet and create fundraising boards for each of the companies.

In May 1975 an article in the *New York Times* announced a "radical reorganization" of City Center of Music and Drama. The reorganization was designed to bring in "new leadership" and devise ways for City Center to overcome its financial problems. City Center executive director Norman Singer had resigned his position the previous year, and Richard Clurman was set to turn in his resignation as chairman of the board at the June meeting.

As it happened, Mazzola had met a man named John Samuels III, who in July 1975 was appointed chairman of City Center. Within a matter of months he was also named chairman of the board of City Opera and chairman of the board of City Ballet. Though Mazzola and the Lincoln Center board were obviously quite impressed with Samuels, it seemed a bit risky that City Center, City Opera, and City Ballet would give a completely unknown person so much power—especially since the three boards were supposed to be separate entities. (In late 1978, with Mazzola's support, Samuels was also appointed chairman of the Lincoln Center Theater.)

Samuels was new to town. He had apparently made his mark in business only a few years before, in late 1973, when he and two partners acquired a coal mine in the wake of the Arab oil embargo. Within a year he had purchased another dozen companies including two additional coal mines, a couple of insurance companies, and a Wall Street bond firm. He also acquired the Ronald and Marietta Tree townhouse on East Seventy-Ninth Street and the old Cunard luxury shipping line headquarters in the Battery for office space.

A July 26, 1975, article in the *New York Times* announcing Samuels's appointment as chairman of the City Center board made mention of his coal conglomerate ICM Carbonim, which "is said to have grossed more than $360 million in sales last year."

It's always been a matter of speculation exactly how much money Samuels gave to City Opera. An early and grand gesture in 1975 was a check for $1 million. That, of course, was enough to land him the chairmanship of our board. From then on he made a series of so-called soft pledges, making a "commitment" to donate money but as far as I know he never followed through with hard cash. That got us in trouble with the folks at the Ford Foundation because of their matching-gift stipulation. I recall a board meeting where Samuels was asked about a pledge he had made, and he told all of us seated at the table that "the check was in the mail." I muttered, "I bet it is," and the City Center controller, Ralph Falcone, who was sitting next to me, whispered, "Shush!"

Samuels was not well grounded in opera and did not know a great deal about the history of our company. On January 28, 1979, nearly four years after he had assumed the chairmanship of our company, Mr. Samuels stated in a *New York Times* article that it was "a terrible shame that the Met, and not City Opera, had produced *Dialogues of the Carmelites* and *The Bartered Bride*." In point of fact, Laszlo Halasz had brought *The Bartered Bride* into our company's repertory in 1945, and I had produced *Dialogues of the Carmelites* during our first season at Lincoln Center. "What Makes Samuels Run On?" was the headline of music critic Leighton Kerner's *Village Voice* column a few days later, in which Kerner commented on the *Times* interview: "'Ignorance is bliss,' said the old philosopher, but recent sprayings by the chairman of the New York City Opera suggest that the proverb might be changed to Ignorance is Samuels."

John Samuels was determined to shake things up. He knew he couldn't tangle with Lincoln Kirstein and George Balanchine—the New York City Ballet was sacrosanct—so he turned his sights to our company. To get the attention he so desired, Samuels would have to do something dramatic—like get rid of me.

The fall 1975 season had been planned long before Samuels arrived. Carol Neblett and John Alexander reprised the roles they had originated the previous spring in Corsaro's haunting multipictorial production of Korngold's *Die tote Stadt*, an unexpected hit that—like Janacek's *The Makropoulos Affair*, also a Corsaro production, with Maralin Niska in her spellbinding performance as the 337-year-old femme fatale Emilia Marty—made stunning use of Ronald Chase's projected film images. *Makropoulos* had screens with pictures of Niska playing out the story of Emilia Marty. The medium was ideal (and relatively inexpensive), and Niska was extraordinary, inhabiting the role with every fiber of her being. Corsaro, of course, was in his element as he worked with Maralin to bring out her complex character.

That same season we also presented City Opera's first performances of Donizetti's *The Daughter of the Regiment* (for Sills) and unveiled a new production of *Die Meistersinger*. When I had originally announced that we would mount the Wagner opera in an English translation (by John Gutman) there was an outcry from our subscribers, many of them European émigrés who had been attending City Opera since our early days at the old Mecca Temple. I received letters and phone calls: "How dare you do an English translation?" I implored our patrons to "Come and see it and then make your decision." John Cox's production was exquisite and atmospheric, designed by Carl Toms in warm shades of brown and green, with soft golden lighting by our own Hans Sondheimer. The outstanding cast was led by Norman Bailey (in his only company appearance) as Hans Sachs, Johanna Meier as Eva, John Alexander as Walther, and James Billings—who was equal parts hilarious, despicable, and pitiful—as Beckmesser. My prediction proved correct: Gutman's translation was superb and easily understood. Some people said it was a pleasure for once to hear the audience laugh at the proper moments, and those who didn't know German were thrilled to finally understand what Sachs's long monologues were about!

I still consider *Meistersinger* to be one of the pinnacles of our achievement. I loved conducting it, and one of my few regrets is that I did not get to conduct more Wagner throughout my career.

On October 27, 1975, we held a memorial tribute for Norman Treigle, who had tragically died the previous February. Sills hosted and I conducted the evening, and company members present and past including Phyllis Curtin, who had always been very close to Norman, performed selections from operas closely associated with him. There was not a dry eye in the house when we played a recording of Norman himself performing "Tal di ciascuno" from *Giulio Cesare*.

The following spring we brought to New York (from the Washington Opera Society) a gorgeous staging, by Ian Strasfogel, of Monteverdi's *Il ritorno d'Ulisse in patria*, with Richard Stilwell as Ulysses and Frederica von Stade in her company debut as Penelope. Although I did not conduct this production (Mario Bernardi was the sensitive conductor), I was to work with Flicka—the childhood name by which Von Stade is known—many times over the years in opera houses here and abroad. In 1979 we collaborated on a lovely recording of Massenet's *Cendrillon* for CBS—alas, the only time I was to conduct this opera—and in 1987 I conducted her television Christmas special. (We filmed the program in Austria in the summer, with the local fire brigade providing the "shredded foam" snow.) Most recently, in 2004 Flicka and I performed together in Buenos Aires in a light-hearted *Merry Widow* with Tom Allen.

Our other new productions in spring 1976 were more of a mixed bag. Donizetti's *Lucrezia Borgia*, imported from San Diego, was a misstep for all involved; the production was not meant for our house, and Sills was not in top form. *Ashmedai*, an allegory by the Israeli composer Josef Tal, fared better—at least with the critics. I knew that *Ashmedai* was not going to be an audience pleaser and that to succeed it needed a strong production, so I invited Broadway's Hal Prince to direct it. I was certain he was the right man for the task—that he could get the most dramatic and imaginative rendition of the work. I was right; the staging was magnificent. (The astringent music, unfortunately, did not play well with a few members of our audience, who walked out halfway through.) Prince enjoyed his operatic outing and went on to direct many operas in houses around the world. When we bumped into each other in 2010 at the New York City Opera dress rehearsal of Bernstein's *A Quiet Place* Hal quipped, "You're the one who got me into this goddamn business!"

During the first week of September 1976, I received a letter from Beverly, who was in San Francisco rehearsing for the season opener at the San Francisco Opera: a new production of Massenet's *Thaïs* directed by Tito Capobianco and underwritten by Cyril Magnin.

Julius dear, Right away you should know it's a serious letter because of the dignified way I start it—and because normally I would be on the phone telling this to you. But since I know how persuasive you can be I'm taking the chicken way out and writing.

I have agonized—well maybe not agonized—maybe a little brooding is closer—and have decided to do something that I've never done with you before. I'm going

⌄ to change my mind—I'd like to withdraw from "Rosenkavalier" in '78. There
are several reasons, all of which I think are valid. First and most important, my
voice isn't ready for it—I had thought that as I got older it would get heavier
and darker. Listening to myself in "Thaïs," that's not the case—so I would
have to "manufacture" a middle register sound which would be difficult—and
unwise—since immediately before the premiere I would be involved in 12 performances of "Thaïs" [NOTE: In 1978 Sills ultimately performed 11 perfor-
⌄ mances of *Thaïs* at the Met and on the Met spring tour]—exactly the time
period where I would—or should—be singing the Marsh. into my voice.

The second reason is that I would be involved in these "Thaïs" performances
for 3 months prior to the premiere and you would be in Europe so the dream
of preparing it together has evaporated as well. The third reason is that I'd like
to consider this a postponement—I still will do my first Marsh. with you whenever you'd like it—but at a future date—and perhaps by then we'll have a new
production and a thoroughly new concept rather than a redirected one—I'd
like to propose in that same period of time repeats of "Pirata"—and a revival of
"Puritani"—I really am so sorry to do this—but to sum it all up—it's too soon
for my voice to handle.

Hope "Pirata" doesn't make you shudder—Is Alexander available?—Di
Giuseppe would make a very teensy pirate—It's not all <u>that</u> florid so I don't
think we have to think about him. I know you'd like to give him something—
but please not with me—please. Please give Rita my love—kiss Rachel [my first
grandchild] for me. As always I love you very much. Bev.

Beverly never sang the Marschallin. (And *Il pirata*, by the way, did not
make it into the company repertory.) She was smart enough to know the
role wasn't vocally right for her, especially at that stage of her career. With
some regrets we replaced the revival of *Rosenkavalier*—planned for our
spring 1978 season—with a new production of *The Merry Widow* starring Beverly and directed by Capobianco, imported from San Diego.

Most of the time in the bel canto repertory Beverly's partner had been
Enrico Di Giuseppe, who had the high notes and the flexibility. He was,
however, much shorter than Sills—and we had a standing joke about the
dearth of available tenors who were "tall enough for her." She and I even
exchanged little missives in the form of five-line limericks. We once had an
exchange about Richard Cassilly—rhyming "Cassilly" with "assilly." Dick was
as tall as Sills but unfortunately did not have a voice suited to bel canto.

It was in the fall of 1976 that things began to unravel. Although the season
started as planned, the house was full of a strange energy—nervous, but not
a healthy energy. Many company members felt a strike was imminent.

Negotiations had been going on all summer, and continued the first
four weeks of the season. But then it came. The strike, which canceled

all performances from September 28 to October 18, took a huge toll on the company. This time around, the unions were not so kind to us. They were banking on the fact that we had our new board chairman to help us. But instead of raising new money from new sources, John Samuels was intent on raising ticket prices. I reminded him that he was supposed to raise money from outside sources—not penalize our loyal patrons.

We had scheduled three new productions that season: Offenbach's *La belle Hélène* (which opened a week before the strike began), *The Barber of Seville*, and Menotti's *The Saint of Bleecker Street*. Though both *Barber* (directed and conducted by Sarah Caldwell) and *Saint* (directed by Menotti's amanuensis Frank Rizzo) were fine productions, we had nothing truly smashing to offer, like the *Anna Bolena* that had opened directly after the 1973 strike.

One of the newest and most active board members at that time was David Lloyd-Jacob, the chairman of Amcon and a cultured and knowledgeable man. As my relationship with Samuels began to seriously deteriorate, I was able to communicate with him only through Lloyd-Jacob.

In February 1977 Samuels and Lloyd-Jacob dropped by my office and we had a discussion during which they complained that City Opera was being run like a "mom and pop store." I remember the exact wording, because until then I had not heard that term. They told me I needed to get rid of senior staff members like John White, who was "senile and old-fashioned." I kept my cool and responded that I knew how to handle my staff—and that I certainly did not like their interference in internal matters.

(Apparently White had been calling Lloyd-Jacob at night at home and making a nuisance of himself, much as he used to call me at two in the morning when I was dealing with Kennedy Center matters. "Did I wake you?" he would ask during these late-night calls. "No, I had to get up to answer the phone anyway," I would say, as though it were an Abbott and Costello routine. The late-night calls continued even when I was conducting in Europe.)

To avoid further confrontations of this sort, a few weeks later I told Lloyd-Jacob of the plan I had been hatching: "When Beverly retires at fifty, she would take over the co-directorship of the company with me—and a few years later, I would fully withdraw and she would be completely in charge." At first Lloyd-Jacob was taken aback by this talk of a "diarchy." But as I talked about how "right" and triumphant the plan would be—"Beverly would still be there for her public" (albeit in a radical turnabout as company director), and she would be a fantastic fund-raiser!—I could see Lloyd-Jacob was becoming interested. "Does she have taste?" he asked. "Of course, and I'll be there beside her!" was my quick response.

It was around that time that John Samuels decided to convert the men's room on the orchestra level of the State Theater into a patron's room—complete with Chinese panels to be donated by Samuels himself. When

City Opera received the bills for the construction of the space (which the company had nicknamed "John's john"), there was no money to pay for the work. It became evident to me that people had made soft pledges that were not fulfilled.

In March 1977 Rolf Liebermann, the intendant of the Paris Opera, came backstage to see me after a performance of *Mefistofele* and gave a bit of unsolicited advice: "Julius, you've done everything you can do at City Opera. You must get out of here."

The palace revolution at City Opera took place in May 1977 while Beverly and I were in Paris recording Charpentier's *Louise.* On Samuels's orders, a "white paper" was drawn up by Robert Walker. In this plan, John White did not exist at all (apparently he would be the first to be eliminated). A newly organized development and marketing department would be installed. The mom and pop store would be replaced by a superstore. It's especially interesting to note that the size of our administrative staff when Baum was still alive was no more than ten people. (At the State Theater our core administration team included, in addition to myself, John White, and Felix Popper, Ruth Hider, Dan Rule, Joan Baekeland, Saba McWilliams, for a time Rosalind Nadell, and later Bruce Maza, Robert Walker, and Susan Woelzl.) When Samuels became chairman, the staff doubled in size.

The presence of such a "restructuring report"—drawn up without my knowledge, let alone consent—indicated that my own departure was not far off. What John Samuels overlooked was the fact that in 1968 I had been given tenure, which meant that they could not simply get rid of me. I would have to formally and voluntarily resign my directorship.

Sills and I had agreed that we would aim for 1980 as the year to begin our codirectorship, but by late '77 I realized that I no longer wanted to remain at the helm of City Opera. The battles with Samuels were becoming more frequent. When I got sick and tired of the shenanigans, I talked to Sills to find out if she was ready to enact our plan. Fortunately she was ready and willing. On January 9, 1978, we held a press conference at which John Samuels and I announced that in the fall of 1980 Beverly would retire as a singer and become codirector of City Opera with me. Although our exact roles in the partnership had not yet been fleshed out, Beverly announced to the assembled reporters, "Window dressing I'm not going to be. Julius knows that. I have strong opinions about our opera company."

I had a pleasant respite that spring. *Poppea* opened in Paris on March 17, 1978, with nine additional performances scheduled through April.

At City Opera that spring, I was conducting *Mefistofele, Figaro, Meistersinger,* and a new production of *The Merry Widow* with Sills and Titus. So it was that each week from early February to late April '78, I was in New York half a week and in Paris the other half. I became a regular on Air France, setting some sort of record when I made sixteen transatlantic crossings in twenty-one days.

I was running on adrenaline, conducting in Paris on Friday night and returning to New York for a performance on Saturday and another on Sunday. All these years later, friends and colleagues such as Johanna Meier and Matthew Epstein can still recall that my coloring in those days was "a ghastly shade of gray-green," but once I stepped into the pit and gave the downbeat I was alive again. My growing disenchantment with Samuels made the Paris performances all that much sweeter.

Late in the spring of 1978 I was offered the music directorship of the Buffalo Philharmonic. It was a most tempting offer. The orchestra dates back to 1935, and its prestigious list of past music directors includes William Steinberg, Josef Krips, Lukas Foss, and Michael Tilson Thomas. The Buffalo Philharmonic had originally invited me to replace Foss when he left in 1971. I certainly wasn't ready to make the switch then, but by the middle of 1978 my patience had worn thin.

There were two confrontations in particular that drove the final nails into the coffin. One involved ticket prices; the other dealt with scheduling. We were in horrible financial shape, and in an effort to help correct that, I offered to mount—at the beginning of our fall 1978 season—fourteen consecutive performances of our company's first production of Victor Herbert's *Naughty Marietta*, a work that I knew would have high attendance and would bring in money. We had done Lehár; we had done Johann Strauss; we had done Gilbert and Sullivan, and Offenbach. So why not do a lighter work by an American like Victor Herbert?

I had originally extended an invitation to the veteran Broadway director George Abbott, who loved Victor Herbert, to direct our production. When Samuels found out my intention to invite the great Mr. Abbott, he ridiculed me, pointing out the director's advanced years. (Abbott was ninety at the time; ironically, he was to direct one more show on Broadway before dying at the ripe old age of 107.) Not wanting another altercation, I dropped the idea and instead asked Gerald Freedman to direct *Naughty Marietta*, starring a young Gianna Rolandi.

Naughty Marietta was a huge success, playing to near-capacity crowds between August 31 and September 10, 1978. By then, John Samuels had already raised our ticket prices twice in one year—something I had always been strongly opposed to. In fall 1978 our orchestra and first ring tickets jumped from $12.50 to $16. After the season ended, Samuels announced yet another price hike—a 25 percent increase for spring 1979, which would bring the top price to $20. His defense to the *New York Times* on November 16, 1978: "At $20, an orchestra seat for the City Opera costs less than a Broadway musical." (A year later when Sills took over the company, Samuels was forced to return ticket prices to their former levels.)

So many unpleasant things were happening at the end of 1978, but in the midst of all the upheaval there was also a happy moment: my conducting debut at the Met on Saturday evening, October 7, 1978. Less than a week earlier I had received a phone call from Joan Ingpen, the Met's music administrator, asking if I could help out and take on the task of conducting for an indisposed Richard Bonynge. The opera was *Werther*, one of my favorites. I had to check and see if I was free. Luckily I could accept, but some of the rehearsals were overlapping with my City Opera schedule. The Met orchestra was very cooperative in accommodating me, even agreeing to change the time of one of the rehearsals (something they had never done before). That particular weekend of my Met debut was a whirlwind of sorts, since I was also conducting three performances at my own house: *The Marriage of Figaro* on Friday night, the Sunday matinee of *The Turk in Italy*, and Sunday night's *Pelléas et Mélisande*. (I reveled in the variety of the repertory.)

The cast for the Met's production of *Werther* was wonderful: Domingo, Elena Obraztsova, Dominic Cossa, and Betsy Norden. I thoroughly enjoyed my Met debut—the first of 268 appearances I was to make with that company over the next three and a half decades.

The next day George Jellinek wrote the following review for the New York Times News Service:

> Julius Rudel, long-time general director of the New York City Opera company, made his Met debut and all the principal singers were heard in their roles here for the first time. Aside from emphasizing the good relationship between New York's two major opera companies, the invitation extended to Rudel was a wise decision—clearly endorsed by the warm ovation which greeted his appearance in the pit. For the past many years he has proved his affinity for French opera not only on stage, but also in an impressive list of major recordings. Taking over *Werther* on short notice to replace the indisposed Richard Bonynge, Rudel controlled the stage action with the skill of the thoroughly experienced craftsman he is. He paced the music with clarity and a thorough understanding of the restraint with which Massenet counterbalanced the over-sentimentality of his literary source, but whipped up plenty of excitement for the passionate climaxes.

At the time of my Met debut I had finalized my decision to become the director of the Buffalo Philharmonic, although only my family knew of my plans. In November of 1978 I invited Beverly for another dinner at Scandia—once again during our annual Los Angeles tour (but this time just the two of us). I asked her, "Would you be able to take over sooner?" Without a pause she said, "Yes." A feeling of relief overtook me, and I ordered outrageous desserts.

The next morning I bought a dozen beautiful red roses and delivered them myself to her hotel with a note: "Thank you for giving me my freedom." Then I called New York and asked my office to have Samuels come to my apartment the following Saturday.

And so John Samuels dropped by my apartment on December 2, a few hours before I flew to Washington to conduct the Kennedy Center Honors. He arrived at the scheduled time. After keeping him waiting for a good half hour in my lobby, I asked the doorman to send Samuels up—and told him I planned to quit "any and all" administrative duties. I had accepted the music directorship of the Buffalo Philharmonic and would resign the directorship of City Opera on June 30, 1979, when my contract expired, although I would remain as principal conductor, as Beverly had requested. Samuels at first seemed taken aback by my news but recovered quickly and displayed no emotion.

The board meeting was scheduled for December 13, after the company returned from the annual Los Angeles tour. We would announce my resignation then.

Samuels said, "How can we keep it quiet?" I replied, "Only Beverly and you and I know, and we don't have to open our mouths about it." We shook hands on it.

Well, somebody did talk.

Bill Zakariasen, the music critic for the *Daily News* and a former member of the New York City Opera chorus, broke the story in the *Daily News* on December 12, the night before the board meeting. I was attending Beverly's performance in *Don Pasquale* at the Met that evening. At intermission, a reporter came over to Rita and me and asked for a comment on the front page article in the next morning's *Daily News*. At that moment my painstakingly devised plan to stage my resignation on my own terms went out the window. I hid my consternation from the reporter and said, "No comment."

But inside I was saying to myself, "That son of a bitch!"

When I arrived home at eleven o'clock I tried to call the *Times*'s Abe Rosenthal, who I considered to be my friend. I also tried to phone Harold Schonberg. There was no answer at either man's house.

The following morning's headline in the *New York Times*—in a story written by Harold Schonberg—spelled disaster: "City Opera Ousting Rudel and Installing Miss Sills as Director." I could barely drink my coffee as I read those glaring words.

The board meeting was scheduled for ten o'clock, with a press conference to follow at eleven. When I arrived at the State Theater shortly before the board meeting, some members of the press were already milling around; I sent my secretary out to tell Mr. Schonberg that I'd like him to come to my office at 10:45. At the board meeting, which Beverly and I both attended, John Samuels announced my resignation with a single sentence. Several of the board members were hearing this news for the first time; others had heard it the previous night on the eleven o'clock news.

I don't remember what I said during the meeting besides announcing my resignation. I wanted to keep my dignity (in spite of the one-two punch I had received from the *Times*) and did not want to come out the loser in this. I really had a blackout of sorts. The only thing I can recall is that throughout the meeting Sills remained uncharacteristically silent, never once reminding the board members that I had tenure and that the decision to leave was entirely mine. From that moment on our friendship was marred. My wife never again spoke to Beverly.

The board meeting ended, and Schonberg arrived at my office promptly at 10:45. First off, I excoriated him: "How could you do that without checking with me first?" He was silent. The damage was done, although the *Times*—perhaps acknowledging their error—had changed the front-page headline in the later editions: "Rudel Ready to Leave Top City Opera Post; Miss Sills Will Step In." Coincidentally, that same morning there was also a piece in the *Times* about Lincoln Center Theater, of which John Samuels was the Chairman: "Beaumont Theater Will Reopen with a 5-Member Directorate." (This highfalutin plan to have five directors on board—among them Woody Allen and Sarah Caldwell—never got off the ground.)

After the press conference, a group of City Opera members gathered in the canteen. Somebody later told me that it was as though they were present at "the divorce of a great marriage that everybody thought would last forever." It seemed to everyone that something was happening beyond our control that was foreign to the company and that was going to change us irreparably.

Fortunately I didn't have time for wallowing. Kurt Herbert Adler, director of the San Francisco Opera, behaved like a true mensch, contacting me as soon as he heard the news and inviting me to conduct *Pelléas* at SFO in the fall of 1979. (Though Adler, Bing, and I had been referred to for years as "The Viennese Mafia," it wasn't until my resignation that Kurt became a friend and even a father figure to me.)

Unfortunately Beverly was not helpful in getting John Samuels to sign my new contract as principal conductor, and ultimately I had to hire a lawyer to get the contract signed. Beverly subsequently wrote in her 1987 autobiography, "During the first six months of 1979, when Julius and I were codirectors . . ." We were *never* codirectors; our original plan had been eclipsed by Samuels's actions.

In addition, she made some negative remarks in articles in *New York* magazine and the *New York Times Sunday Magazine*—complaining, among other things, that during those transition months from January to June 1979, I wouldn't let her use my office, which wasn't exactly true. In a barely disguised effort to humiliate me, Samuels had asked me to give up the director's office space during the spring 1979 season so that incoming director Beverly could have an office. I said, "I can't direct the opera from a dressing room." Which is what Samuels wanted. He wanted me to move into the conductors' dressing room. When I threatened to resign immediately, he backed off.

I had a full schedule that season, conducting our revivals of *Figaro*, *Mefistofele*, *Manon*, and *The Turk in Italy* (a light romp starring Beverly) along with the world premiere of Argento's *Miss Havisham's Fire*. In addition, I had to oversee another new production: a double bill of Purcell's *Dido and Aeneas* and Richard Strauss's ballet *Le bourgeois gentilhomme* (with Rudolf Nureyev, Patricia McBride, and Jean-Pierre Bonnefous), both conducted by Cal Stewart Kellogg. The Purcell work was directed by Corsaro; George Balanchine and Jerry Robbins choreographed *Le bourgeois gentilhomme*. The board was quite critical of my budget for the production, but I told them that since Balanchine was *donating* his services to us I could hardly deny him his choice of a costume and set designer, Rouben Ter-Arutunian.

Beverly, who was only appearing in one City Opera production that season (and touring with the Met in *Don Pasquale*), spent the spring months "learning the ropes." The previous summer, when she had first joined the New York City Opera board (and when she and I were still planning our joint directorship), Marty Oppenheimer of the City Opera board had invited John White, Beverly, and me to his law offices for an informational meeting. In the course of the meeting he verified what we already knew: that Samuels was moving into high gear and instituting all kinds of changes—even though the company had no money. With such a vivid memory of that meeting etched in my mind, I've always found Sills's claim that John and I had kept the true financial facts from her a bit disingenuous.

On April 29, 1979, the very day that I conducted my last performance as general director of the company—Argento's *Miss Havisham's Fire*—there was a bit of high drama: a front-page story written by reporter Ann Crittenden in the *New York Times* about John Samuels and the fact that his financial empire was crashing and burning. The headline: "Cultural Impresario's Businesses Tumble Into Debt and Disarray."

In February 1980 Samuels announced that he intended to resign his New York City Opera chairmanship later that year but he ended up staying longer, finally stepping down as chairman of the City Opera board in May 1981.

꩜꩜

The final world premiere of my directorship was *Miss Havisham's Fire*, a melodious and dramatic opera by Dominick Argento. We were all very excited as we rehearsed for the opening. I realized this was a major new work with one big flaw. The last scene of the opera needed cutting and restructuring. Although Dominick was amenable, the librettist John Olon-Scrymgeour absolutely refused to do this.

On opening night exactly what I feared would happen did indeed happen. I could tell in the first two acts that the audience was "with us." But then the last scene began and as it rambled on, I could palpably feel that we were losing them. At one point there was even some giggling. We had lost them. Still, even this could not detract from the well-done performances of the entire cast, led by Rita Shane and Gianna Rolandi. (And I was happy to learn of the subsequent success of the revamped work at Opera Theatre of St. Louis in 2001.)

What are my memories of my last performance as general director? The house was packed. When I entered the pit, I was met by a wall of cheers. At the end of the performance, when I came out for my curtain call, the applause was quite possibly the loudest I have ever heard. Then the curtain rose, and onstage was the entire company including Sills along with another fan, the celebrated soprano Licia Albanese. Everyone was cheering, and I was stunned and teary-eyed. With the goings-on of the past year, I had no idea such an outpouring of emotion and—dare I say—love was going to occur that night.

17

LIFE AFTER NEW YORK CITY OPERA

A funny thing happened during our annual tour to Los Angeles in November 1977. It seems that Paramount Pictures was shooting a film in San Francisco, a comedy starring Goldie Hawn, Chevy Chase, and Dudley Moore. The climax of the film was to take place in the San Francisco Opera House during a performance of Gilbert and Sullivan's *The Mikado*. It was expected that the San Francisco Opera would perform the needed music. Apparently the San Francisco Opera was unable to accommodate the request, so the producers of the film called us and, while we weren't touring with *The Mikado*, we were performing *Madama Butterfly*. I suggested that we use the sets from Puccini's tragedy to represent Sullivan's Japan. Also, we had singers who could do the required parts and *Mikado* was a score I knew well. Contracts were signed, and within days, on our day off, the film company was transporting New York City Opera to San Francisco to shoot this one scene and to record the music. It was a delightful experience and showed just how flexible our company was. The movie, *Foul Play*, was released late in 1978, just prior to the announcement of my resignation from City Opera. What I hadn't known at the time was that our little side-trip into the San Francisco Opera House had angered that company's general director, Kurt Herbert Adler. How ironic it now seems that the first call I received following my resignation from City Opera came from Adler—inviting me to conduct at San Francisco Opera. And what an invitation it was! A new production of Debussy's *Pelléas et Mélisande*, an opera I love and a cast that was ideal starring Maria Ewing, Dale Duesing, and an old City Opera friend, Michael Devlin.

At the time I was far too preoccupied with the issues surrounding my resignation to even begin to appreciate the new journey I was about to embark on, a journey that to some degree actually began with my Met debut conducting *Werther* in October 1978. (There was no way I could have predicted at that time that my Met career would span nearly thirty years and include more than 250 performances of operas ranging from Handel's *Samson* to Poulenc's *Dialogues of the Carmelites*.) I had also by that time agreed to become the Music Director of the Buffalo Philharmonic, a fine orchestra with a rich tradition. Making the position even sweeter was the fact that it reunited me with the orchestra's splendid concert master, Charlie Haupt, who had started in the City Opera orchestra and had been my concertmaster for many summers at Caramoor.

Looking back, I realize how free I felt once I was out of City Opera. I could step onto any podium and not worry about fundraising or who was covering a small role or union negotiations. I could make music, unencumbered, and as my own international career blossomed, I reconnected with many of the singers who'd begun their careers with me at City Opera.

It seemed quite appropriate that two of the cast at my Met debut were City Opera stalwarts, Dominic Cossa and Plácido Domingo; in fact, many of the important engagements that followed reunited me with Plácido. Working with him was always an unmitigated delight. His musicianship is unwavering and everything he does on stage is well-conceived and adds to the beauty and completeness of the interpretation. My only regret is that Plácido and I didn't record more together, and what is especially sad is that no recording of him singing Ginastera's *Don Rodrigo* was ever made.

I worked with so many wonderful artists during the thirty years of guest-conducting that followed my City Opera resignation that it's difficult to even begin to recount them all. But as my career expanded and I went from city to city—Paris, Vienna, Chicago, Tel Aviv, Copenhagen, Barcelona, Madrid, Seoul, Los Angeles, San Francisco, Buenos Aires, London, Prague, Munich, Houston, Tokyo—those musical relationships often developed into lasting friendships. There is Sherrill Milnes, who began at City Opera, and with whom I worked in Paris and Buenos Aires. And Sam Ramey—imagine my delight upon arriving in Vienna to conduct *Carmen* to find that he was the Escamillo! There were Met performances with other friends, including Alfredo Kraus, Catherine Malfitano, Tatiana Troyanos, Kiri Te Kanawa, Maralin Niska, Ermano Mauro, Paul Plishka, Diana Soviero, Frederica von Stade, Régine Crespin, Johnny Alexander, Joyce Castle, Dwayne Croft, and James Morris.

As for Jim Morris, who remains a dear friend and an artist for whom I have tremendous respect, I am proud to say that I not only conducted his professional debut when, barely out of his teens, he sang the part of Crespel in a Baltimore production of *Tales of Hoffmann* starring Sills, Treigle, and Domingo in 1967, but I conducted one of the productions that launched his amazing journey as a Wagner singer. It was Thanksgiving 1984 and Jim and I were in Houston where he was to sing his first Dutchman. The production itself was just so-so, but being able to guide Jim through the challenges of that demanding part was simply musical joy.

Sometimes life has a bizarre way of imitating art; there are moments that, when seen in isolation, are merely additional experiences, but when you step back you realize that those particular moments may have had more importance. There are two engagements that in many ways brought my career full circle.

In November of 2005 I was invited to return to Vienna Staatsoper to lead a performance of *Tosca* as part of the Fiftieth Anniversary season marking the postwar rebuilding of the opera house. When I arrived, I was flooded by memories and emotions, feelings I had not permitted myself to feel previously. First of all, this was the opera house where my journey had begun, and marking the anniversary of the reopening made it impossible to ignore thoughts of what this house had endured since my first visit to it in 1924. Ghosts of singers, conductors, directors, and shadows of productions that had helped shape me were all around. Furthermore, the *Tosca* production was the one the house had been using since the fifties, and the constancy of that only heightened my sense of living in the past. I've conducted *Tosca* hundreds of times in houses all over the world, and that night, as I stood on the podium before the members of the Vienna Philharmonic, I grew nervous, not for what I was about to do, but for all that had happened. After the performance, my son Tony and I went to the Sacher Restaurant for supper. We spoke little. How I wish that Rita had lived long enough to share this with me.

About a year later I had another full-circle moment; Paul Kellogg, who had announced that he would be stepping down as general director of New York City Opera, wanted me to return before he left. After much thought and discussion with my compassionate manager William Guerri, I agreed to lead a new production of Mozart's *Così fan tutte*. The cast was a wonderful group of young singers (including a soprano, Julianna Di Giacomo, who— true to City Opera tradition—jumped in at the eleventh hour for an ailing colleague) and, while I wasn't crazy about the production, it would do. I was energized by the rehearsals and when I conducted the first orchestra reading I was pleased to see many familiar faces. Conducting Mozart is itself healing, and in each performance his music allowed me to enjoy the experience I had initially dreaded. It was a good run, and I was pleased to work with young singers (as I had been doing for the past several summers at the Aspen Music Festival) and to see how the model we had built for City Opera, though scaled back, was still working. It was only after the run ended that I realized it had been a quarter of a century since I last conducted at New York City Opera.

Epilogue

When the New York State Theater (that is what I will always call it) reopened in November of 2009, George Steel asked me to lead a performance of the Revival Meeting scene from Carlisle Floyd's *Susannah* with Sam Ramey as Olin Blitch. I agreed, but during the limited time I was there for rehearsals, it was easy to see that the foundation that had sustained City Opera had eroded to the point of nonsustainability. There was no core group of singers; the systems we had built were gone; there was no appreciation of how an opera company runs and attracts a loyal audience.

Now I understand completely how the actions of ill-informed board members can destroy a company. It probably started in 1978 with John Samuels, and was momentarily halted during Christopher Keene's directorship, but what the board of New York City Opera allowed to happen, or more accurately, precipitated is well-nigh criminal. I am at the stage of life where anger is not a frequently felt emotion, but when George Steel, whose knowledge of opera is limited (to put it kindly), announced that City Opera would leave Lincoln Center, I was enraged.

There is so much I could say, in frustration and sadness, but I will close with the op-ed piece that ran in the *New York Times* on June 7, 2011. Within it are the beliefs and ideas that helped me grow a company, discover wonderful artists, and have an amazing, unimaginable life in music.

The People's Opera, in Peril
By Julius Rudel

The New York City Opera was born in 1943, a year after I graduated from the Mannes Music School. Laszlo Halasz, the company's first music director, hired me as a rehearsal pianist and vocal coach. I was 22 and had arrived in the United States five years earlier, after Hitler took over my native Austria.

That an opera company could be created while World War II raged spoke to America's best aspirations. Mayor Fiorello H. La Guardia called it "the people's opera," in contrast to the older Metropolitan Opera, and from the beginning, it was. It brought opera to the masses, including immigrants like myself. It exposed audiences to innovative and challenging works. It showcased the talents of American singers and composers.

Today, City Opera, to which I devoted some of the best years of my conducting career, is fighting to survive. Last month, it revealed plans to leave Lincoln Center, its home for the last 45 years, and to perform at various, unspecified locations around New York. It slashed its $31 million budget and laid off nearly a quarter of its administrative staff members. And it declined to say what operas it will put on next season, where they will be performed, or how they will be financed. The vague plans put forward would leave the company not even a shadow of what it was intended to be—and became.

Some have blamed the company's woes on its Lincoln Center location, citing the expense and the proximity to the Met. But I believe the location has become a scapegoat for the hardships of a company that has suffered from inconsistent leadership by its board and a failure to engage in the smart programming and strategic planning that companies need to survive in hard times. I cannot sit by and watch as the legacy that was built by a company, if not a family, of talented, dedicated people is cast aside.

In 1965, when we considered moving from our first home (New York City Center, on West 55th Street) to the New York State Theater (now the David H.

Koch Theater) at Lincoln Center, I was apprehensive, fearing that we might be forced to abandon the qualities that had allowed us to grow. I was wrong.

From our first night in our new home—Feb. 22, 1966, the North American premiere of Alberto Ginastera's "Don Rodrigo," starring a 25-year-old Plácido Domingo—the benefits were apparent: the ambience, the proximity to other institutions (including, yes, the Met), and the attention the international music press lavished on the new arts complex. That attention helped us to attract, despite our low fees, top-flight singers, conductors and directors.

The new space and new technologies also allowed us to put on memorable productions of Arrigo Boito's "Mefistofele," Leos Janacek's "Makropulos Case" and Erich Wolfgang Korngold's "Tote Stadt," among others. We presented new works and reinterpreted old ones to sold-out houses. At its peak, we presented 200 performances a year in New York and undertook annual tours to Los Angeles and Washington.

We also developed teams of ensemble singers, many of whom went on to major international careers—Beverly Sills, Norman Treigle, Phyllis Curtin, Beverly Wolff, Samuel Ramey, Catherine Malfitano and many, many others—and helped establish the American opera singer as a force to be reckoned with. If we had become the traveling band that is currently being proposed, many of those careers might never have blossomed.

Indeed, Lincoln Center solidified the company's place not as New York's *second* opera company, but as New York's *other* opera company. We were never thought of, and never thought of ourselves, as a lesser Met.

Over 68 years, I have seen City Opera thrive and I've seen it struggle. I realize that today's economic climate and changing paradigms in the arts pose monumental challenges. Opera companies everywhere face the question of how to attract and retain audiences; keeping the opera experience fresh and meaningful, making certain that what is presented is first-class, and experimenting with innovative repertory and productions that steadily build audiences are vital to assure opera's survival.

Once before, in 1956, City Opera faced the threat of bankruptcy, but instead of retrenching and cutting, the board boldly moved forward, securing the financing we needed to stabilize the company and then grow. The current board must reconsider its decision and demonstrate the commitment and vision its predecessors had.

If the board and management of City Opera cannot finance, produce and support full seasons of new works and standard operas in interesting productions with first-rate casts as we once did, they should be replaced, so that 68 years from now no one will wonder what ever became of City Opera.

There is something to be said for longevity. Since leaving New York City Opera, I've enjoyed my life as a peripatetic conductor. I count myself lucky to have had a career that has spanned six decades and two continents—and several worlds of music. I have conducted in the world's great opera houses and symphony halls, and have worked with literally thousands of the greatest artists of our time. I've been involved with creating exciting productions, and have had the incredible privilege of spending my life bringing great composers' masterpieces to new audiences.

In the end, for me, it's always about the music.

Maria Jeritza, whom I had seen and cheered as a child from the fourth gallery of the Vienna Staatsoper, later moved to the United States, where she married a very wealthy businessman and settled down to a life of baronial splendor in—of all places—Newark, New Jersey! She became a real fan and friend of mine and would come to many New York City Opera performances and sit in the first row directly behind me, always dramatically costumed.

Not infrequently she would invite Rita and me to dinner at her home; occasionally her guests included another former Metropolitan Opera diva, Anna Case. Both women by then were in their late seventies. Naturally the conversation would often center on musical happenings. One night in 1965 we had been discussing the new production of *The Tales of Hoffmann* that I had conducted at New York City Opera when suddenly, Anna Case started to hum the famous "Barcarolle" from *Hoffmann* and Jeritza joined in. Just the two of them, sans accompaniment.

A piece of the past came up and smiled at me.

APPENDIX

The Three American Seasons of New York City Opera

WP   World Premiere

AP   American Premiere

NYCOP   New York City Opera Premiere

REP   Revival of a production in the New York City Opera repertory

NP   New production of an opera previously performed at
            New York City Opera

d   New York City Opera debut artist

Season 1 (April 3–May 11, 1958)

NYCOP. *The Ballad of Baby Doe* (Moore/J. Latouche)
April 3, 1958 (plus 3 additional performances that season)
Sills, Lipton, Krebs, Baisley, Rodgers (d), LeSawyer, Andrea, Alpert, Lockard; Cassel, Hecht, Fried, Ludgin, Kaldenberg, DeLon (d), Del Monte, Newman, Hoel, Elliot (d), Sliker (d), Dennison (d); Buckley, Rosing, Oenslager (d)

NYCOP. *Tale for a Deaf Ear* (Bucci/Bucci)
April 6, 1958 (2)
On a double bill with *Trouble in Tahiti*
Neway, Bower, Venora (d); Chapman, Cassilly, Newman; Gamson, Pollock, Sylbert

NYCOP. *Trouble in Tahiti* (Bernstein/Bernstein)
April 6, 1958 (2)
Wolff (d), Collier; Atkinson (d), Metcalf (d), Kolk (d); Bernstein (d), Pollock, Nomikos

NYCOP. *Lost in the Stars* (Weill/M. Anderson)
April 9, 1958 (12)
Carter (d)*, Le Noire (d); Winters, Gossett (d); Rudel, Quintero (d), Nomikos
*Shirley Carter subsequently changed her name to Shirley Verrett

NYCOP. *The Taming of the Shrew* (Giannini/D. Fee)
April 13, 1958 (2)
Curtin, Stolin (d); Cassel, Alexander, Ukena (d), Watson (d); Adler, Webster, Barratt (d)

NP. *Regina* (Blitzstein/Blitzstein)
April 17, 1958 (2)
Lewis, Carron, Strine (d), Brice (d); Hecht, Renan, Driscoll, Irving (d), Frierson (d); Krachmalnick (d), Shumlin (d), Bay

REP. *The Old Maid and the Thief* (Menotti/Menotti)
April 20, 1958 (2)
Moody, Kobart, Bower; Reardon; Whallon (d), Butler, Condell
On a double bill with *The Medium*

REP. *The Medium* (Menotti/Menotti)
April 20, 1958 (2)
Turner, Carroll (d), LeSawyer, Sanders; Scott (d), Newman; Whallon (d), Butler, Armistead

WP. *The Good Soldier Schweik* (Kurka/L. Allen)
April 23, 1958 (1)
LeSawyer, Kobart, Baisley, Collier; Kelley, Atkinson, Renan, Irving, Watson, Fried, Ludgin, Hecht, Ruddy, Sliker, DeLon, Wendler; Rudel, Capalbo (d), Nomikos

NP. *Susannah* (Floyd/Floyd)
April 30, 1958 (1)
Curtin, Sanders, LeSawyer, Moody, Kobart; Chapman, Cassilly, Kaldenberg, Newman, DeLon, Driscoll, Hecht; Rudel, Corsaro (d), Sylbert

Season 2 (March 30–May 3, 1959)

NYCOP. *Maria Golovin* (Menotti/Menotti)
March 30, 1959 (1)
Kombrink (d), Neway, Sarfaty; Cross (d), Kelley, Ludgin, Sechler (d); Grossman, Browning (d), Ter-Arutunian

NYCOP. *Street Scene* (Weill/L. Hughes)
April 2, 1959 (6)
Carron, Scott, Kobart, Dussault (d) Lee (d), Chapman, Poleri, Storch, Fried, DeLon, Tone (d), Krachmalnik, Machiz (d), Sylbert

REP. *The Ballad of Baby Doe* (Moore/J. Latouche)
April 3, 1959 (2)
Sills, Bible, Krebs; Cassel, Hecht; Buckley, Field, Oenslager

AP. *The Scarf* (Hoiby/H. Duncan)
April 5, 1959 (2)
Neway; Cross, Druary; Stanger (d), Browning, Ter-Arutunian
On a double bill with *The Devil and Daniel Webster*

NYCOP. *The Devil and Daniel Webster* (Moore/S. V. Benét)
April 5, 1959 (2)
Bishop; Cassel, Kelley, Hecht; Goberman (d), Houseman (d), Ter-Arutunian

NYCOP. *Wuthering Heights* (Floyd/Floyd)
April 9, 1959 (2)
Curtin, Moody, Neway; Reardon, Crain, Porretta, Voketaitis, Williams, DeLon; Rudel, D. Mann, Polakov

NYCOP. *He Who Gets Slapped* (Ward/B. Stambler)
April 12, 1959 (1)
Sarfaty, Venora; Atkinson, Ludgin, Porretta, Kelley, Renan, Bruns (d), Dooley (d); Buckley, Pollock, Nomikos

NYCOP. *The Triumph of Saint Joan* (Dello Joio/Dello Joio)
April 16, 1959 (1)
Venora; Watson, Harrell, Ludgin, Voketaitis, DeLon; Grossman, Quintero, Hays (d)
On a double bill with *The Medium*

REP. *The Medium* (Menotti/Menotti)
April 16, 1959 (1)
Turner, Clements (d), LeSawyer, Sarfaty; Perez (d), Newman; Torkanowsky (d), Pollock, Armistead

REP. *Susannah* (Floyd/Floyd)
April 18, 1959 (1)
Curtin, Kobart, LeSawyer, Moody, Sarfaty; Hecht, Cassilly, Kaldenberg, Ludgin, DeLon, Williams, Voketaitis; Rudel, Corsaro, Sylbert

REP. *Regina* (Blitzstein/Blitzstein)
April 19, 1959 (1)
Lewis, Carron, Moser (d), Brice; Hecht, Renan, Driscoll, Irving, Frierson; Krachmalnick, Shumlin, Bay

WP. *Six Characters in Search of an Author* (Weisgall/D. Johnston)
April 26, 1959 (1)
Bishop, Neway, Kobart, Sarfaty, Sills, Darian, Mannion (d); Ukena, Trehy (d), Timberlake (d), Voketaitis, Williams, Macurdy, McChesney; Levin (d), Ball (d), Smith (d)

Season 3 (February 11–21, 1960)

This abbreviated season was followed by a US tour to nineteen cities during which four of these operas (*The Ballad of Baby Doe*, *Six Characters in Search of an Author*, *Street Scene*, and *Susannah*) were performed.

NYCOP. *The Cradle Will Rock* (Blitzstein/Blitzstein)
February 11, 1960 (3)
Grimes (d), Kobart, Dussault, Ginn (d), Johnston (d); Atkinson, Riggs, Voketaitis, Harrold, Timberlake, Macurdy, Hecht, Smith, Porretta, Del Monte, Kerns, Stern, Fried, Griffis (d), Wager (d), Cowles (d), Bruns; Engel (d), Da Silva (d), Hays

REP. *Susannah* (Floyd/Floyd)
February 12, 1960 (0)
Curtin, Kobart, LeSawyer, Clements, Sarfaty; Treigle, Cassilly, Kaldenberg, Ludgin, Stern, Fried, Voketaitis; Rudel, Corsaro, Sylbert

REP. *Street Scene* (Weill/L. Hughes)
February 13, 1960 (2)
Carron, Clements, Kobart, Viracola, Lee; Atkins, Porretta, Stern, Fried, DeLon, Tone; Rudel, Machiz, Sylbert

REP. *The Ballad of Baby Doe* (Moore/J. LaTouche)
February 14, 1960 (m) (2)
Sills, Bible, Krebs; Cassel, Hecht; Buckley, Field, Oenslager

REP. *The Consul* (Menotti/Menotti)
February 14, 1960 (e) (1)
Neway, Sachs (d), Sarfaty, Marlo, Di Gerlando; Ludgin, Hecht, Voketaitis, Harrold, Merriman; Torkanowsky, Menotti, Armistead

REP. *Six Characters in Search of an Author* (Weisgall/D. Johnston)
February 18, 1960 (0)
Bishop, Kraft (d), Kobart, Sarfaty, Sills, Clements, Krebs; Ukena, Trehy, Timberlake, Voketaitis, Williams, Macurdy, Fried; Rudel, Ball, Smith

INDEX

As a seventeen-year-old Jewish boy, Julius Rudel escaped from Austria after the Nazi invasion and moved to New York, where he began his career as an unpaid musical assistant and worked his way up through the ranks of the newly formed New York City Opera, being named in 1957 as the company's general director and principal conductor. Later, he became the first artistic director of the Kennedy Center in Washington, DC.

In his twenty-two-year leadership of New York City Opera, Rudel challenged audiences with new and unusual repertoire—including fifteen world premieres and three seasons consisting entirely of American operas—turning the popularly priced "People's Opera" into the most influential and daring opera company in the United States.

Rudel writes in detail of his unusual repertoire choices and of the political battles behind New York City Opera's move to Lincoln Center in 1966, and he reminisces about his legendary collaborations with Beverly Sills (on Handel's *Giulio Cesare* and Donizetti's "Three Queens") and Plácido Domingo (on Ginastera's *Don Rodrigo*)—and about his work with other extraordinary talents including Norman Treigle, Phyllis Curtin, William Ball, Frank Corsaro, Tito Capobianco, Leopold Stokowski, Leonard Bernstein, Harold Prince, and Gian Carlo Menotti.

First and Lasting Impressions gives a rare personal look into Julius Rudel's career as a conductor and administrator during the glory years of New York City Opera.

Julius Rudel was general director and principal conductor of New York City Opera from 1957 to 1979, and since that time has been a frequent guest conductor at the Metropolitan Opera and many of the world's other great opera houses.

Rebecca Paller, a curator at the Paley Center for Media in New York, has written about the arts for publications including *Opera News*, *Opera*, *Vogue*, *Playbill*, *Symphony*, and *American Theatre*.

"In his remarkable career at New York City Opera, Julius Rudel enriched and enlarged the lives of music-loving New Yorkers. This book, coauthored with Rebecca Paller, is a fascinating account of how his devotion to music—*music*, not marketing—helped shape an era. I am particularly happy to have Maestro Rudel's version of his long and complicated working relationship with Beverly Sills."

—Brian Kellow, features editor, *Opera News*

"Julius Rudel offers us direct insight into his rise through the ranks to become the director of one of America's most vibrant cultural institutions in the twentieth century, the New York City Opera. Evident on nearly every page is that same abiding dedication, guiding spirit, and bold imagination that helped transplant a largely foreign art form and root it deep in America's artistic soil. This book will prove fascinating to opera singers and lovers of opera, especially American opera, not to mention interested teachers, pianists, voice coaches, and orchestra and choral conductors."

—Michael V. Pisani, Vassar College